Quizlet 사용법

▶ 온라인 학습사이트
Quizlet 바로가기

스마트폰, 태블릿, 컴퓨터에서 재미있고 효과적인 어휘 공부를 할 수 있는 학습 사이트!
Flash Card와 Spell Check, 게임 등의 서비스를 제공하며, 미국에서는 이미 주요 교육 수단으로 자리잡은 학습 시스템

01 Quizlet 사용방법

Step 1. 네이버 QR 인식기 또는 별도의 QR 인식기를 실행시켜
페이지 상단의 QR코드를 인식합니다.

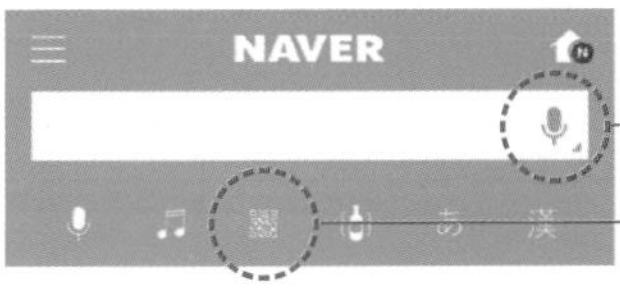

ⓐ 네이버 앱에서 마이크 아이콘 클릭합니다.

ⓑ QR 코드 인식기를 클릭합니다.

Step 2. 원하는 학습 일차를 선택합니다.

Step 3. 원하는 어휘의 MP3 음원을 선택하여 듣습니다.

KB011626

02 Quizlet의 다양한 학습기능

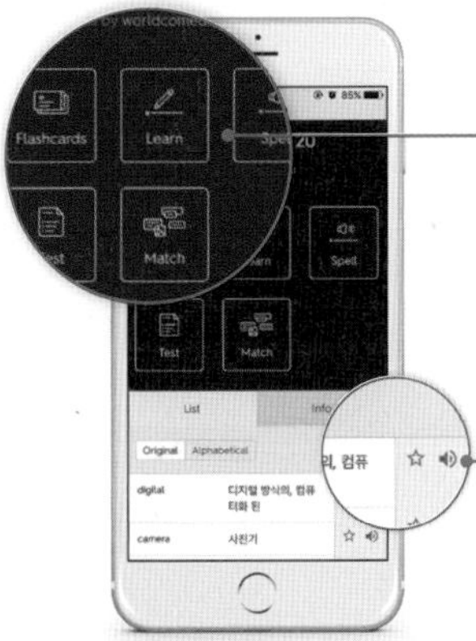

STUDY와 PLAY를 통해 다양한 방식으로 재밌게 학습할 수 있습니다.

- STUDY : Flashcard, Learn, Spell, Test
- PLAY : Match

단어 혹은 스피커 버튼을 누르면 음성을 들을 수 있습니다.

* Google Play에서 Quizlet 어플리케이션 다운로드 및 이용이 가능합니다.

QR 코드 사용법

보다 쉽고 간편하게 접근할 수 있는 학습 방법!
QR코드 인식을 통한 Word Max 6단계 시리즈 음원 바로 듣고 학습하기

01 네이버 앱을 통해 QR코드 사용하기

Step 1. 네이버 QR 인식기 또는 별도의 QR 인식기를 실행시킵니다.

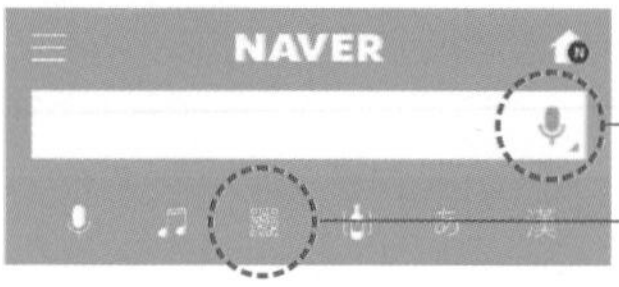

ⓐ 네이버 앱에서 마이크 아이콘 클릭합니다.
ⓑ QR 코드 인식기를 클릭합니다.

Step 2. 내지의 QR 코드를 인식합니다.

Step 3. MP3 음원이 유튜브를 통해 다운로드 없이 이용 가능합니다.

WORD MAX 2 5300

WorldCom Edu

WORD MAX 5300 2

초판	2016년 10월 31일
지은이	김 지 훈, 김 채 원
영문검수	Kenneth Drenen
책임편집	신 은 진
편집팀	월드컴 에듀 편집팀
펴낸이	임 병 업
디자인	임 예 슬, 김 지 현, 차 지 원
펴낸곳	(주)월드컴 에듀
등록	2016년 10월 31일
주소	서울시 강남구 언주로 120, 912호 (도곡동, 인스토피아)
전화	02)3273-4300 (대표)
팩스	02)3273-4303
홈페이지	www.wcbooks.co.kr
이메일	wc4300@wcbooks.co.kr

WORD MAX 5300 여는 글

언어를 배울 때 어휘 학습은 모든 언어 학습자가 가장 먼저 시작하는 분야이면서 동시에 가장 숙달하기 어려운 분야입니다. 이는 문법이나 읽기, 듣기와는 다른 어휘 학습의 독특한 측면이며 다른 학습 방식이 필요한 이유이기도 합니다. 수능을 비롯한 최근의 영어 시험 경향은 결국 어휘사용능력이 전반적인 문제 해결의 핵심 요소가 되고 있습니다.
WORD MAX 5300은 최신 경향에 맞추어 가장 효율적인 어휘 학습 방식을 제공하고자 합니다.

WORD MAX 5300시리즈는 과학적인 방법으로 최대의 효과를 얻을 수 있도록 어휘를 엄선했습니다.

WORD MAX 5300시리즈는 총 6권의 수준별 구성으로 최신 출제 경향과 엄선된 예문 및 다양하고 풍부한 리뷰 테스트를 통해 어휘 활용 능력을 최대화 할 수 있도록 구성했습니다.
최근 12년의 수능 및 각종 시험 기출 문제와 교과서 자료를 중심으로 자체 데이터베이스를 통해 학습 대상 어휘를 엄선했습니다. 특히 기출 빈도와 출제 예상도를 고려하여 선정한 어휘들은 효율적인 어휘 학습을 도와 줄 것입니다.

단계별로 세분화되고 실용성 있는 어휘 학습 환경을 제공합니다.

Level 1~3은 핵심적인 어휘를 풍부한 예문과 리뷰 테스트를 통해 예비중학 과정부터 중등 내신 대비까지 학생들의 기본적 영어 능력 향상에 도움이 되도록 구성했습니다.
Level 4~6은 최근 12년간의 수학능력시험, 모의고사, 학력평가의 기출문제를 토대로 어휘를 선정하였습니다. 더불어 각 어휘의 출제 맥락을 연구하고 수준별 분류 및 보정과정을 통해 단순 어휘 학습을 넘어 전반적인 영어 활용 능력을 향상 시킬 수 있게 구성했습니다.

다양한 어휘 활용 연습 기회를 제공하여 전반적인 영어 실력의 향상을 목표로 합니다.

WORD MAX 5300시리즈는 일일 테스트를 비롯한 Review Test의 총 8개 섹션의 다양한 테스트를 통해 학습한 어휘를 완전히 이해하고 활용할 수 있도록 했습니다. 쓰임에 따라 다양한 뜻을 가진 어휘들과 이에 대한 실용성 높은 예문들은 영어 사용 능력 향상에 확실한 도움이 될 것입니다.

어휘 학습 방법에 대한 이견은 많지만 어휘 학습 대상 선정의 중요성에 대해서는 연구자와 일선 교육자 모두 공감하고 있습니다. WORD MAX 5300시리즈를 충실히 학습한다면 어휘를 학습하는 재미 뿐만 아니라 영어 전반에서 실력 향상을 성취 할 수 있을 것이라 자부합니다.

WORD MAX 5300시리즈와 함께 어휘 학습에 최고의 결과를 얻을 수 있기를 기원합니다.

- 월드컴 에듀 편집팀 일동

구성 및 활용

1 단계별 30일 구성의 계획적 어휘 학습!

'단어 → 어구 → 예문' 순으로 자연스럽게 확장되는 학습을 통해 어휘력을 향상합니다.

하루 25개
단계별 30일 구성

유의어, 반의어, 연관 단어 등의
제시를 통해 어휘력을 확장합니다.

다양한 예문을 통해
표제어를 응용 학습합니다.

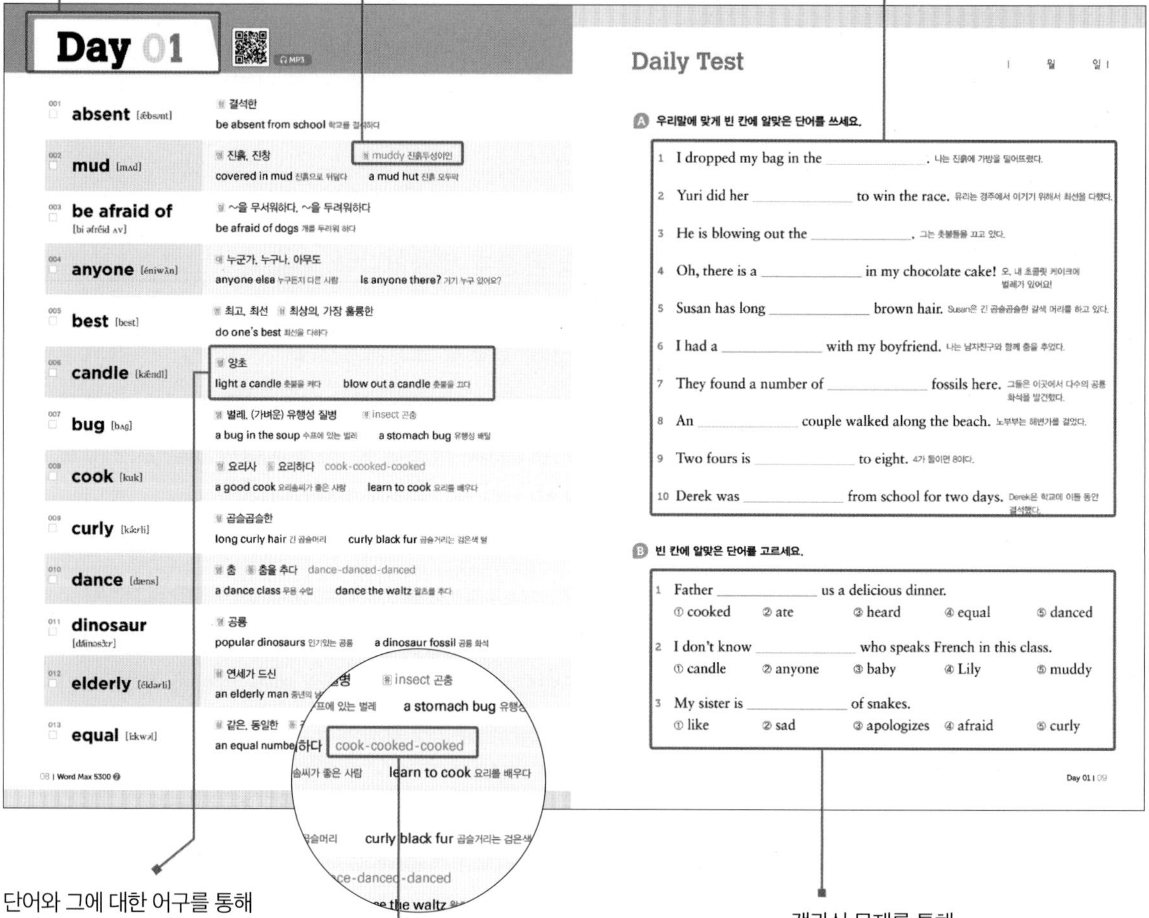

단어와 그에 대한 어구를 통해
다양한 어휘 학습을 가능하게 합니다.

동사의 3단 변화형과 비교형 제시를 통해
시제별 동사 형태를 연습합니다.

객관식 문제를 통해
내신대비 어휘학습을 가능하게 합니다.

2 Review Test 7가지 유형으로 학습 점검하기!

2일마다 학습한 어휘를 다양한 유형의 문제를 통해 반복 학습합니다.

어구 빈칸 완성
우리말에 따라 어구를 완성합니다

영영 풀이
보기에서 영영 풀이에 해당하는 단어를 찾아 봅니다.

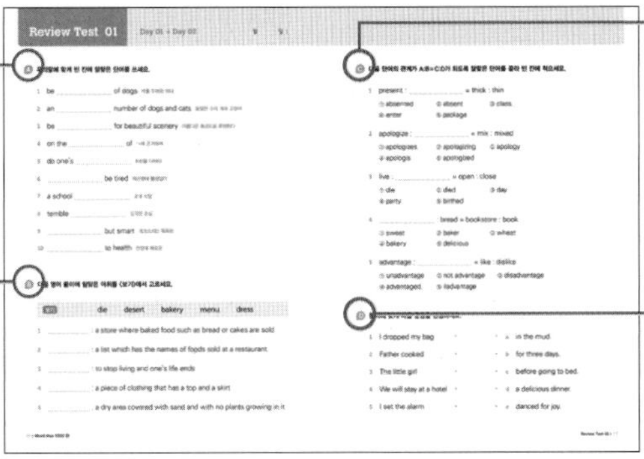

어휘 관계 파악
단어 간의 관계를 파악하여 알맞은 단어를 찾아봅니다.

문장 연결 완성
문맥상 알맞은 문장끼리 연결하여 완성된 문장을 학습합니다.

영영 어휘활용
문장에서 문맥상 알맞은 단어를 선택합니다.

문장 완성
우리말에 따라 보기에서 알맞은 단어를 골라 문장을 완성합니다.

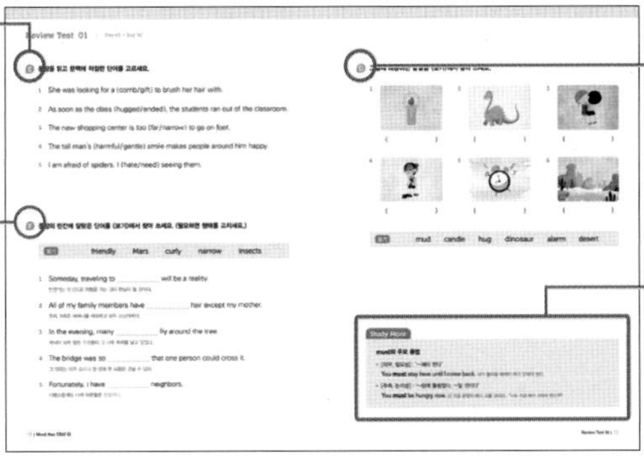

그림-단어 연결
각 그림에 알맞은 단어를 찾아봅니다.

Study More
표제어에 대한 확장된 개념을 제시함으로써 다양한 관점에서 어휘력을 향상 시킬 수 있습니다.

3 Work Book

워크북을 활용하여 단어의 철자와 뜻을 한번 더 반복 학습합니다.

쓰기 노트

일일 테스트

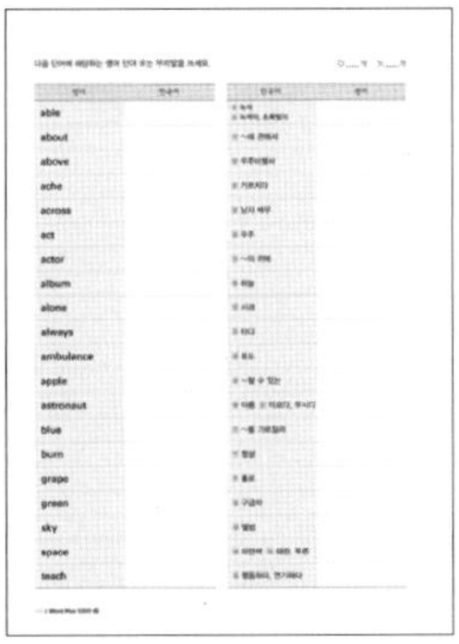

목차

★ 책 속의 책 Workbook 제공

WORD MAX 2 5300

Day 01

MP3

001 **absent** [ǽbsənt]
형 결석한
be absent from school 학교를 결석하다

002 **mud** [mʌd]
명 진흙, 진창　　형 muddy 진흙투성이인
covered in mud 진흙으로 뒤덮다　　a mud hut 진흙 오두막

003 **be afraid of** [bi əfréid ʌv]
형 ~을 무서워하다, ~을 두려워하다
be afraid of dogs 개를 두려워 하다

004 **anyone** [éniwʌ̀n]
대 누군가, 누구나, 아무도
anyone else 누구든지 다른 사람　　Is anyone there? 거기 누구 있어요?

005 **best** [best]
명 최고, 최선　형 최상의, 가장 훌륭한
do one's best 최선을 다하다

006 **candle** [kǽndl]
명 양초
light a candle 촛불을 켜다　　blow out a candle 촛불을 끄다

007 **bug** [bʌg]
명 벌레, (가벼운) 유행성 질병　　유 insect 곤충
a bug in the soup 수프에 있는 벌레　　a stomach bug 유행성 배탈

008 **cook** [kuk]
명 요리사　동 요리하다　cook-cooked-cooked
a good cook 요리솜씨가 좋은 사람　　learn to cook 요리를 배우다

009 **curly** [kə́ːrli]
형 곱슬곱슬한
long curly hair 긴 곱슬머리　　curly black fur 곱슬거리는 검은색 털

010 **dance** [dæns]
명 춤　동 춤을 추다　dance-danced-danced
a dance class 무용 수업　　dance the waltz 왈츠를 추다

011 **dinosaur** [dáinəsɔ̀ːr]
명 공룡
popular dinosaurs 인기있는 공룡　　a dinosaur fossil 공룡 화석

012 **elderly** [éldərli]
형 연세가 드신
an elderly man 중년의 남자　　an elderly couple 연세가 많으신 부부

013 **equal** [íːkwəl]
형 같은, 동일한　동 같다　　부 equally 똑같이, 동등하게
an equal number of dogs and cats 동일한 수의 개와 고양이

Daily Test

| 월 일 |

A 우리말에 맞게 빈 칸에 알맞은 단어를 쓰세요.

1 I dropped my bag in the ________________. 나는 진흙에 가방을 떨어뜨렸다.

2 Yuri did her ________________ to win the race. 유리는 경주에서 이기기 위해서 최선을 다했다.

3 He is blowing out the ________________. 그는 촛불들을 끄고 있다.

4 Oh, there is a ________________ in my chocolate cake! 오, 내 초콜릿 케이크에 벌레가 있어요!

5 Susan has long ________________ brown hair. Susan은 긴 곱슬곱슬한 갈색 머리를 하고 있다.

6 I had a ________________ with my boyfriend. 나는 남자친구와 함께 춤을 추었다.

7 They found a number of ________________ fossils here. 그들은 이곳에서 다수의 공룡 화석을 발견했다.

8 An ________________ couple walked along the beach. 노부부는 해변가를 걸었다.

9 Two fours is ________________ to eight. 4가 둘이면 8이다.

10 Derek was ________________ from school for two days. Derek은 학교에 이틀 동안 결석했다.

B 빈 칸에 알맞은 단어를 고르세요.

1 Father ________________ us a delicious dinner.

① cooked ② ate ③ heard ④ equal ⑤ danced

2 I don't know ________________ who speaks French in this class.

① candle ② anyone ③ baby ④ Lily ⑤ muddy

3 My sister is ________________ of snakes.

① like ② sad ③ apologizes ④ afraid ⑤ curly

Day 01

MP3

014 famous [féiməs]
형 유명한 유 well-known 잘 알려진
be famous for beautiful scenery 아름다운 풍경으로 유명하다

015 finger [fíŋgər]
명 손가락
the ring finger 약지 the index finger 집게 손가락

016 gift [gift]
명 선물 유 present 선물
a gift from Grandmother 할머니가 주신 선물

017 hotel [houtél]
명 호텔
hotel guests 호텔 투숙객 stay at a hotel 호텔에 머무르다

018 glasses [glæsiz]
명 안경
a pair of glasses 안경 wear glasses 안경을 쓰다

019 hug [hʌg]
동 껴안다 hug-hugged-hugged
hug each other 서로 껴안다 hug tightly 꽉 껴안다

020 job [dʒab]
명 직업, 일, 책임
get a job 직장을 얻다 do a good job 일을 잘 하다

021 leg [leg]
명 다리
a left leg 왼쪽 다리 break a leg 다리가 부러지다

022 Mars [mɑːrz]
명 화성
on Mars 화성에 the movie about Mars 화성에 관한 영화

023 menu [ménjuː]
명 (식당, 식사의) 메뉴
look at the menu 메뉴를 보다 bring a menu 메뉴를 가져오다

024 apologize [əpálədʒàiz]
동 사과하다 apologize-apologized-apologized
apologize to ~에게 사과하다 apologize for ~에 대해 사과하다

025 narrow [nǽrou]
형 좁은 반 wide 넓은
a narrow sidewalk 좁은 인도 narrow-minded 속이 좁은

Daily Test

| 월 일 |

A **우리말에 맞게 빈 칸에 알맞은 단어를 쓰세요.**

1 The picture is a ______________ from my uncle. 저 그림은 우리 삼촌이 주신 선물이다.

2 We will stay at a ______________ for three days. 우리는 3일 동안 호텔에 머무를 것이다.

3 He is wearing ______________. 그는 안경을 쓰고 있다.

4 She ______________ her daughter tightly. 그녀는 딸을 꽉 껴안았다.

5 She got a new ______________ last month. 그녀는 지난 달에 새로운 직장을 얻었다.

6 Kihyuk broke his ______________ yesterday. 기혁이는 어제 다리가 부러졌다.

7 We watched the movie about ______________. 우리는 화성에 관한 영화를 보았다.

8 I'll bring the ______________ for you. 당신을 위해 메뉴를 가져다 줄게요.

9 He ______________ for being rude to her. 그는 그녀에게 무례했던 것에 대해 사과했다.

10 He walked through the ______________ paths of the park.
그는 공원의 좁은 길을 따라 걸었다.

B **빈 칸에 알맞은 단어를 고르세요.**

1 She is ______________ for taking unique pictures.
① gift ② hugs ③ equal ④ curly ⑤ famous

2 Yuri was often ______________ from school.
① attend ② absent ③ bug ④ narrow ⑤ elderly

Day 02

MP3

026 □ **friendly** [fréndli]

형 친절한, 상냥한

a friendly smile 친절한 웃음 friendly neighbors 친절한 이웃

027 □ **bakery** [béikəri]

명 빵집 *baker 명 제빵사

a nearby bakery 근처 빵집 work at a bakery 빵집에서 일하다

028 □ **must** [mʌst]

조 ~해야 한다, ~임이 틀림없다

must be tired 피곤함에 틀림없다 must sleep now 지금 자야 한다

029 □ **alarm** [əlɑ́ːrm]

명 자명종, 경보기 동 놀라게 하다 alarm-alarmed-alarmed

set the alarm 자명종을 맞추다 ring the alarm 경보를 울리다

030 □ **away** [əwéi]

부 떨어져, 사라져

go away 떠나다 push away 밀어 젖히다

031 □ **basis** [béisəs]

명 기초, 근거

the basis of your opinion 당신 의견의 근거

032 □ **cafeteria** [kæ̀fətíəriə]

명 카페테리아(셀프 서비스 식당), 구내식당

a school cafeteria 교내 식당 in the cafeteria 구내 식당에서

033 □ **comb** [koʊm]

명 빗 동 빗다 comb-combed-combed

a plastic comb 플라스틱 빗 comb your hair 머리를 빗다

034 □ **damage** [dǽmidʒ]

명 손상 동 손상을 주다 damage-damaged-damaged

terrible damage 심각한 손상

035 □ **desert** [dézərt]

명 사막

the Sahara Desert 사하라 사막 a huge desert 거대한 사막

036 □ **dress** [dres]

명 드레스, 옷 동 옷을 입다 dress-dressed-dressed

change my dress 옷을 갈아입다 dress up 격식에 맞게 차려 입다

037 □ **end** [end]

동 끝내다 end-ended-ended

end a meeting 미팅을 끝내다 end a sentence 문장을 끝내다/마치다

038 □ **far** [fɑːr]

부 멀리 형 먼 far-farther-farthest

far away 멀리 떨어진 far from the school 학교로부터 멀리

Daily Test

| 월 일 |

A 우리말에 맞게 빈 칸에 알맞은 단어를 쓰세요.

1 Sam is ______________ and funny. Sam은 친절하고 재미 있다.

2 There is a big ______________ across the street. 길 건너에 큰 빵집이 있다.

3 Students ______________ pass the graduation exam. 학생들은 졸업시험을 꼭 통과해야 한다.

4 I set the ______________ before going to bed. 나는 자기 전에 자명종을 맞추어 놓았다.

5 What's the ______________ of your opinion? 당신 의견의 근거는 무엇인가요?

6 Insu is waiting for his friend in front of the school ______________. 인수는 교내식당 앞에서 친구를 기다리고 있다.

7 The fire ______________ the building last night. 지난 밤 불길이 건물을 손상시켰다.

8 You don't need to ______________ up for the party. 파티를 위해 굳이 차려 입지 않아도 된다.

9 We will meet at the ______________ of the month. 우리는 이번 달 말에 만날 것이다.

10 The shopping center is ______________ from the subway station. 쇼핑센터는 지하철역에서 멀다.

B 빈 칸에 알맞은 단어를 고르세요.

1 They went ______________ without saying good bye.
① away ② friendly ③ famous ④ basis ⑤ end

2 Don't forget to ______________ your hair!
① long ② comb ③ dress ④ apologize ⑤ curly

3 Camels live in the ______________.
① sea ② desert ③ lake ④ cafeteria ⑤ dessert

Day 02

MP3

039 □ **film** [film]
명 영화, 카메라 필름
watch a film 영화를 보다 / a roll of film 필름 한 통

040 □ **die** [dai]
동 죽다 die-died-died / 명 death 죽음
die slowly 서서히 죽다 / die from cancer 암으로 죽다

041 □ **gentle** [dʒéntl]
형 온화한, 순한, 조용한 / 부 gently 온화하게
a gentle man 온화한 남자 / his gentle voice 그의 조용한 목소리

042 □ **harmful** [hά:rmfəl]
형 해로운
harmful to health 건강에 해로운 / a harmful habit 해로운 습관

043 □ **hate** [heit]
동 몹시 싫어하다, 미워하다
hate each other 서로 미워하다 / hate carrots 당근을 싫어하다

044 □ **insect** [ínsekt]
명 곤충 / 유 bug 벌레
a common insect 흔한 곤충 / a harmful insect 해로운 곤충

045 □ **joy** [dʒɔi]
명 기쁨
dance for joy 기뻐서 춤을 추다 / a great joy 큰 기쁨

046 □ **knife** [naif]
명 칼 동 칼로 베다 / 복 knives
a pocket knife 접이식 칼 / a steak knife 스테이크용 칼

047 □ **lazy** [léizi]
형 게으른
a lazy boy 게으른 소년 / lazy but smart 게으르지만 똑똑한

048 □ **miracle** [mírəkl]
명 기적 / 형 miraculous 기적같은
a miracle cure 기적의 치유법 / do a miracle 기적을 행하다

049 □ **advantage** [ədvǽntidʒ]
명 이점, 이익 / 반 disadvantage 불이익, 약점
a great advantage 엄청난 장점 / an advantage over ~보다 유리한 점

050 □ **need** [ni:d]
동 필요로 하다 명 필요 need-needed-needed
need a break 휴식이 필요하다 / need to study 공부할 필요가 있다

Daily Test

| 월 일 |

A 우리말에 맞게 빈 칸에 알맞은 단어를 쓰세요.

1 The ________________ made us cry. 그 영화가 우리를 울게 했다.

2 She ________________ from lung cancer last year. 그녀는 폐암으로 작년에 죽었다.

3 His voice is ________________ and quiet. 그의 목소리는 온화하고 조용하다.

4 My son ________________ carrots. 내 아들은 당근을 싫어한다.

5 I'm so afraid of ________________. 나는 곤충을 정말 무서워한다.

6 What a ________________ boy he is! 그는 얼마나 게으른 소년인지!

7 Many people believed that John did a ________________.
많은 사람들이 John이 기적을 행했다고 믿었다.

8 This new car has many ________________. 이 새로운 자동차는 많은 장점들이 있다.

9 You ________________ to study English hard. 너는 영어 공부를 열심히 할 필요가 있다.

10 The little girl danced for ________________. 그 어린 소녀는 기뻐서 춤을 췄다.

B 빈 칸에 알맞은 단어를 고르세요.

1 Junk food is ________________ to your health.
① far ② gentle ③ full ④ narrow ⑤ harmful

2 You should be careful when you use a sharp ________________.
① dance ② knife ③ joy ④ miracle ⑤ insect

Review Test 01

A 우리말에 맞게 빈 칸에 알맞은 단어를 쓰세요.

1 be ________________ of dogs 개를 두려워 하다

2 an ________________ number of dogs and cats 동일한 수의 개와 고양이

3 be ________________ for beautiful scenery 아름다운 풍경으로 유명하다

4 on the ________________ of ~에 근거하여

5 do one's ________________ 최선을 다하다

6 ________________ be tired 피곤함에 틀림없다

7 a school ________________ 교내 식당

8 terrible ________________ 심각한 손상

9 ________________ but smart 게으르지만 똑똑한

10 ________________ to health 건강에 해로운

B 다음 영어 풀이에 알맞은 어휘를 〈보기〉에서 고르세요.

보기	die	desert	bakery	menu	dress

1 ____________ : a store where baked food such as bread or cakes are sold

2 ____________ : a list which has the names of foods sold at a restaurant

3 ____________ : to stop living and one's life ends

4 ____________ : a piece of clothing that has a top and a skirt

5 ____________ : a dry area covered with sand and with no plants growing in it

C 다음 단어의 관계가 A:B=C:D가 되도록 알맞은 단어를 골라 빈 칸에 적으세요.

1 present : ________________ = thick : thin

① absented ② absent ③ class
④ enter ⑤ package

2 apologize : ________________ = mix : mixed

① apologizes ② apologizing ③ apology
④ apologis ⑤ apologized

3 live : ________________ = open : close

① die ② died ③ day
④ party ⑤ birthed

4 ________________ : bread = bookstore : book

① sweet ② baker ③ wheat
④ bakery ⑤ delicious

5 advantage : ________________ = like : dislike

① unadvantage ② not advantage ③ disadvantage
④ advantaged ⑤ iladvantage

D 문맥에 맞게 다음 문장을 완성하세요.

1 I dropped my bag •	• a in the mud.
2 Father cooked •	• b for three days.
3 The little girl •	• c before going to bed.
4 We will stay at a hotel •	• d a delicious dinner.
5 I set the alarm •	• e danced for joy.

E 문장을 읽고 문맥에 적절한 단어를 고르세요.

1 She was looking for a (comb/gift) to brush her hair with.

2 As soon as the class (hugged/ended), the students ran out of the classroom.

3 The new shopping center is too (far/narrow) to go on foot.

4 The tall man's (harmful/gentle) smile makes people around him happy.

5 I am afraid of spiders. I (hate/need) seeing them.

F 문장의 빈칸에 알맞은 단어를 〈보기〉에서 찾아 쓰세요. (필요하면 형태를 고치세요.)

보기	friendly	Mars	curly	narrow	insects

1 Someday, traveling to ____________ will be a reality.
언젠가는 화성으로 여행을 가는 것이 현실이 될 것이다.

2 All of my family members have ____________ hair except my mother.
우리 가족은 어머니를 제외하고 모두 곱슬머리다.

3 In the evening, many ____________ fly around the tree.
저녁이 되자 많은 곤충들이 그 나무 주위를 날고 있었다.

4 The bridge was so ____________ that one person could cross it.
그 다리는 아주 좁아서 한 번에 한 사람만 건널 수 있었다.

5 Fortunately, I have ____________ neighbors.
다행스럽게도 나의 이웃들은 친절하다.

G 그림에 해당하는 낱말을 〈보기〉에서 골라 쓰세요.

1 

(　　　　　　　　)

2 

(　　　　　　　　)

3 

(　　　　　　　　)

4 

(　　　　　　　　)

5 

(　　　　　　　　)

6 

(　　　　　　　　)

보기 mud candle hug dinosaur alarm desert

Study More

must의 주요 용법

- [의무, 필요성] : '~해야 한다'
  You **must** stay here until I come back. 내가 돌아올 때까지 여기 있어야 한다.
- [추측, 논리성] : '~임에 틀림없다, ~일 것이다'
  You **must** be hungry now. 넌 지금 분명히 배가 고플 것이다. *너는 지금 배가 고파야 한다(X)

Day 03

MP3

051 copy [kápi]

명 복사(본) 동 복사하다 copy-copied-copied

make a copy 복사하다 a copycat 남의 것을 따라하는 사람

052 part [pɑːrt]

명 일부, 부분, 부품 형 partial 부분적인

a part of the town 마을의 한 부분 a body part 신체 부위

053 repair [ripέər]

동 수리하다 repair-repaired-repaired

repair a car 차를 수리하다 repair a monitor 모니터를 수리하다

054 around [əráund]

부 주위에 전 주변에

all around 사방에서 sit around the table 식탁에 둘러앉다

055 bookmark [bʊkmɑːrkʌv]

명 책갈피, 북마크 동 북마크를 하다

mark the page with a bookmark 그 페이지에 책갈피로 표시하다

056 bitter [bítər]

형 맛이 쓴, 쓰라린

a bitter taste 쓴 맛 a bitter experience 쓰리린 경험

057 cloth [klɔːθ]

명 천, 옷감

cotton cloth 면 소재의 옷감 a wet cloth 젖은 천

058 cousin [kʌ́zən]

명 사촌

a distant cousin 먼 사촌 play with cousins 사촌과 함께 놀다

059 down [daun]

부 아래로

look down 내려다 보다 jump down 뛰어 내리다

060 fact [fækt]

명 사실

a surprising fact 놀라운 사실 in fact 사실은

061 variety [vəraiəti]

명 여러 가지, 갖가지 형 various 여러 가지의, 다양한

a variety of 다양한~ a variety of ways 다양한 방식

062 fashion [fǽʃən]

명 유행, 패션

the latest fashion style 최신 유행 스타일

063 handsome [hǽnsəm]

형 잘생긴, 멋진 반 ugly 못생긴

a handsome face 잘생긴 얼굴 a handsome actor 잘생긴 배우

Daily Test

| 월 일 |

Ⓐ 우리말에 맞게 빈 칸에 알맞은 단어를 쓰세요.

1 I remember that ______________ of the novel. 나는 소설의 그 부분을 기억한다.

2 Some people ______________ the road last night. 지난 밤 몇몇 사람들이 도로를 보수했다.

3 There are many people ______________ the statue. 그 조각상 주변에는 많은 사람들이 있다.

4 She placed a ______________ on the page she was reading. 그녀는 그녀가 읽고 있는 페이지에 책갈피를 두었다.

5 Good medicine tastes ______________. 좋은 약은 입에 쓰다.

6 Mom covered the table with a white ______________. 엄마는 식탁을 하얀 천으로 덮었다.

7 Suzi played with her ______________ last week. 지난 주에 수지는 그녀의 사촌들과 놀았다.

8 I heard some interesting ______________ about dogs. 나는 개에 대한 흥미로운 사실들을 들었다.

9 There were a ______________ of opinions in the meeting. 회의에서 갖가지 의견들이 있었다.

10 He was a ______________ and polite actor. 그는 잘생기고 예의 바른 영화배우다.

Ⓑ 빈 칸에 알맞은 단어를 고르세요.

1 The woman is making a ______________ of her essay.

① letter ② cousin ③ copy ④ fact ⑤ nature

2 The leaves of the trees are falling ______________.

① next ② in ③ on ④ down ⑤ to

3 Short curly hair is out of ______________ this year.

① around ② machine ③ lamp ④ fashion ⑤ false

Day 03

MP3

064 **guest** [gest]

명 손님

a special guest 특별 손님 Chinese guests 중국인 손님들

065 **hall** [hɔːl]

명 (모임이나 공연을 위한)공간, 건물, 홀

a student hall 학생회관 a concert hall 콘서트 홀

066 **hero** [híː(ː)ərou]

명 영웅 형 heroic 영웅적인

a war hero 전쟁 영웅 a heroic myth 영웅 신화

067 **lamp** [læmp]

명 등, 램프 유 light 전등

a desk lamp 탁상용 스탠드 a safety lamp 안전용 램프

068 **limit** [límit]

명 한계 동 제한하다 limit-limited-limited

an age limit 나이 제한 limit speed 속도를 제한하다

069 **machine** [məʃíːn]

명 기계

a washing machine 세탁기 a sewing machine 재봉틀

070 **nature** [néitʃər]

명 자연, 본성 형 natural 자연의, 천연의

the laws of nature 자연의 법칙 human nature 인간의 본성

071 **never** [névər]

부 결코 ~않는

never watch a horror movie 절대 공포영화를 보지 않는다

072 **outdoor** [áutdɔ̀ːr]

형 야외의 반 indoor 실내의

outdoor activities 야외 활동 outdoor clothing 야외 의류

073 **false** [fɔːls]

형 틀린

a false answer 틀린 답 false information 잘못된 정보

074 **pen** [pen]

명 펜

a pen and paper 펜과 종이 a fountain pen 만년필

075 **photo** [fóutou]

명 사진 복 photos

a color photo 컬러 사진 take a photo 사진을 찍다

Daily Test

| 월 일 |

A **우리말에 맞게 빈 칸에 알맞은 단어를 쓰세요.**

1 Go straight and turn left, then you will see the student ________________
쭉 가서 왼쪽으로 돌면, 학생회관이 있습니다.

2 'Iron Man' is my favorite film ________________. 아이언맨은 내가 좋아하는 영화 속 영웅이다.

3 The ________________ is on the table. 스탠드가 탁자 위에 있다.

4 Mom bought a new sewing ________________. 엄마는 새 재봉틀을 사셨다.

5 I sometimes spend time in ________________. 나는 때때로 자연에서 시간을 보낸다.

6 Sean ________________ watches horror movies alone.
Sean은 절대 혼자서 공포영화를 보지 않는다.

7 My favorite ________________ activity is hiking. 내가 가장 좋아하는 야외활동은 하이킹이다.

8 Write the words with a blue ________________. 그 단어들은 푸른 색 펜으로 쓰세요.

9 He took some beautiful ________________ in Hawaii.
그는 하와이에서 아름다운 사진들을 찍었다.

10 The rumor was ________________. 그 소문은 사실이 아니었다.

B **빈 칸에 알맞은 단어를 고르세요.**

1 We will have a special ________________ tonight.

① guest ② proud ③ outdoor ④ repair ⑤ friendly

2 The speed ________________ is 70km/h on this road.

① hour ② limit ③ around ④ score ⑤ part

Day 04

MP3

076 correct [kərékt]
형 맞는, 정확한 동 바로잡다 correct-corrected-corrected
a correct answer 정답 correct errors 틀린 곳을 고치다

077 pretty [príti]
형 예쁜, 매력적인 pretty-prettier-prettiest
a pretty girl 예쁜 소녀 a pretty flower 예쁜 꽃

078 be about to [bi əbáut tu]
~을 막 하려고 하다
be about to leave 막 떠나려 하다.

079 balance [bǽləns]
명 균형 동 균형을 유지하다 balance-balanced-balanced
keep a balance 균형을 맞추다

080 award [əwɔ́ːrd]
명 상 동 수여하다 award-awarded-awarded
win an award 상을 받다 award a gold medal 금메달을 수여하다

081 careless [kέərlis]
형 부주의한, 경솔한 반 careful 조심스러운
a careless mistake 경솔한 실수 a careless driver 부주의한 운전자

082 class [klæs]
명 학급, 수업
a music class 음악 수업 in class 수업 중

083 elementary [èləméntəri]
형 초급의 유 basic 기초적인
an elementary school 초등학교 elementary education 초등 교육

084 exact [igzǽkt]
형 정확한 부 exactly 정확하게
the exact time 정확한 시간 an exact date 정확한 날짜

085 skirt [skəːrt]
명 치마
wear a white skirt 흰 치마를 입다 a short skirt 짧은 치마

086 flight [flait]
명 비행
a comfortable flight 편안한 비행 a flight attendant 비행 승무원

087 gold [gould]
명 금 형 금빛의
a gold ring 금 반지 decorate with gold 금으로 장식하다

088 glove [glʌv]
명 장갑
a pair of gloves 장갑 한 켤레 wear gloves 장갑을 끼다

Daily Test

| 월 일 |

Ⓐ 우리말에 맞게 빈 칸에 알맞은 단어를 쓰세요.

1 Check these sentences and ______________ the errors.
이 문장들을 확인하고 틀린 곳을 고치세요.

2 There are many ______________ flowers in the garden.
정원에는 예쁜 꽃들이 많이 있다.

3 He won an ______________ for dancing. 그는 댄스 경연대회에서 상을 받았다.

4 The bus driver was very ______________. 버스 운전사는 매우 부주의했다.

5 My sister and I are in the same ______________ at school.
언니와 나는 학교에서 같은 반이다.

6 My sister is an ______________ school student. 내 여동생은 초등학생이다.

7 Can you tell me the ______________ time of the accident?
그 사고의 정확한 시간을 말해 줄 수 있나요?

8 Sarah wears a short blue ______________. Sarah는 짧은 파란색 치마를 입고 있다.

9 He gave a ______________ ring to his girlfriend. 그는 여자친구에게 금반지를 주었다.

10 It's too cold. You should wear ______________. 너무 추워. 넌 장갑을 껴야 해.

Ⓑ 빈 칸에 알맞은 단어를 고르세요.

1 Amy was ______________ to call her mother.
① careless ② exact ③ pretty ④ about ⑤ on

2 What time is your next ______________ to LA?
① fight ② error ③ flight ④ running ⑤ hotel

3 He can ______________ on one leg.
① balance ② exact ③ run ④ hero ⑤ correct

Day 04

MP3

089 **household** [háushòuld]
명 가정
a large household 대가족 a whole household 온 가족

090 **hunt** [hʌnt]
명 사냥 동 사냥하다 hunt-hunted-hunted
hunt for ~을 사냥하다 hunt for a rabbit 토끼를 사냥하다

091 **item** [áitem]
명 항목, 물품 유 article 물품
old items 오래된 물품들 item by item 항목마다

092 **lean** [liːn]
동 기울다, ~에 기대다 lean-leaned-leaned
lean against the wall 벽에 기대다 lean back 뒤로 젖히다

093 **a lot of** [ə lɑt ʌv]
대 많은
a lot of people 많은 사람들 a lot of time 많은 시간

094 **mosquito** [məskíːtou]
명 모기
set up a mosquito net 모기장을 치다 a mosquito bite 모기에 물린 곳

095 **parents** [perənts]
명 부모
live with her parents 그녀의 부모님과 함께 살다

096 **passport** [pǽspɔːrt]
명 여권
get a passport 여권을 발급받다 a passport photo 여권 사진

097 **understand** [ʌ̀ndərstǽnd]
동 이해하다 understand-understood-understood
understand German 독일어를 이해하다 understand well 잘 이해하다

098 **clever** [klévər]
형 영리한, 똑똑한 clever-cleverer-cleverest
a clever boy 영리한 소년 clever animals 영리한 동물들

099 **quickly** [kwíkli]
부 빨리, 빠르게 형 quick 빠른
run quickly 빨리 달리다 talk quickly 빠르게 말하다

100 **ready** [rédi]
형 준비된
get ready 준비하다 get ready for school 학교 갈 준비를 하다

Daily Test

| 월 일 |

A 우리말에 맞게 빈 칸에 알맞은 단어를 쓰세요.

1 The whole ______________ was at home last night. 지난 밤에 온 가족이 집에 있었다.

2 The hunters ______________ for seals. 사냥꾼들은 물개를 사냥했다.

3 She checked all the ______________ on the list. 그녀는 목록의 항목들을 모두 점검했다.

4 A ______________ of people are talking about the movie. 많은 사람들이 그 영화에 대해서 이야기한다.

5 My ______________ are special to me. 부모님은 내게 특별하다.

6 I ______________ what you're saying. 네가 무슨 말을 하는지 이해한다.

7 Dogs are ______________ animals. 개는 영리한 동물이다.

8 He sent the letter ______________. 그는 빨리 편지를 보냈다.

9 They are getting ______________ to get married. 그들은 결혼할 준비를 하고 있다.

10 Father set up a ______________ net. 아빠가 모기장을 쳐 주셨다.

B 빈 칸에 알맞은 단어를 고르세요.

1 She ______________ against the wall.
① hunted ② clever ③ leaned ④ understood ⑤ hit

2 You need a ______________ to travel to foreign countries.
① household ② passport ③ money ④ mosquito ⑤ cleaver

Review Test 02

Day 03 + Day 04 | 월 일 |

A 우리말에 맞게 빈 칸에 알맞은 단어를 쓰세요.

1 get a ______________ 여권을 발급받다

2 mark the page with a ______________ 그 페이지에 책갈피로 표시하다

3 a surprising ______________ 놀라운 사실

4 ______________ the speed 속도를 제한하다

5 human ______________ 인간의 본성

6 get ______________ for school 학교 갈 준비를 하다

7 an ______________ date 정확한 날짜

8 ______________ back 뒤로 젖히다

9 ______________ German 독일어를 이해하다

10 take a ______________ 사진을 찍다

B 다음 영어 풀이에 알맞은 어휘를 〈보기〉에서 고르세요.

보기	item	cousin	guest	glove	lamp

1 ____________ : the son or daughter of your uncle or aunt

2 ____________ : a person who is invited to visit or stay at your house

3 ____________ : a device that makes light from gas or electricity

4 ____________ : a hand covering worn to cover or protect each of your fingers

5 ____________ : a particular thing that is in a group or list and can be counted

C 다음 단어의 관계가 A:B=C:D가 되도록 알맞은 단어를 골라 빈 칸에 적으세요.

1 copy : ________________ = fry : fried

① copyed ② copyes ③ copied
④ copies ⑤ copited

2 ________________ : mistake = make : cookie

① correct ② difficult ③ wrong
④ jump ⑤ correction

3 clever : ________________ = short : shortest

① clvered ② clevering ③ clevers
④ cleverest ⑤ cleverrest

4 true : ________________ = dry : wet

① story ② rumor ③ sentence
④ honest ⑤ false

5 ________________ : car = drink : juice

① dream ② repair ③ wheel
④ black ⑤ handle

D 문맥에 맞게 다음 문장을 완성하세요.

1 There are many people •	• a a new sewing machine.
2 Sarah wears •	• b with a white cloth.
3 Mom bought •	• c a short blue skirt.
4 Mom covered the table •	• d a mosquito net.
5 Father set up •	• e around the statue.

E 문장을 읽고 문맥에 적절한 단어를 고르세요.

1 I wrapped my mother's birthday gift in (pretty/careless) paper.

2 It took quite (ready/long) for me to read the book.

3 The man said that he had (never/lot) seen such a nice painting before.

4 Tonight we will talk (about/around) the science problem.

5 This book gives a (lot/glove) of information on France.

F 문장의 빈칸에 알맞은 단어를 〈보기〉에서 찾아 쓰세요. (필요하면 형태를 고치세요.)

보기	flight	bitter	careless	elementary	hero

1 Because the medicine had a ____________ taste, I did not feel like taking it.
그 약은 쓴 맛이 나서 나는 그것을 먹고 싶은 기분이 들지 않았다.

2 After a ten-hour ____________, we landed in Paris.
10시간의 비행 끝에 우리는 파리에 착륙했다.

3 The ____________ of the match was the goalkeeper.
그 시합의 영웅은 골키퍼였다.

4 It was ____________ of him to speak in such a rude manner.
그렇게 불손한 태도로 말하다니 그는 경솔하다.

5 These days Sohee is taking an ____________ Spanish course.
요즘 소희는 초급 스페인어 강좌를 수강하고 있다.

G 그림과 낱말이 잘못 짝지어진 것을 고르세요. ·· (　　　　　　)

ⓐ

down

ⓑ

pen

ⓒ

run

ⓓ

gold

H 낱말과 어울리는 그림을 연결하세요.

1 quickly •　　　　• ⓐ 

2 mosquitos •　　　　• ⓑ 

Study More

pretty의 여러 의미

- [형용사] : '예쁜, 매력적인'

  a **pretty** face 귀여운 얼굴　a **pretty** garden 예쁜 정원

- [부사] : '꽤, 아주, 매우'

  be **pretty** hungry 꽤 배가 고프다　be **pretty** hard to explain 설명하기 꽤 어렵다

Day 05

MP3

101 dig [dig]
동 파다 dig-dug-dug
dig a hole 구멍을 파다 dig down ~을 파 내려가다

102 romance [roumǽns]
명 연애(감정), 로맨스
a romance with a beautiful princess 아름다운 공주와의 연애

103 forecast [fɔ́ːrkæ̀st]
명 예측 동 예측하다 forecast-forecast-forecast
weather forecast 일기 예보 forecast heavy rain 폭우를 예측하다

104 amazing [əméiziŋ]
형 놀라운 부 amazingly 놀랄만큼
an amazing story 놀라운 이야기 an amazing discovery 놀라운 발견

105 battery [bǽtəri]
명 건전지, 배터리
replace the batteries 건전지를 교체하다 a car battery 자동차 배터리

106 bow [bau]
동 고개를 숙이다, 절하다 bow-bowed-bowed
bow before the king 왕에게 허리 숙여 절하다

107 close [klous]
형 가까이의, 친한 동 닫다 close-closed-closed
a close friend 가까운 친구 close the window 창문을 닫다

108 concert [kánsə(ː)rt]
명 연주회, 콘서트
a rock concert 락 콘서트 go to a concert 연주회에 가다

109 diary [dáiəri]
명 일기
keep a diary / write a diary 일기를 쓰다 a travel diary 여행 일지

110 even [íːvən]
부 ~조차(도), 훨씬 형 짝수의
even on weekends 주말까지도 even numbers 짝수

111 fare [fɛər]
명 요금 유 charge 요금
bus fare 버스 요금 pay the fare 차비를 내다

112 collect [kəlékt]
동 모으다, 수집하다 collect-collected-collected
collect stamps 우표를 수집하다 collect information 정보를 모으다

113 heat [hiːt]
명 열, 더위 동 가열하다 heat-heated-heated
the heat of the Sun 태양의 열 heat the water 물을 데우다

Daily Test

| 월 일 |

A 우리말에 맞게 빈 칸에 알맞은 단어를 쓰세요.

1 Jane dreamed about a ______________ with a handsome boy.
Jane은 잘생긴 소년과의 연애를 꿈꿨다.

2 Heavy snow is ______________ for tomorrow. 폭설이 내일 예상됩니다.

3 It's really an ______________ thing! 정말 놀라운 일이구나!

4 Rick is replacing a car ______________. Rick은 자동차 배터리를 교체 중이다.

5 The servants ______________ before the king. 하인들이 왕에게 허리 숙여 절했다.

6 Is the department store ______________ to your house?
백화점이 너희 집에서 가깝니?

7 I'll go to the ______________ with Jane tomorrow.
나는 Jane과 내일 연주회에 갈 것이다.

8 I usually write in my ______________ every night. 나는 대개 매일 밤 일기를 쓴다.

9 Peter works ______________ on weekends. Peter는 주말에도 일한다.

10 Minji ______________ water to take a bath. 민지는 목욕을 하기 위해 물을 데웠다.

B 빈 칸에 알맞은 단어를 고르세요.

1 The dog ______________ a hole in the garden.
① stands ② collected ③ dug ④ even ⑤ hung

2 What is the ______________ from Busan to Seoul?
① fare ② distant ③ day ④ far ⑤ street

3 Sue is ______________ stamps.
① closing ② collecting ③ amazing ④ forecasting ⑤ bowing

Day 05

MP3

114 **human** [hjúːmən]
형 인간의
the human body 인체 human being 인간, 사람

115 **jog** [dʒαg]
동 조깅하다 jog-jogged-jogged
go jogging 조깅하러 가다 jog in the evening 저녁에 조깅하다

116 **level** [lévəl]
명 정도, 수준, 단계
a low English level 낮은 단계의 영어 happiness level 행복 수준

117 **lizard** [lízərd]
명 도마뱀
find a lizard 도마뱀을 발견하다 scared of lizards 도마뱀을 무서워하는

118 **mind** [maind]
명 마음, 정신
an active mind 활기찬 정신 mind and body 몸과 마음

119 **month** [mʌnθ]
명 월, 달 monthly 형 매월의 부 매월
the month of July 7월 three months old 생후 3개월

120 **pimple** [pímpl]
명 여드름
pop a pimple 여드름을 짜다 a pimple on the cheek 뺨 위의 여드름

121 **powder** [páudər]
명 가루
rice powder 쌀가루 curry powder 카레 가루

122 **quiet** [kwáiət]
형 조용한, 한적한 부 quietly 조용히
keep quiet 조용히 하다 a quiet place 조용한 장소

123 **recipe** [résəpìː]
명 조리법, 요리법
a recipe for spaghetti 스파게티 만드는 법 a recipe book 요리책

124 **remember** [rimémbər]
동 기억하다 remember-remembered-remembered
remember his birthday 그의 생일을 기억하다

125 **return** [ritə́ːrn]
동 돌아오다, 돌려주다 return-returned-returned
return from a journey 여행에서 돌아오다

Daily Test

| 월 일 |

A 우리말에 맞게 빈 칸에 알맞은 단어를 쓰세요.

1 Some ______________ activities destroy the environment. 몇몇 인간의 활동들은 환경을 파괴한다.

2 Aaron usually ______________ in the morning. Aaron은 대개 아침에 조깅을 한다.

3 The happiness ______________ is different from country to country. 행복 수준은 나라마다 다르다.

4 I found the ______________ under the rock. 나는 바위 밑에서 도마뱀을 발견했다.

5 The baby is four ______________ old. 그 아기는 생후 4개월이 되었다.

6 We need some rice ______________ to make noodles. 우리는 국수를 만들기 위해 쌀가루가 필요하다.

7 Keep ______________ when you are in the library. 도서관에 있을 때는 조용히 해라.

8 He couldn't ______________ my name. 그는 내 이름을 기억하지 못했다.

9 Kate will ______________ from her journey after three months. Kate는 3개월 후에 여행에서 돌아올 것이다.

10 Linda has a ______________ on her nose. Linda는 코 위에 여드름이 났다.

B 빈 칸에 알맞은 단어를 고르세요.

1 Out of sight, out of ______________.

① mind ② eyes ③ hearts ④ brain ⑤ height

2 I want the ______________ for chocolate cake.

① lizard ② ways ③ pimple ④ recipe ⑤ jogging

Day 06

MP3

126 **difficulty** [dífəkʌ̀lti]

명 어려움

have difficulty writing in English 영어로 쓰는 데 어려움을 겪다

127 **loud** [laud]

형 (소리가) 큰, 시끄러운 부 loudly 크게

a loud voice 큰 목소리 clap loudly 크게 손뼉 치다

128 **admire** [ədmáiər]

동 존경하다, 칭찬하다 admire-admired-admired

admire his courage 그의 용기를 칭찬하다

129 **bin** [bin]

명 쓰레기통

a waste bin 쓰레기통 empty the trash bin 쓰레기통을 비우다

130 **be aware of** [bi əwɛ́ər ʌv]

형 ~을 알고 있다, ~을 알아차리다

be aware of the problem 그 문제에 대해 알고 있다

131 **build** [bild]

동 짓다, 건설하다 build-built-built

build a house 집을 짓다 build a bridge 다리를 건설하다

132 **comedy** [kámidi]

명 코미디, 희극 형 comic 희극의, 우스꽝스러운

a comedy show 코미디 쇼 play in a comedy 희극에 출연하다

133 **daily** [déili]

형 매일의

a daily newspaper 일간 신문 daily life 일상 생활

134 **engineer** [èndʒəníər]

명 기사, 기술자

a computer engineer 컴퓨터 기술자 a railway engineer 철도 기사

135 **especially** [ispéʃəli]

부 특히, 유난히

especially difficult 특히 어려운 especially for you 특별히 너를 위해서

136 **excite** [iksáit]

동 들뜨게 하다, 흥분시키다 명 excitement 흥분, 신남

excite the crowd 군중을 들뜨게 하다 excite envy 질투심을 자극하다

137 **fine** [fain]

형 좋은 명 벌금

fine clothes 좋은 옷 a parking fine 주차 벌금

138 **hard** [hɑːrd]

형 단단한, 굳은 부 열심히, 힘껏

a hard rock 단단한 돌 study hard 열심히 공부하다

Daily Test

| 월 일 |

A 우리말에 맞게 빈 칸에 알맞은 단어를 쓰세요.

1 The audience clapped ______________. 관객들은 크게 박수 쳤다.

2 We ______________ King Sejong. 우리는 세종대왕을 존경한다.

3 Yoonji is ______________ of the purpose of the meeting. 윤지는 모임의 목적에 대해 알고 있다.

4 We will ______________ a new concert hall here next year. 우리는 내년에 이 곳에 새로운 콘서트 홀을 지을 예정이다.

5 I like to watch ______________ shows at night. 나는 밤에 코미디 쇼를 보는 것을 좋아한다.

6 Father usually reads a ______________ newspaper in the morning. 아버지는 아침에 주로 일간 신문을 읽는다.

7 I called a computer ______________ to fix my computer. 컴퓨터를 고치기 위해 나는 컴퓨터 기술자에게 전화를 걸었다.

8 Last Saturday was ______________ cold. 지난 토요일은 유난히 추웠다.

9 Jane was so ______________ about her trip to Europe. Jane은 유럽으로의 여행에 매우 들떠있었다.

10 I don't care about the accident. I'm ______________. 나는 그 사고를 신경쓰지 않아. 괜찮아.

B 빈 칸에 알맞은 단어를 고르세요.

1 Jinsu had ______________ writing in English.
① difficulty ② hard ③ difficult ④ building ⑤ strong

2 We should empty the trash ______________.
① garage ② bin ③ ball ④ round ⑤ away

3 She studied very ______________ to pass the exam.
① hardly ② daily ③ difficulty ④ hard ⑤ strongly

Day 06

MP3

139	**inform** [infɔ́:rm]	동 알리다, 통지하다 inform-informed-informed inform the manager 관리자에게 알리다
140	**knock** [nɑk]	동 두드리다, 노크하다 명 노크 소리 knock-knocked-knocked knock on the door 문을 노크하다
141	**lie** [lai]	명 거짓말 tell a lie 거짓말하다 a white lie 악의없는 거짓말
142	**leaf** [li:f]	명 낙엽, 잎 복 leaves dead leaves 낙엽 tea leaves 찻잎
143	**monster** [mɑ́nstər]	명 괴물 a scary monster 무서운 괴물 like a monster 괴물처럼
144	**polite** [pəláit]	형 예의바른, 정중한 반 impolite 예의없는 a polite attitude 예의바른 태도 polite to others 다른 이에게 예의바르다
145	**plan** [plæn]	명 계획 동 계획을 짜다 plan-planned-planned a holiday plan 휴가 계획 plan a party 파티를 계획하다
146	**powerful** [páuərfəl]	형 강한, 강력한 a powerful leader 강력한 지도자 a powerful engine 강력한 엔진
147	**relieve** [rilí:v]	동 안도시키다, 완화하다 relieve-relieved-relieved relieve stress 스트레스를 없애주다 relieve pain 고통을 완화시키다
148	**rude** [ru:d]	형 무례한 유 impolite 예의없는 a rude question 무례한 질문 rude behavior 무례한 행동
149	**sad** [sæd]	형 슬픈 유 unhappy 불행한, 슬픈 a sad movie 슬픈 영화 look sad 슬퍼 보이다
150	**sand** [sænd]	명 모래 a sandcastle 모래성 a grain of sand 한 알의 모래

Daily Test

| 월 일 |

A 우리말에 맞게 빈 칸에 알맞은 단어를 쓰세요.

1 Please ______________ us of how to get to the station. 우리에게 그 역에 가는 방법을 알려주세요.

2 Don't tell a ______________. 거짓말 하지마.

3 There are many dead ______________ on the street. 길가에 낙엽들이 많이 있다.

4 She acts like a ______________. 그녀는 괴물처럼 행동했다.

5 Amy is always ______________ to others. Amy는 항상 다른 이에게 예의바르다.

6 He is a rich and ______________ man. 그는 부유하고 강한 사람이다.

7 She was ______________ to hear the news. 그 소식은 그녀를 안도시켰다.

8 Harry's behavior was very ______________. Harry의 태도는 매우 무례했다.

9 You look so ______________. What's wrong? 너 슬퍼 보이는구나. 무슨 일 있니?

10 Children are making a ______________ on the beach. 해변가에서 아이들이 모래성을 만들고 있다.

B 빈 칸에 알맞은 단어를 고르세요.

1 What's your ______________ for the summer vacation?

① value ② inform ③ plan ④ leaf ⑤ knock

2 I ______________ on the door twice and waited.

① rolled ② made ③ cried ④ admired ⑤ knocked

A 우리말에 맞게 빈 칸에 알맞은 단어를 쓰세요.

1 weather ________________ 일기 예보

2 tell a ________________ 거짓말을 하다

3 ________________ and body 몸과 마음

4 a ________________ leader 강력한 지도자

5 a ________________ attitude 정중한 태도

6 a parking ________________ 주차 벌금

7 ________________ his courage 그의 용기를 칭찬하다

8 ________________ difficult 특히 어려운

9 ________________ stress 스트레스를 없애주다

10 a grain of ________________ 한 알의 모래

B 다음 영어 풀이에 알맞은 어휘를 〈보기〉에서 고르세요.

보기	concert	diary	jog	battery	comedy

1 ____________ : a book where you write down your experience or thoughts daily

2 ____________ : a public performance of music or dance before an audience

3 ____________ : to run slowly for exercise or pleasure

4 ____________ : a light and funny drama or show which makes people laugh

5 ____________ : a device that makes and stores electricity

C 다음 단어의 관계가 A:B=C:D가 되도록 알맞은 단어를 골라 빈 칸에 적으세요.

1 difficult : ________________ = hungry : hunger

① difficults ② difficulty ③ difficulted
④ difficulties ⑤ different

2 plan : ________________ = go : went

① plan ② plans ③ planed
④ plant ⑤ planned

3 ________________ : book = fly : kite

① return ② thick ③ call
④ English ⑤ Korean

4 ________________ : postcards = clean : cups

① tradition ② American ③ post office
④ collect ⑤ stamp

5 leaf : ________________ = knife : knives

① leafs ② leafies ③ leaves
④ leaffes ⑤ leafves

D 문맥에 맞게 다음 문장을 완성하세요.

1	Jane dreamed about a romance •	• a	of the purpose of the meeting.
2	We need some rice •	• b	destroy the environment.
3	Please inform us of •	• c	how to get to the station.
4	Some human activities •	• d	powder to make noodles.
5	Yoonji is aware •	• e	with a handsome boy.

E 문장을 읽고 문맥에 적절한 단어를 고르세요.

1 He (bowed/forecast) politely to the principal.

2 He never (knocks/heats) on a door before he enters a room.

3 George did not (relieve/remember) where he put his student card.

4 The soup is cold now. (Aware/Heat) it up before you eat it.

5 The singer's performance on stage (excited/returned) the audience.

F 문장의 빈칸에 알맞은 단어를 〈보기〉에서 찾아 쓰세요. (필요하면 형태를 고치세요.)

보기	loudly	rude	lizard	recipe	amazing

1 The scientist finally made a(n) ____________ discovery.
그 과학자는 마침내 놀라운 발견을 했다.

2 His ____________ behavior made people avoid talking to him.
그의 무례한 행동은 사람들이 그와 이야기하는 것을 피하게 만들었다.

3 Body language is the most important means of communication to ____________.
몸짓 언어는 도마뱀들에게는 제일 중요한 소통 수단이다.

4 The cook did not want to talk about his ____________ for the dish.
요리사는 그 요리에 대한 조리법에 대해 이야기 하고 싶지 않았다.

5 Jongmin's mother told him not to speak ____________ in public places.
종민의 어머니는 그에게 공공장소에게 크게 이야기 하지 말라고 했다.

G 그림에 해당하는 낱말을 〈보기〉에서 골라 쓰세요.

1 

(　　　　　　)

2 

(　　　　　　)

3 

(　　　　　　)

4 

(　　　　　　)

5 

(　　　　　　)

6 

(　　　　　　)

보기 quiet dig difficulty closed sad pimples

Study More

혼동하기 쉬운 말 fare vs. fair

- [fare] 명 교통 요금 유 charge, cost, fee
  a bus **fare** 버스 요금 a single **fare** 1회 승차 요금 an adult **fare** 성인 요금
- [fair] 형 공정한, 공평한 반 unfair
  a **fair** competition 공평한 경쟁 **fair** treatment 공평한 대우 a **fair** teacher 공평한 선생님

Day 07

MP3

151 **stand** [stænd]
동 서다 stand-stood-stood
stand up 서다 stand in line 일렬로 서다

152 **line** [lain]
명 선
a straight line 직선 line up 줄을 서다

153 **advice** [ədváis]
명 조언, 충고 동 advise 충고하다
good advice 좋은 충고 give advice 충고를 하다

154 **ancient** [éinʃənt]
형 고대의
an ancient story 고대 이야기 an ancient kingdom 고대의 왕국

155 **base** [beis]
명 기초, 기반 유 foundation 기초, 근거, 토대
the base of the building 건물의 기반

156 **breath** [breθ]
명 입김, 숨
a deep breath 깊은 숨 hold your breath 숨을 참다

157 **company** [kʌ́mpəni]
명 회사, 단체 유 firm 회사
a toy company 장난감 회사 a dance company 무용단

158 **curry** [kə́:ri]
명 카레, 카레 요리
curry and rice 카레라이스 spicy curry 매운 카레 요리

159 **drama** [drá:mə]
명 드라마, 연극 형 dramatic 극적인, 인상적인
a historical drama 역사극 a drama school 연극 학교

160 **environment** [inváiərənmənt]
명 자연환경, (주변의) 환경 형 environmental 환경의
protect the environment 환경을 보호하다

161 **fantastic** [fæntǽstik]
형 환상적인
a fantastic movie 환상적인 영화 a fantastic time 환상적인 시간

162 **gray** [grei]
형 회색의 명 회색
paint in gray 회색으로 칠하다 a dark gray door 짙은 회색 문

163 **guess** [ges]
명 추측 동 추측하다 guess-guessed-guessed
guess the answer 답을 추측하다 take a guess 추측하다

Daily Test

| 월 일 |

A 우리말에 맞게 빈 칸에 알맞은 단어를 쓰세요.

1 The students are ______________ in line. 학생들이 일렬로 서 있다.

2 She usually gives me good ______________. 그녀는 자주 내게 좋은 충고를 해준다.

3 He wrote a novel about an ______________ kingdom. 그는 고대 왕국에 대한 소설을 썼다.

4 He works at the largest clothing ______________ in the world. 그는 세계에서 제일 큰 의류회사에서 일한다.

5 Tom likes spicy chicken ______________. Tom은 매운 닭고기 카레를 좋아한다.

6 Jieun is interested in historical ______________. 지은이는 역사극에 흥미를 가지고 있다.

7 We should protect the ______________. 우리는 환경을 보호해야 한다.

8 We had a ______________ time in LA. 우리는 LA에서 환상적인 시간을 보냈다.

9 The girl is wearing a ______________ skirt. 그 소녀는 회색 치마를 입고 있다.

10 James ______________ the right answer. James는 정답을 추측해냈다.

B 빈 칸에 알맞은 단어를 고르세요.

1 The boy is drawing a straight ______________.
① circle ② round ③ advice ④ line ⑤ lock

2 The ______________ of the tower is made from steel.
① breath ② base ③ company ④ advice ⑤ humor

3 Nick held his ______________ and dove into the pool.
① minute ② breath ③ guess ④ eyes ⑤ deaf

Day 07

MP3

164 **humorous** [hjúːmərəs]

형 재미있는, 유머가 넘치는 명 humor 유머, 해학

a humorous story 재미있는 이야기 a humorous writer 유머가 있는 작가

165 **lake** [leik]

명 호수

by a lake 호수 옆에서 swim in the lake 호수에서 수영하다

166 **danger** [déindʒər]

명 위험 형 dangerous 위험한

danger of fire 불의 위험 be in danger of ~할 위험이 있다

167 **lock** [lɑk]

동 잠그다 명 자물쇠 lock-locked-locked

lock the door 문을 잠그다 a metal lock 금속 자물쇠

168 **motto** [mɑ́tou]

명 좌우명

a family motto 가훈 a school motto 교훈

169 **pill** [pil]

명 알약

a headache pill 두통약 a vitamin pill 비타민 알약

170 **process** [prɑ́ses]

명 과정, 절차 유 procedure 절차, 방법

a simple process 간단한 과정 a production process 생산 과정

171 **regret** [rigrét]

명 후회 동 후회하다 regret-regretted-regretted

regret fighting with friends 친구와 싸운 것을 후회하다

172 **sale** [seil]

명 판매, 세일

a year-end sale 연말 세일 a car on sale 판매중인 차

173 **sauce** [sɔːs]

명 소스, 향신료

tomato sauce 토마토 소스 sweet sauce 달콤한 소스

174 **science** [sáiəns]

명 과학 형 scientific 과학적인

pass the science exam 과학시험을 통과하다

175 **smart** [smɑːrt]

형 현명한, 똑똑한 반 stupid 어리석은

a smart student 똑똑한 학생 look smart 똑똑해 보이다

Daily Test

| 월 일 |

A 우리말에 맞게 빈 칸에 알맞은 단어를 쓰세요.

1 He is handsome and ________________. 그는 잘생겼고 유머가 넘친다.

2 Boys are swimming in the ________________. 소년들이 호수에서 수영하고 있다.

3 Oh, I forgot to ________________ the door. 오. 나 문 잠그는 것을 깜빡했어.

4 My ________________ is 'live honestly'. 내 좌우명은 '정직하게 살자' 이다.

5 The doctor told him to take two ________________ a day.
의사는 그에게 하루에 알약 두 알을 먹으라고 했다.

6 The ________________ of making kimchi is complex. 김치를 만드는 과정은 복잡하다.

7 The dress will be on ________________ soon. 저 드레스는 곧 판매 될 것이다.

8 What is your favorite ________________? 어떤 소스를 가장 좋아하세요?

9 I was happy because I passed the ________________ exam.
나는 과학 시험을 통과했기 때문에 행복했다.

10 Ellen looks so ________________. Ellen은 꽤 똑똑해 보인다.

B 빈 칸에 알맞은 단어를 고르세요.

1 Some animals are in ________________ of losing their homes.

① motto ② dangerous ③ danger ④ safe ⑤ smart

2 I ________________ eating the spicy sauce.

① lock ② sale ③ regret ④ humor ⑤ sad

Day 08

MP3

176 **spend** [spend]

동 쓰다, 소비하다 spend-spent-spent

spend money 돈을 쓰다 spend the weekend 주말을 보내다

177 **dessert** [dizə́ːrt]

명 디저트, 후식

a sweet dessert 달콤한 후식 serve dessert 디저트를 내놓다

178 **miss** [mis]

동 그리워하다 miss-missed-missed

miss my old friends 내 오랜 친구들을 그리워하다

179 **aisle** [ail]

명 통로

an aisle seat 통로 쪽 좌석 in the aisle 통로에

180 **bacteria** [bæktí(ː)əriə]

명 박테리아, 세균

kill the bacteria 세균을 죽이다 dangerous bacteria 위험한 박테리아

181 **cheer** [tʃiər]

동 환호하다, 응원하다 명 환호 cheer-cheered-cheered

cheer up 격려하다 words of cheer 격려의 말

182 **couple** [kʌ́pl]

명 두 개의, 둘의

a couple of~ 한 쌍의~ a couple of cups 컵 두 개

183 **relax** [rilǽks]

동 휴식을 취하다, 긴장을 풀다 relax-relaxed-relaxed

relax in the room 방에서 쉬다 Just relax. 긴장을 풀어라.

184 **empty** [émpti]

형 텅 빈 동 비우다 empty-emptied-emptied

an empty box 빈 상자 empty the glass 잔을 비우다

185 **example** [igzǽmpl]

명 예시, 본보기 유 instance 보기

a good example 좋은 본보기 for example 예를 들어

186 **trouble** [trʌ́bl]

명 문제, 골칫거리

big trouble 큰 문제, 곤경 a troublemaker 말썽꾸러기

187 **floor** [flɔːr]

명 층, 바닥

the second floor 2층 a concrete floor 콘크리트 바닥

188 **hang** [hæŋ]

동 걸다 hang-hung-hung

hang your coat in the closet 옷장에 코트를 걸다

Daily Test

| 월 일 |

A 우리말에 맞게 빈 칸에 알맞은 단어를 쓰세요.

1 We will ______________ the weekend in Paris. 우리는 주말을 파리에서 보낼 것이다.

2 I don't ______________ her. 난 그녀가 그립지 않다.

3 The statue is at the end of the ______________. 그 조각상은 통로 끝에 있다.

4 There is a variety of ______________ in the pond. 이 연못에는 다양한 박테리아가 있다.

5 Stretching helps to ______________ your muscles. 스트레칭은 근육의 긴장을 푸는 것을 도와준다.

6 You should ______________ the box before going to bed. 자러 가기 전에 저 박스를 비워야 한다.

7 He gave an ______________ of a good novel. 그는 좋은 소설의 예를 들었다.

8 Tell us about your ______________. 우리에게 너의 고민을 얘기해봐.

9 Mary lives on the third ______________. Mary는 3층에 살고 있다.

10 ______________ the picture on the wall. 그 그림을 벽에 걸어라.

B 빈 칸에 알맞은 단어를 고르세요.

1 I ate some cookies for ______________.

① aisle ② desert ③ trouble ④ dessert ⑤ picnic

2 ______________ up! You can do it.

① Come ② Cheer ③ Empty ④ Dessert ⑤ Hang

3 I bought a ______________ of pencils.

① piece ② couple ③ packs ④ couples ⑤ boxes

Day 08

MP3

189 **instead of** [instéd ʌv]

전 ~대신에

eat bread instead of rice 밥 대신에 빵을 먹다

190 **kingdom** [kíŋdəm]

명 왕국

the United Kingdom 영국　a small kingdom 작은 왕국

191 **list** [list]

명 목록　동 목록을 작성하다

a shopping list 쇼핑 목록　make a list 목록을 만들다

192 **mask** [mæsk]

명 가면, 탈

wear a mask 가면을 쓰다　a gas mask 가스 마스크

193 **note** [nout]

명 메모, 편지　유 memo 메모

write a note 짧은 편지를 쓰다　a brief note 짧은 편지

194 **raise** [reiz]

동 들어올리다, 올리다, 모으다　raise-raised-raised

raise your hand 손을 들다　raise prices 가격을 올리다

195 **pose** [pouz]

동 자세를 취하다　명 자세　pose-posed-posed

pose for a photograph 사진을 위해 포즈를 취하다

196 **ordinary** [ɔ́:rdənèri]

형 보통의, 일반적인　반 extraordinary 탁월한

an ordinary day 보통 날　ordinary people 일반인

197 **rule** [ru:l]

명 규칙

follow the rules 규칙을 따르다　break a rule 규칙을 어기다

198 **scare** [skεər]

동 겁주다, 겁내다　형 scared 겁먹은

scare his sister 그의 여동생을 겁주다　be scared of ~을 두려워하다

199 **shadow** [ʃǽdou]

명 그림자

a dark shadow 어두운 그림자　cast a shadow 그림자를 드리우다

200 **sleepy** [slí:pi]

형 졸린

a sleepy baby 졸린 아기　feel sleepy 졸리다

Daily Test

| 월 일 |

A 우리말에 맞게 빈 칸에 알맞은 단어를 쓰세요.

1 A beautiful princess lives in a small ______________. 아름다운 공주가 작은 왕국에 살고 있다.

2 Let's make a shopping ______________ before going to the market. 가게에 가기 전에 쇼핑목록을 만들자.

3 She is wearing a blue ______________. 그녀는 파란 가면을 쓰고 있다.

4 Youngjin wrote a ______________ to his girlfriend. 영진은 그의 여자친구에게 짧은 편지를 썼다.

5 They ______________ in front of the tower for a group photograph. 그들은 탑 앞에서 단체 사진을 위해 자세를 취했다.

6 I don't want to live an ______________ life. 나는 평범한 삶을 살고 싶지 않다.

7 Students should follow school ______________. 학생들은 교칙을 지켜야 한다.

8 A big spider ______________ many people in the woods. 큰 거미가 숲에 있는 사람들을 겁나게 했다.

9 The tall building cast a ______________ across the sidewalk. 큰 건물이 인도 위에 그림자를 드리우고 있다.

10 I feel ______________. I want to go to bed. 난 졸려. 자러 가고 싶어요.

B 빈 칸에 알맞은 단어를 고르세요.

1 I want to drink coffee ______________ of coke.

① instead ② however ③ afraid ④ like ⑤ and

2 Jaehan ______________ money for the blind.

① corrected ② posed ③ raised ④ missed ⑤ hung

Review Test 04

A 우리말에 맞게 빈 칸에 알맞은 단어를 쓰세요.

1 ________________ for a photograph 사진을 위해 포즈를 취하다

2 protect the ________________ 환경을 보호하다

3 a school ________________ 교훈

4 ________________ fighting with friends 친구와 싸운 것을 후회하다

5 look ________________ 똑똑해 보이다

6 big ________________ 큰 문제

7 an ________________ seat 통로 쪽 좌석

8 feel ________________ 졸리다

9 eat bread ________________ of rice 밥 대신에 빵을 먹다

10 a dark ________________ 어두운 그림자

B 다음 영어 풀이에 알맞은 어휘를 〈보기〉에서 고르세요.

보기	company	curry	drama	couple	mask

1 ____________ : an organization that makes money by selling products or services

2 ____________ : something that covers or hides your face

3 ____________ : a story written to be played on stage or TV

4 ____________ : any of two things that go together or belong to the same kind

5 ____________ : an Indian food made with many kinds of spices and usually eaten with rice

C 다음 단어의 관계가 A:B=C:D가 되도록 알맞은 단어를 골라 빈 칸에 적으세요.

1 danger : ________________ = humor : humorous

① dangerous ② dangers ③ dangerly
④ dangeric ⑤ dangerish

2 spend : ________________ = take : took

① spended ② money ③ spent
④ spends ⑤ time

3 ________________ : sit = hard : soft

① seat ② chair ③ leg
④ get ⑤ stand

4 round : cookie = ________________ : life

① live ② lifes ③ your
④ ordinary ⑤ frankly

5 ________________ : door = listen : radio

① bus ② fast ③ pose
④ lock ⑤ Korean

D 문맥에 맞게 다음 문장을 완성하세요.

1	Stretching helps •	• a	historical dramas.
2	A beautiful princess lives •	• b	in a small kingdom.
3	Students should follow •	• c	to relax your muscles.
4	Jieun is interested in •	• d	to his girlfriend.
5	Youngjin wrote a note •	• e	school rules.

E 문장을 읽고 문맥에 적절한 단어를 고르세요.

1 Suzie took her teacher's (process/advice) for Spanish study.

2 These days, people eat bread in the morning (instead/example) of rice.

3 Here is a new word for today. Can you (pose/guess) the meaning of the word?

4 If you are going to go shopping now, why don't you make a (list/sale) of items you need to buy?

5 Sam is a friendly student. For (example/note), he likes to help his friends.

F 문장의 빈칸에 알맞은 단어를 〈보기〉에서 찾아 쓰세요. (필요하면 형태를 고치세요.)

보기	humorous	raise	ancient	line	process

1 People began to ____________ up to enter the concert hall.
사람들은 콘서트 홀에 입장하기 위해 줄을 서기 시작했다.

2 Jamie is a ____________ and friendly boy.
Jamie는 유쾌하고 친절한 소년이다.

3 The new history teacher taught us about the ____________ history of East Asia.
새로 오신 역사 선생님께서 동아시아의 고대 역사에 대해 가르쳐 주셨다.

4 Making a new software program alone may be a long ____________.
새로운 소프트웨어 프로그램을 혼자서 만드는 것은 긴 과정일 수 있다.

5 Some museums in the city ____________ their admission fees.
시내의 몇몇 박물관은 입장료를 올렸다.

G 그림과 낱말이 <u>잘못</u> 짝지어진 것을 고르세요. ·· (　　　　　　)

ⓐ

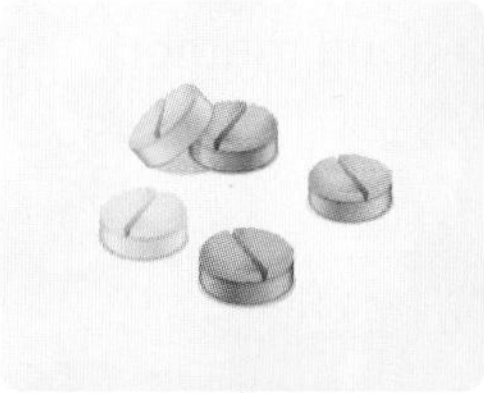

pill

ⓑ

science

ⓒ

desert

ⓓ

empty

H 낱말과 어울리는 그림을 연결하세요.

1 hang •

• ⓐ 

2 scare •

• ⓑ 

Study More

혼동하기 쉬운 말 raise vs. rise

- [raise] : '~을 들어 올리다 (to raise something)'　[rise] : '~이 오르다 (something rises)'
  The boy **raised** his arms above his head. 소년은 양팔을 위로 올렸다.
  The water temperature is **rising.** 물 온도가 올라가고 있다.
- Rise your arms. (X)　The airplane raised into the sky. (X)

Day 09

MP3

201 **recommend** [rèkəménd]
동 추천하다 recommend-recommended-recommended
recommend a hospital 병원을 추천하다

202 **memory** [méməri]
명 기억(력), 추억
happy memories 행복한 추억 have a good memory 기억력이 좋다

203 **alike** [əláik]
형 비슷한 부 비슷하게
look alike 닮아 보이다 treat alike 차별없이 대우하다

204 **article** [á:rtikl]
명 기사, 물품
a newspaper article 신문기사 read an article 기사를 읽다

205 **asleep** [əslí:p]
형 잠이 든, 자고 있는
fall asleep 잠들다 be fast asleep 깊이 잠들다

206 **cause** [kɔ:z]
명 이유, 원인 동 ~을 일으키다 cause-caused-caused
cause and effect 원인과 결과 cause damage 손상을 일으키다

207 **chat** [tʃæt]
동 담소를 나누다, 수다를 떨다 chat-chatted-chatted
have a chat with friends 친구들과 잡담하다

208 **costume** [kástju:m]
명 의상, 복장
traditional costume 전통 의상 formal costumes 격식 있는 의상

209 **decrease** [dí:kri:s]
동 감소하다 명 감소 decrease-decreased-decreased
decrease sharply 급격하게 줄어들다

210 **emperor** [émpərər]
명 황제 +empire 명 제국
the Roman Emperor 로마 황제 the emperor system 황제 제도

211 **fat** [fæt]
명 지방 형 뚱뚱한 fat-fatter-fattest
fat meat 지방이 많은 고기 vegetable fat 식물성 지방

212 **grass** [græs]
명 풀, 잔디
cut the grass 잔디를 깎다 play in the grass 잔디에서 놀다

213 **ground** [graund]
명 땅, 용지
on the ground 땅바닥에서 a football ground 축구장

Daily Test

| 월 일 |

A 우리말에 맞게 빈 칸에 알맞은 단어를 쓰세요.

1 Jin has a good ______________. Jin은 기억력이 좋다.

2 They look ______________. 그들은 닮았다.

3 I read an ______________ about air pollution. 나는 대기 오염에 관한 기사를 읽었다.

4 The baby fell ______________ on the bed. 아기는 침대 위에서 잠이 들었다.

5 A storm can ______________ terrible damage. 폭풍은 심각한 손상을 일으킬 수 있다.

6 We had a long ______________ last night. 우리는 지난 밤 많은 이야기를 했다.

7 You should ______________ speed. 너는 속도를 줄여야 한다.

8 He was the last ______________ of Rome. 그는 로마의 마지막 황제였다.

9 Some dogs are playing on the ______________. 강아지들이 잔디에서 놀고 있다.

10 The boy picked up a book that was on the ______________.
소년은 땅바닥에 있는 책을 주웠다.

B 빈 칸에 알맞은 단어를 고르세요.

1 A Hanbok is a Korean traditional ______________.
① article ② costume ③ classic ④ grass ⑤ ground

2 You should do exercise to avoid becoming ______________.
① asleep ② chat ③ fat ④ adult ⑤ healthy

3 Can you ______________ a book to read?
① decrease ② hear ③ read ④ recommend ⑤ made

Day 09

MP3

214 □ **hint** [hint]

명 힌트, 암시

give a hint 힌트를 주다　take a hint 힌트를 알아차리다

215 □ **lead** [led]

동 안내하다　lead-led-led　유 guide 안내하다

lead the class 학급을 이끌다　lead the country 나라를 이끌다

216 □ **lend** [lend]

동 빌려주다　lend-lent-lent

lend some money 돈을 빌려주다　lend a pen 펜을 빌려주다

217 □ **possible** [pάsəbl]

형 가능한　반 impossible 불가능한

a possible reason 가능한 이유　as soon as possible 가능한 빨리

218 □ **order** [ɔ́:rdər]

동 명령하다, 주문하다　명 명령　order-ordered-ordered

order a coffee 커피를 주문하다　follow an order 명령을 따르다

219 □ **captain** [kǽptən]

명 주장, 선장

captain of a soccer team 축구팀 주장

220 □ **prepare** [pripέər]

동 준비하다　prepare-prepared-prepared　명 preparation 준비

prepare for Helen's birthday party Helen의 생일파티를 준비하다

221 □ **record** [rékərd]

동 녹음하다, 기록하다　명 기록, 음반　record-recorded-recorded

record your voice 당신의 목소리를 녹음하다

222 □ **scene** [si:n]

명 (영화, 연극 등의) 장면, 경치, 풍경

the last scene of this movie 이 영화의 마지막 장면

223 □ **war** [wɔ:r]

명 전쟁　+battle 명 전투

a war hero 전쟁 영웅　a terrible war 끔찍한 전쟁

224 □ **snake** [sneik]

명 뱀

a snake on the sand 모래 위에 있는 뱀　hate snakes 뱀을 싫어하다

225 □ **song** [sɔ(:)ŋ]

명 노래

folk songs 민요　pop songs 대중 가요

Daily Test

| 월 일 |

A 우리말에 맞게 빈 칸에 알맞은 단어를 쓰세요.

1 The teacher gave some ______________ to his students.
선생님은 그의 학생들에게 약간의 힌트를 주었다.

2 He will ______________ our company from next month.
그는 다음 달부터 우리 회사를 이끌 것이다.

3 Can you ______________ me your car tomorrow? 내일 차를 빌려줄 수 있니?

4 I ______________ bread and coffee. 나는 빵과 커피를 주문했다.

5 People are ______________ to celebrate Christmas.
사람들은 크리스마스를 기념하기 위해 준비하고 있다.

6 Jimmy set a new American baseball ______________.
Jimmy는 미국 야구에서 새로운 기록을 세웠다.

7 He is practicing the last ______________ of 'Hamlet'.
그는 '햄릿'의 마지막 장면을 연습하고 있다.

8 Many people were killed during World ______________ II.
세계 2차 대전 동안에 많은 사람들이 죽었다.

9 I'm so afraid of ______________. 나는 뱀을 매우 무서워한다.

10 He is good at singing folk ______________. 그는 민요를 잘 부른다.

B 빈 칸에 알맞은 단어를 고르세요.

1 Please call us as soon as ______________.
① asleep ② possible ③ impossible ④ order ⑤ alike

2 My father was a ______________ of a ship.
① captain ② scene ③ man ④ reader ⑤ mission

Day 10

MP3

226 **overcome** [òuvərkʌ́m]
동 극복하다 overcome-overcame-overcome
overcome differences 차이를 극복하다

227 **host** [houst]
명 주최자 동 (행사, 파티 등을) 주최하다 host-hosted-hosted
a kind and generous host 친절하고 관대한 주인

228 **snowy** [snóui]
형 눈이 오는
a snowy day 눈이 오는 날 a snowy mountain 눈 덮인 산

229 **among** [əmʌ́ŋ]
전 ~의 사이에
among the trees 나무들 사이에 among students 학생들 사이에

230 **beg** [beg]
동 간청(애원)하다, 구걸하다 beg-begged-begged
beg for help 도움을 간청하다 beg for money 돈을 구걸하다

231 **change** [tʃeindʒ]
명 변화 동 변하다 change-changed-changed
change your mind 마음을 바꾸다 need a change 변화가 필요하다

232 **classical** [klǽsikl]
형 고전의, 고전적인 +classic 형 최고 수준의, 대표적인
a classical ballet 고전 발레 classical novel 고전 소설

233 **confident** [kɑ́nfidənt]
형 자신감 있는 명 confidence 자신(감)
a confident girl 자신감 있는 소녀 be confident of ~에 자신있다

234 **short** [ʃɔːrt]
형 짧은 short-shorter-shortest
a short story 짧은 이야기 a short skirt 짧은 치마

235 **drawer** [drɔːr]
명 서랍
the top drawer 윗서랍 an empty drawer 빈 서랍

236 **flood** [flʌd]
명 홍수 동 범람하다, 물에 잠기다 flood-flooded-flooded
a dangerous flood 위험한 홍수 flood a village 마을을 물에 잠기게 하다

237 **giant** [dʒáiənt]
형 거대한 명 거인
a giant house 거대한 집 a giant in the movie 영화 속 거인

238 **serious** [sí(ː)əriəs]
형 심각한 부 seriously 심각하게
a serious problem 심각한 문제 serious damage 심각한 손상

Daily Test

| 월 일 |

A 우리말에 맞게 빈 칸에 알맞은 단어를 쓰세요.

1 I should ______________ my fear of flying. 나는 비행에 대한 공포를 극복해야 한다.

2 We climbed to the top of the ______________ hill.
우리는 눈 오는 언덕 꼭대기에 올라갔다.

3 A small lake was seen ______________ the trees. 나무들 사이로 작은 호수가 보였다.

4 She needs to ______________ her hair style. 그녀는 머리스타일을 바꿀 필요가 있다.

5 We are ______________ of winning the soccer game.
우리는 축구경기에서 이길 자신이 있다.

6 I heard a ______________ story about the universe.
나는 우주에 대한 짧은 이야기를 들었다.

7 Susan opened her white ______________. Susan은 그녀의 흰 서랍을 열었다.

8 Yujin lost her house because of the ______________.
유진은 홍수 때문에 그녀의 집을 잃었다.

9 I want to live in a ______________ house. 나는 거대한 집에서 살고 싶다.

10 She has a ______________ problem with her health. 그녀는 건강에 심각한 문제가 있다.

B 빈 칸에 알맞은 단어를 고르세요.

1 Seoul ______________ the Olympics in 1988.
① made ② closed ③ overcome ④ hosted ⑤ visited

2 He is reading a ______________ novel.
① classical ② before ③ class ④ among ⑤ snowy

3 The man in the street ______________ for food.
① hosted ② begged ③ serious ④ bagged ⑤ nodded

Day 10

MP3

239 laugh [læf]
명 웃음 동 웃다 laugh-laughed-laughed
laugh at ~을 비웃다 laugh at his accent 그의 말투를 비웃다

240 light [lait]
명 빛, 전등 형 밝은 유 bright 밝은
a light bulb 전구 a light color 밝은 색

241 marathon [mǽrəθɑ̀n]
명 마라톤
the LA Marathon LA 마라톤 run a marathon 마라톤을 뛰다

242 nod [nɑd]
동 (고개를) 끄덕이다 명 끄덕임 nod-nodded-nodded
nod one's head 고개를 끄덕이다

243 palm [pɑːm]
명 손바닥
open your palm 손바닥을 펴다 on the right palm 오른쪽 손바닥 위에

244 praise [preiz]
동 칭찬하다 명 칭찬 praise-praised-praised
praise for her courage 그녀의 용기를 칭찬하다

245 prison [prízən]
명 감옥
escape from a prison 감옥에서 탈출하다 in prison 수감 중이다

246 roll [roul]
명 두루마리, 통 동 굴리다, 구르다 roll-rolled-rolled
a roll of paper 종이 한 통 roll a ball 공을 굴리다

247 schedule [skédʒuːl]
명 일정 유 timetable 시간표
a train schedule 열차 시간표 on schedule 일정대로

248 difference [dífərəns]
명 차이
a small difference 작은 차이 learn the difference 차이를 배우다

249 steak [steik]
명 스테이크
pork steak 돼지고기 스테이크 a steak knife 스테이크용 칼

250 straight [streit]
형 곧은 부 똑바로
short straight hair 짧고 곧은 머리 walk straight 똑바로 걷다

Daily Test

| 월 일 |

A 우리말에 맞게 빈 칸에 알맞은 단어를 쓰세요.

1 There is a street ______________ in front of my house.
우리 집 앞에는 가로등이 있다.

2 Juhyung won the Japan ______________ last month.
주형은 지난 달에 일본 마라톤에서 우승했다.

3 She ______________ to Harry. 그녀는 Harry에게 고개를 끄덕였다.

4 He put some candies in my left ______________. 그는 내 왼쪽 손바닥에 사탕을 주었다.

5 We ______________ James for his kind attitude. 우리는 James의 친절한 태도를 칭찬했다.

6 The boy is ______________ a ball in the playground.
소년은 운동장에서 공을 굴리고 있다.

7 The performance will start on ______________. 공연은 예정대로 시작 할 겁니다.

8 I can't tell the ______________ between the two designs.
나는 두 디자인의 차이점을 모르겠다.

9 Today's dinner is beef ______________. 오늘 저녁은 소고기 스테이크에요.

10 He looked me ______________ in the eye. 그는 내 눈을 똑바로 쳐다보았다.

B 빈 칸에 알맞은 단어를 고르세요.

1 Some people ______________ at my new coat.
① laughter ② palm ③ saw ④ changed ⑤ laughed

2 The woman spent three years in ______________ for her crime.
① person ② prison ③ schedule ④ marathon ⑤ lake

Review Test 05 Day 09 + Day 10 | 월 일 |

A 우리말에 맞게 빈 칸에 알맞은 단어를 쓰세요.

1 escape from a ________________ 감옥에서 탈출하다

2 treat ________________ 차별없이 대우하다

3 ________________ and effect 원인과 결과

4 follow an ________________ 명령을 따르다

5 ________________ for Helen's birthday party Helen의 생일파티를 준비하다

6 on ________________ 일정대로

7 ________________ the trees 나무들 사이에

8 ________________ at ~을 비웃다

9 open your ________________ 손바닥을 펴다

10 walk ________________ 똑바로 걷다

B 다음 영어 풀이에 알맞은 어휘를 〈보기〉에서 고르세요.

보기	steak	emperor	giant	captain	costume

1 ____________ : clothing that a group of people wear for a particular purpose

2 ____________ : someone who is very tall, strong, and powerful

3 ____________ : a person who rules a group of nations or peoples

4 ____________ : a person who commands and controls a ship or an airplane

5 ____________ : a thick and flat slice of meat, usually of beef

C 다음 단어의 관계가 A:B=C:D가 되도록 알맞은 단어를 골라 빈 칸에 적으세요.

1 overcome : ________________ = break : broke

① overcomed ② overcame ③ overcomes
④ overcoming ⑤ overcamed

2 possible : ________________ = polite : impolite

① unpossible ② ilpossible ③ expossible
④ impossible ⑤ inpossible

3 ________________ : movie = move : box

① recommend ② horror ③ British
④ good ⑤ escape

4 happy : happiness = different : ________________

① differ ② differenty ③ differents
④ differently ⑤ difference

5 serious : ________________ = brave : bravely

① serial ② seriously ③ seriouslly
④ seriousness ⑤ seriouses

D 문맥에 맞게 다음 문장을 완성하세요.

1	Can you lend	a	begged for food.
2	She needs to change	b	her hair style.
3	Jimmy set a new	c	me your car tomorrow?
4	The man in the street	d	a book that was on the ground.
5	The boy picked up	e	American baseball record.

E 문장을 읽고 문맥에 적절한 단어를 고르세요.

1 Yunji is doing a lot of exercise to keep her from getting (fat/serious).

2 Tommy, this question is too difficult. Can you give me a (host/hint)?

3 Hannah, I forgot to bring my pencil case. Can you (lend/lead) me a pencil?

4 The teacher (praised/regretted) his students for keeping the classroom clean.

5 After the weather got cold, the number of people running in the morning (decreased/flooded).

F 문장의 빈칸에 알맞은 단어를 〈보기〉에서 찾아 쓰세요. (필요하면 형태를 고치세요.)

보기	confident	nod	drawer	host	article

1 He signalled his agreement by ____________ his head.
그는 고개를 끄덕여서 동의를 표시했다.

2 Brian is ____________ about finishing the project on time.
Brian은 프로젝트를 제 시간에 끝내는 것을 자신하고 있다.

3 The ____________ of the party told us that we could bring our parents with us.
그 파티의 주최자는 우리에게 부모님도 데려 올 수 있다고 말했다.

4 Today's newspapers are full of ____________ about the accident.
오늘 자 신문들은 모두 그 사고에 대한 기사들로 가득하다.

5 I keep my socks and towels in the bottom ____________ of my closet.
나는 양말과 수건은 옷장 맨 아래 서랍에 보관한다.

G 그림에 해당하는 낱말을 〈보기〉에서 골라 쓰세요.

1 
(　　　　　　)

2 
(　　　　　　)

3 
(　　　　　　)

4 
(　　　　　　)

5 
(　　　　　　)

6 
(　　　　　　)

보기 roll flood snowy light war marathon

Study More

'사이'를 나타내는 between vs. among의 구별

- [between] : 주로 '두 개의 독립된 혹은 동등한 자격을 가진 개체일 때'
- [among] : 주로 '집합적인 성격을 가지는 개체와 구성원의 자격이 일정하지 않을 때'
- [비교] : **between** you and me (O) vs. among you and me (X)
  between the members of the group (X) vs. **among** the members of the group (O)
  an agreement (**between**/~~among~~) Korea, Japan, and China 한국, 일본, 중국 사이의 동의
  *독립적이며 동등한 자격을 가진 개체에 대해서는 between 사용 가능

Day 11

MP3

251 **access** [ǽksès]
동 접근하다, 접속하다 명 접근 형 accessible 접근 가능한
easy to access 접근하기 쉬운 access the Internet 인터넷에 접속하다

252 **mushroom** [mʌ́ʃru(:)m]
명 버섯
fresh mushrooms 신선한 버섯 mushroom soup 버섯 수프

253 **ability** [əbíləti]
명 능력, 역량 유 capability 능력, 역량
ability in music 음악적 역량 unique ability 독특한 능력

254 **pale** [peil]
형 (얼굴) 창백한, 색이 옅은 pale-paler-palest
a pale face 창백한 얼굴 pale blue 옅은 파랑색

255 **avoid** [əvɔ́id]
동 피하다 avoid-avoided-avoided
avoid the war 전쟁을 피하다 avoid a big accident 큰 사고를 피하다

256 **blanket** [blǽŋkit]
명 담요
a warm blanket 따뜻한 담요 pull up a blanket 담요를 덮다

257 **coffee** [kɔ́(:)fi]
명 커피
a cup of coffee 커피 한 잔 make coffee 커피를 끓이다

258 **diet** [dáiət]
명 식사, 다이어트
a healthy diet 건강한 식사 go on a diet 다이어트를 하다

259 **download** [dáunlòud]
동 파일을 내려받다 download-downloaded-downloaded
download songs from the Internet 인터넷에서 노래를 내려받다

260 **enough** [inʌ́f]
형 충분한 부 충분히
enough money 충분한 돈 strangely enough 기이하게도

261 **field** [fi:ld]
명 들판, 분야
a football field 축구장 in the music field 음악 분야에서

262 **glory** [glɔ́:ri]
명 영광, 명예, 영예 형 glorious 영광스러운
a moment of glory 영광의 순간 gain glory 명예를 얻다

263 **have** [həv]
동 먹다, 마시다 have-had-had
have breakfast 아침을 먹다 have delicious food 맛있는 음식을 먹다

Daily Test

| 월 일 |

A 우리말에 맞게 빈 칸에 알맞은 단어를 쓰세요.

1 We need some fresh ______________ to cook for dinner.
우리는 저녁 식사 준비를 위해서 신선한 버섯들이 필요하다.

2 Jina painted the wall in ______________ blue. Jina는 벽을 옅은 파랑색으로 칠했다.

3 We should ______________ the war. 우리는 전쟁을 피해야 한다.

4 He gave us some ______________. 그는 우리에게 담요 몇 벌을 주었다.

5 Cindy is drinking a cup of ______________. Cindy는 커피를 마시고 있다.

6 I ______________ a train schedule from the Internet.
나는 인터넷에서 열차 시간표를 내려받았다.

7 I don't have ______________ time to study. 나는 공부할 시간이 충분하지 않다.

8 Amy is famous in the medical ______________. Amy는 의학 분야에서 유명하다.

9 Soldiers fought for ______________ and victory. 병사들은 명예와 승리를 위해 싸웠다.

10 I want to ______________ sweet things. 나는 달콤한 게 먹고 싶어요.

B 빈 칸에 알맞은 단어를 고르세요.

1 It's easy to ______________ the Internet in this school.
① field ② access ③ blank ④ jump ⑤ roll

2 He has a great ______________ in math.
① able ② enough ③ ability ④ mushrooms ⑤ jump

3 Mary decided to go on a ______________.
① glory ② diet ③ coffee ④ health ⑤ field

Day 11

MP3

264 **mayor** [méiər]
명 시장
the mayor of Seoul 서울시장 a new mayor 새로운 시장

265 **master** [mǽstər]
동 완전히 익히다 명 대가, 주인 master-mastered-mastered
master the piano 피아노를 익히다 a chess master 체스 대가

266 **medal** [médəl]
명 메달
a bronze medal 동메달 a medal winner 메달리스트

267 **midnight** [mídnàit]
명 한밤중, 자정
study until midnight 자정까지 공부하다 a midnight snack 야식

268 **pot** [pɑt]
명 냄비, 솥, 병
a soup pot 수프 냄비 a flower pot 화분

269 **piece** [piːs]
명 한 부분, 조각
a piece of 하나의 a piece of cake 케이크 한 조각

270 **relationship** [riléiʃənʃìp]
명 관계
a close relationship 긴밀한 관계 build a relationship 관계를 맺다

271 **save** [seiv]
동 구하다, 모으다, 저축하다 save-saved-saved
save money 돈을 모으다 save one's life ~의 생명을 구하다

272 **soon** [suːn]
부 곧, 머지않아 soon-sooner-soonest
See you soon! 곧 만나자! sooner or later 조만간

273 **stamp** [stæmp]
명 우표, 도장
collect stamps 우표를 모으다 get a stamp 도장을 받다

274 **stress** [stres]
명 스트레스, 압박, 긴장
stress level 스트레스 지수 under a lot of stress 스트레스를 받다

275 **style** [stail]
명 방식, 스타일 형 stylish 유행을 따르는, 멋진
a style of writing 글을 쓰는 방식 a new hair style 새로운 머리 스타일

Daily Test

| 월 일 |

A 우리말에 맞게 빈 칸에 알맞은 단어를 쓰세요.

1 The dog really loved his ______________. 그 개는 그의 주인을 굉장히 좋아했다.

2 Sue wants to win a gold ______________ in the PyeongChang Olympics. Sue는 평창 올림픽에서 금메달을 따기 원한다.

3 It started to snow around ______________. 자정 무렵에 눈이 내리기 시작했다.

4 Boil some water in the ______________. 냄비에 물을 좀 끓이세요.

5 Juna and I keep a good ______________. Juna와 나는 좋은 관계를 유지하고 있다.

6 We will take a taxi to ______________ time. 우리는 시간을 아끼기 위해 택시를 탈 거예요.

7 She will ______________ be 15 years old. 그녀는 곧 15살이 될 것이다.

8 You can buy ______________ at the nearby post office. 가까운 우체국에서 우표를 살 수 있다.

9 Many people are under a lot of ______________ these days. 오늘 날 많은 사람들이 스트레스를 받고 있다.

10 I love her ______________ of cooking. 나는 그녀의 요리 방식을 좋아한다.

B 빈 칸에 알맞은 단어를 고르세요.

1 Woojin is the new ______________ of Busan.

① master ② pot ③ stress ④ style ⑤ mayor

2 Can you give me a ______________ of paper?

① pieces ② bottle ③ piece ④ cup ⑤ can

Day 12

MP3

276 **cute** [kju:t]

형 귀여운 cute-cuter-cutest

a cute doll 귀여운 인형 a cute baby 귀여운 아기

277 **manner** [mǽnər]

명 방식, 태도, 예의

a kind manner 친절한 태도 learn table manners 식사 예절을 배우다

278 **special** [spéʃəl]

형 특별한 반 ordinary 일반적인

a special gift 특별한 선물 a special party 특별한 파티

279 **aloud** [əláud]

부 소리 내어, 큰 소리로

speak aloud 큰 소리로 말하다 read aloud 큰 소리로 읽다

280 **basic** [béisik]

형 기본적인, 기초적인

basic information 기초적인 정보 basic steps 기본 단계들

281 **borrow** [bárou]

동 빌리다 borrow-borrowed-borrowed

borrow money 돈을 빌리다 borrow books 책을 빌리다

282 **climate** [kláimit]

명 기후

a warm climate 따뜻한 기후 climate change 기후 변화

283 **complain** [kəmpléin]

동 불평하다, 항의하다 complain-complained-complained

complain about the result 결과에 대해 불평하다

284 **effort** [éfərt]

명 노력, 수고 유 attempt 시도

a lot of effort 많은 노력 make an effort 노력하다

285 **favor** [féivər]

명 호의, 친절, 부탁

return the favor 은혜를 갚다 with favor 호의적으로

286 **full** [ful]

형 가득한, 배가 부른

be full of ~로 가득하다 be full of energy 힘이 가득하다

287 **guide** [gaid]

명 여행 가이드, 안내자 동 안내하다 guide-guided-guided

a tour guide 관광 안내인 a guide to France 프랑스 관광 안내서

288 **increase** [ínkriːs]

명 증가, 인상 동 증가하다 increase-increased-increased

price increase 가격 인상 increase speed 속도를 올리다

Daily Test

| 월 일 |

A **우리말에 맞게 빈 칸에 알맞은 단어를 쓰세요.**

1 Helen's hat is so ______________. Helen의 모자는 귀엽다.

2 She spoke in a friendly ______________. 그녀는 다정한 태도로 말했다.

3 There is a ______________ event for students tomorrow.
내일 학생들을 위한 특별한 행사가 있을 것이다.

4 I read Sam's letter ______________ to my family.
나는 가족들에게 큰 소리로 Sam의 편지를 읽어주었다.

5 Jimmy ______________ a book from Tina. Jimmy는 Tina에게 책을 빌렸다.

6 The ______________ of Korea is wet in summer. 한국의 여름 기후는 습하다.

7 She always ______________ about food. 그녀는 늘 음식에 대해 불평한다.

8 You need to put in a lot of ______________ to win the race.
경주에서 이기기 위해서 많은 노력을 해야 한다.

9 Can I ask you a ______________? 부탁 하나 해도 될까요?

10 She will ______________ us to the museum. 그녀가 우리를 박물관으로 안내해 줄 것이다.

B **빈 칸에 알맞은 단어를 고르세요.**

1 There are four ______________ steps to writing a novel.
① cute ② basic ③ favor ④ effort ⑤ point

2 The hall is ______________ of students.
① quite ② special ③ sample ④ full ⑤ pull

3 The price of books ______________.
① upstairs ② guided ③ increased ④ aloud ⑤ ancient

Day 12

MP3

289 **float** [flout]

동 (물 위에) 뜨다, 떠다니다 float-floated-floated

float on the river 강 위에 떠 다니다　float in the air 공중에 뜨다

290 **attract** [ətrǽkt]

동 끌다, 매혹하다 attract-attracted-attracted

attract attention 주의를 끌다　attract visitors 관광객을 끌다

291 **muscle** [mʌ́sl]

명 근육　형 muscular 근육의, 근육질의

a neck muscle 목 근육　relax a muscle 근육을 이완시키다

292 **point** [pɔint]

명 뾰족한 끝, 요점　동 가리키다, 겨루다

get to the point 본론으로 들어가다　point at a map 지도를 가리키다

293 **protect** [prətékt]

동 보호하다 protect-protected-protected

protect the earth 지구를 보호하다　protect nature 자연을 보호하다

294 **quite** [kwait]

부 꽤, 상당히

quite tall 상당히 키가 큰　quite tired 꽤 피곤한

295 **riddle** [rídl]

명 수수께끼　유 mystery 수수께끼

solve a riddle 수수께끼를 풀다　a difficult riddle 어려운 수수께끼

296 **screen** [skriːn]

명 화면, 스크린

a cinema screen 영화관 스크린　a large screen 대형 화면

297 **solve** [sɑlv]

동 해결하다, (문제를) 풀다 solve-solved-solved

solve a difficult problem 어려운 문제를 풀다

298 **accident** [ǽksidənt]

명 사고, 우연　형 accidental 우연한

a car accident 자동차 사고　by accident 우연히

299 **sample** [sǽmpl]

명 견본, 샘플

a free sample 무료 샘플　a blood sample 혈액 샘플

300 **sudden** [sʌ́dən]

형 갑작스러운

a sudden change 갑작스런 변화　a sudden success 갑작스러운 성공

Daily Test

| 월 일 |

A 우리말에 맞게 빈 칸에 알맞은 단어를 쓰세요.

1 The program ______________ a lot of attention from viewers.
그 프로그램은 많은 사람들로부터 관심을 끌었다.

2 This exercise is helpful to develop the shoulder ______________.
이 운동은 어깨 근육을 키우는 데 도움이 된다.

3 I think Jimin missed the ______________. 내 생각에 지민은 요점을 놓친 것 같다.

4 He is ______________ good at dancing. 그는 꽤 춤을 잘 춘다.

5 Can you solve this ______________? 너 이 수수께끼를 풀 수 있니?

6 I like to watch movies on the large ______________.
나는 대형 화면으로 영화를 보는 것을 좋아한다.

7 Brian failed to ______________ the science problem.
Brian은 그 과학문제를 푸는 데 실패했다.

8 There was a terrible ______________ last night. 지난 밤에 끔찍한 사고가 있었다.

9 Here is a free ______________ from our new menu.
여기 저희의 신 메뉴 무료 시식 샘플이 있어요.

10 We were surprised by the ______________ noise.
우리는 갑작스런 소음때문에 깜짝 놀랐다.

B 빈 칸에 알맞은 단어를 고르세요.

1 The bottle was ______________ on the river.
① floating ② point ③ float ④ floatted ⑤ solving

2 I ______________ my little sister from mosquitos.
① pointed ② solved ③ borrowed ④ protected ⑤ lived

A 우리말에 맞게 빈 칸에 알맞은 단어를 쓰세요.

1 unique ________________ 독특한 능력

2 pull up a ________________ 담요를 덮다

3 ________________ breakfast 아침을 먹다

4 a close ________________ 긴밀한 관계

5 ________________ or later 조만간

6 a difficult ________________ 어려운 수수께끼

7 ________________ about the result 결과에 대해 불평하다

8 ________________ visitors 관광객을 끌다

9 ________________ tall 상당히 키가 큰

10 a blood ________________ 혈액 샘플

B 다음 영어 풀이에 알맞은 어휘를 〈보기〉에서 고르세요.

보기	mayor	pot	basic	climate	piece

1 ____________ : a person who officially governs a city or town

2 ____________ : the usual weather patterns or conditions in an area or place

3 ____________ : a deep and round container used for cooking

4 ____________ : necessary and important to make or understand things

5 ____________ : a thing or part separated or cut from the whole

C 다음 단어의 관계가 A:B=C:D가 되도록 알맞은 단어를 골라 빈 칸에 적으세요.

1 access : ________________ = taste : tasty

① accessible ② accessty ③ accesses
④ accessiblity ⑤ accessed

2 attract : ________________ = visit : visited

① attraction ② attracts ③ attractly
④ attracted ⑤ attractied

3 ________________ : doll = curly : hair

① girl ② cute ③ make
④ ribbon ⑤ play

4 terrible : ________________ = popular : actor

① awful ② last ③ real
④ telephone ⑤ accident

5 make : ________________ = paint : wall

① made ② Olympics ③ effort
④ nod ⑤ concerned

D 문맥에 맞게 다음 문장을 완성하세요.

1	Soldiers fought for	a	a cup of coffee.
2	You can buy stamps	b	glory and victory.
3	We were surprised	c	by the sudden noise.
4	Cindy is drinking	d	on the large screen.
5	I like to watch movies	e	at the nearby post office.

E 문장을 읽고 문맥에 적절한 단어를 고르세요.

1 After seeing a doctor, she (saves/avoids) eating meat.

2 Dan, can I ask you a (riddle/favor)? I need to bring these boxes upstairs.

3 Pam (increased/borrowed) the amount of work she did to make more money.

4 He doesn't have (full/enough) money to buy a new car.

5 If you want to join the club, please (download/master) a membership application form from our website.

F 문장의 빈칸에 알맞은 단어를 〈보기〉에서 찾아 쓰세요. (필요하면 형태를 고치세요.)

보기	complain	special	protect	borrow	manner

1 Bill always ____________ about food.
Bill은 항상 음식에 대해 불평을 한다.

2 You can ____________ up to three books at a time from the school library.
여러분은 학교 도서관에서 책을 한 번에 세 권까지 빌릴 수 있습니다.

3 Today we have a very ____________ guest who will surprise you.
우리는 오늘 여러분을 놀라게 할 특별한 손님이 있습니다.

4 Washing your hands regularly will ____________ you from colds.
손을 자주 씻는 것이 여러분을 감기로부터 보호해 줄 것입니다.

5 My mother praised Matt for his polite ____________.
어머니는 Matt의 예의 바른 태도를 칭찬하셨다.

G 그림과 낱말이 잘못 짝지어진 것을 고르세요. ( )

ⓐ

favor

ⓑ

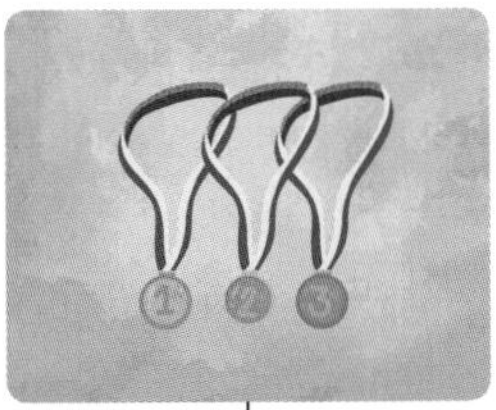

medal

ⓒ

mushrooms

ⓓ

stress

H 낱말과 어울리는 그림을 연결하세요.

1 float •

2 muscles •

• ⓐ

• ⓑ

Study More

piece의 용법

- piece는 주로 불가산명사(e.g. furniture)에 대한 셀 수 있는 단위를 제공한다.
  a **piece of** information/advice/furniture/wood/cloth
  정보 한 가지, 충고 하나, 가구 하나, 나무 한 조각, 옷감 한 조각 *a furniture (X) an information (X)
- 'a piece of cake'는 숙어로서 '아주 쉬운 일, 식은 죽 먹기' 의 뜻이 있다.
  How was the exam?-It was a piece of cake. 시험은 어땠어?-아주 쉬웠어.

Day 13

MP3

301 **tire** [taiər]
명 타이어 동 피곤하게 하다, 지치다 tire-tired-tired
a flat tire 바람 빠진 타이어 tire easily 쉽게 피로해지다

302 **speech** [spiːtʃ]
명 연설 유 address 연설
make a speech / give a speech 연설을 하다

303 **next** [nekst]
형 다음의 부 다음에, 옆에
the next chapter 다음 장 live next door 옆집에 살다

304 **be ashamed of** [bi əʃéimd ʌv]
~을 부끄러워하다
be ashamed of her behavior 그녀의 행동을 부끄러워하다

305 **battle** [bǽtl]
명 전투 동 싸우다 battle-battled-battled
a violent battle 격렬한 전투 battle for freedom 자유를 위해 싸우다

306 **blame** [bleim]
동 ~을 탓하다, 비난하다 blame-blamed-blamed
blame John for the accident 사고에 대해 John을 비난하다

307 **cave** [keiv]
명 동굴
a cave near the ocean 바다 근처에 있는 동굴

308 **connect** [kənékt]
동 연결하다 connect-connected-connected
connect a computer to the Internet 컴퓨터를 인터넷에 연결하다

309 **dense** [dens]
형 빽빽한, 밀집한
a dense forest 빽빽한 숲 a dense fog 짙은 안개

310 **event** [ivént]
명 사건, 행사
a special event 특별한 행사 hold an event 행사를 열다

311 **flash** [flæʃ]
명 섬광, 번쩍임 동 번쩍이다 flash-flashed-flashed
a flash of light 불빛의 번쩍임 flash a light 전등을 비추다

312 **gain** [gein]
동 얻다, 늘다 gain-gained-gained
gain weight 무게가 늘다 gain information 정보를 얻다

313 **ill** [il]
형 아픈, 병 든 ill-worse-worst 명 illness 병, 아픔
feel ill 아프다 be ill from a fever 고열로 앓다

Daily Test

| 월 일 |

A 우리말에 맞게 빈 칸에 알맞은 단어를 쓰세요.

1 Roy made a ______________ on climate change. Roy는 기후 변화에 대한 연설을 했다.

2 Let's go to the theater ______________ time. 다음에는 극장에 가자.

3 Many people ______________ for freedom. 많은 사람들이 자유를 위해 싸웠다.

4 People ______________ him for the terrible accident.
사람들은 그 끔찍한 사고에 대해 그를 비난했다.

5 There is a big ______________ near our village. 우리 마을 근처에 큰 동굴이 있다.

6 The bridge ______________ the two islands. 그 다리는 두 섬을 이어준다.

7 Our school will hold a special ______________ next Monday.
우리 학교는 다음주 월요일에 특별한 행사를 열 예정이다.

8 There was a ______________ of lightening in the dark sky.
어두운 하늘에 번개가 번쩍였다.

9 I want to ______________ new experiences. 나는 새로운 경험을 얻고 싶다.

10 The baby was ______________ from a fever. 그 아기는 고열로 앓았다.

B 빈 칸에 알맞은 단어를 고르세요.

1 He was ______________ because he couldn't sleep well last night.
① happy ② next ③ flash ④ tired ⑤ fever

2 She was ______________ of herself for being late.
① mine ② ashamed ③ blamed ④ mild ⑤ melted

3 A ______________ fog is forecast for tomorrow.
① bright ② flash ③ dense ④ battle ⑤ pork

Day 13

MP3

314	**wolf** [wulf]	명 늑대 / 복 wolves a pack of wolves 늑대 무리 / a lone wolf 혼자 있기를 선호하는 사람
315	**melt** [melt]	동 녹다, 녹이다 melt-melted-melted melt the ice 얼음을 녹이다 / start to melt 녹기 시작하다
316	**mild** [maild]	형 온화한, 순한, 따뜻한 mild-milder-mildest a mild climate 온화한 기후 / a mild soap 순한 비누
317	**parrot** [pǽrət]	명 앵무새 a pet parrot 애완용 앵무새 / play the parrot 남의 흉내를 내다
318	**pork** [pɔːrk]	명 돼지고기 / +beef 명 소고기 roast pork 구운 돼지고기 / pork sausage 돼지고기 소시지
319	**reduce** [ridjúːs]	동 줄이다, 낮추다 reduce-reduced-reduced reduce speed 속도를 줄이다 / reduce weight 무게를 줄이다
320	**rope** [roup]	명 줄, 밧줄 a short rope 짧은 줄 / a jump rope 줄넘기 줄
321	**seem** [siːm]	동 ~처럼 보이다 seem-seemed-seemed seem happy 행복해 보이다 / seem young 어리게 보이다
322	**soil** [sɔil]	명 흙, 토양 rich soil 비옥한 토양 / sandy soil 모래가 많은 토양
323	**adult** [ədʌ́lt]	명 어른, 성인 / 유 grown-up 어른 become an adult 성인이 되다 / an adult learner 성인 학습자
324	**surface** [sə́ːrfis]	명 표면, 수면 the surface of the water 수면 / an even surface 평평한 표면
325	**take** [teik]	동 잡다, 획득하다, 먹다 take-took-taken take her hand 그녀의 손을 잡다 / Take your pick. 골라봐.

Daily Test

| 월 일 |

A 우리말에 맞게 빈 칸에 알맞은 단어를 쓰세요.

1 There are a pack of ______________ in the forest. 숲 속에 늑대 무리가 있다.

2 Boil the water until the chocolate ______________. 초코릿이 녹을 때까지 물을 끓여라.

3 Today is ______________ and sunny. 오늘은 따뜻하고 화창하다.

4 She has a pet ______________. 그녀는 애완용 앵무새가 있다.

5 Jack loves roast ______________. Jack은 구운 돼지고기를 좋아한다.

6 Jane tries to ______________ weight. Jane은 몸무게를 줄이려고 노력한다.

7 This book ______________ interesting. 이 책은 재미있어 보인다.

8 This movie is good for kids and ______________. 이 영화는 아이들과 어른들에게 좋다.

9 Mom cleaned the ______________ of the table with a cloth.
엄마는 천으로 탁자의 표면을 닦았다.

10 The boy ______________ his father's arm. 소년은 자기 아버지의 팔을 잡았다.

B 빈 칸에 알맞은 단어를 고르세요.

1 They tied their boxes with a ______________.
① wolves ② pork ③ cave ④ connection ⑤ rope

2 Flowers can grow well in rich ______________.
① muscle ② soil ③ sky ④ water ⑤ cage

Day 14

MP3

326 **cancel** [kǽnsəl]
동 취소하다 cancel-cancelled-cancelled
cancel a party 파티를 취소하다 cancel a trip 여행을 취소하다

327 **criticize** [kritisaiz]
동 비난하다, 비평하다 criticize-criticized-criticized
criticize the players 선수들을 비난하다

328 **against** [əgénst]
전 ~에 반대하여
be against ~에 반대하다 against violence 폭력에 반대하여

329 **basement** [béismənt]
명 지하실
in a basement 지하실에서 a basement garage 지하 주차장

330 **belong to** [biló(:)ŋ tu]
동 ~에 속하다 belong-belonged-belonged
belong to the same class 같은 반 소속이다

331 **calendar** [kǽləndər]
명 달력
a desk calendar 탁상 달력 check the calendar 달력을 넘겨보다

332 **colorful** [kʌ́lərfəl]
형 다채로운, 화려한
colorful clothes 화려한 옷 colorful leaves 형형색색의 나뭇잎

333 **deliver** [dilívər]
동 배달하다, 연설을 하다 deliver-delivered-delivered
deliver a letter 편지를 배달하다 deliver a lecture 강의를 하다

334 **dew** [dju:]
명 이슬 형 dewy 이슬 맺힌
morning dew 아침 이슬 wet with dew 이슬에 젖은

335 **envelope** [énvəlòup]
명 봉투
an airmail envelope 항공우편 봉투 open an envelope 봉투를 열다

336 **safe** [seif]
형 안전한 명 safety 안전
a safe place 안전한 장소 be safe for children 아이들에게 안전하다

337 **garbage** [gá:rbidʒ]
명 쓰레기 유 rubbish 쓰레기
be full of garbage 쓰레기로 가득 차다 a garbage can 쓰레기 통

338 **jail** [dʒeil]
명 감옥, 투옥 유 prison 감옥, 교도소
released from jail 감옥에서 석방되다 break jail 탈옥하다

Daily Test

| 월 일 |

A 우리말에 맞게 빈 칸에 알맞은 단어를 쓰세요.

1 The man was ______________ for his bad behavior.
그 사람은 좋지 못한 행동때문에 비난 받았다.

2 We are ______________ the war. 우리는 전쟁에 반대한다.

3 They walked down to the ______________. 그들은 지하실로 걸어 내려갔다.

4 Peter and I ______________ to the same soccer club.
Peter와 나는 같은 축구 동아리 소속이다.

5 Look at the ______________ and check Tim's birthday.
달력을 보고 Tim의 생일을 확인해봐.

6 She wears a ______________ skirt today. 그녀는 오늘 화려한 치마를 입었다.

7 The grass was wet with ______________. 잔디가 이슬에 젖어있었다.

8 Grandfather gave me concert tickets in an ______________.
할아버지는 봉투에 콘서트 표를 넣어서 내게 주셨다.

9 This toy is ______________ for children. 이 장난감은 아이들에게 안전하다.

10 The man will be released from ______________ next week.
그 남자는 다음 주에 감옥에서 석방 될 것이다.

B 빈 칸에 알맞은 단어를 고르세요.

1 We ______________ the trip because of the storm.
① went ② liked ③ canceled ④ enjoyed ⑤ planned

2 Mr. Lee will ______________ a lecture on Korean history next Saturday.
① deliver ② like ③ basement ④ dew ⑤ recycle

3 Don't throw your ______________ away here.
① garage ② go ③ garbage ④ surface ⑤ partner

Day 14

MP3

339 **land** [lænd]
명 땅 동 착륙하다 land-landed-landed
flat land 평평한 땅 land safely 안전하게 착륙하다

340 **wave** [weiv]
명 파도, 파장, 흔들기 동 흔들다
ride the waves 파도를 타다 wave flags 깃발을 흔들다

341 **neighbor** [néibər]
명 이웃 사람
invite neighbors 이웃들을 초대하다 a next-door neighbor 옆집 사람

342 **partner** [pá:rtnər]
명 동반자, 동료 유 companion 동반자
a business partner 사업 동반자 a dancing partner 무용 파트너

343 **produce** [prádju:s]
동 생산하다 produce-produced-produced
produce cars 차를 생산하다 produce oil 석유를 생산하다

344 **recycle** [ri:sáikl]
동 재활용하다 recycle-recycled-recycled
recycle paper 종이를 재활용하다 recycle bottles 병을 재활용하다

345 **sail** [seil]
동 항해하다, (배를) 조종하다 sail-sailed-sailed
sail across the ocean 대양을 가로질러 항해하다

346 **set** [set]
동 놓다, (시계를) 맞추다, (표준, 규칙, 기록을) 세우다 set-set-set
set her hat down 그녀의 모자를 내려놓다

347 **sneeze** [sni:z]
동 재채기하다 명 재채기 sneeze-sneezed-sneezed
sneeze all day 하루 종일 재채기 하다 hold a sneeze 재채기를 참다

348 **stupid** [stjú:pid]
형 어리석은 유 foolish 어리석은
a stupid mistake 어리석은 실수 a stupid boy 어리석은 소년

349 **strange** [streindʒ]
형 이상한, 낯선 명 stranger 낯선 사람
a strange thing 이상한 일 a strange place 낯선 장소

350 **tale** [teil]
명 이야기, 설화
a romantic tale 낭만적인 이야기 tales of the Indians 인디언들의 이야기

Daily Test

| 월 일 |

A 우리말에 맞게 빈 칸에 알맞은 단어를 쓰세요.

1 Yuna loves to listen to the sound of the ______________.
유나는 파도 소리 듣는 것을 좋아한다.

2 William is my good ______________. William은 내 좋은 이웃이다.

3 Jungmin is an excellent tennis ______________. 정민은 훌륭한 테니스 상대이다.

4 We should ______________ metal and glass. 우리는 금속과 유리를 재활용해야 한다.

5 My uncle ______________ his ship to Jeju Island.
삼촌은 그의 배를 조종하여 제주도로 갔다.

6 Hyunsuk ______________ the alarm for 6 a.m. 현석은 그의 시계를 아침 6시에 맞추었다.

7 The baby ______________ all night. 아기는 밤새 재채기를 했다.

8 I think it's a very ______________ idea. 나는 그게 아주 어리석은 생각같아.

9 In my dream, I was in a ______________ city. 꿈 속에서 나는 낯선 도시에 있었다.

10 Sarah told her sons ______________ tales.
Sarah는 그녀의 아들들에게 재미있는 이야기를 해주었다.

B 빈 칸에 알맞은 단어를 고르세요.

1 The factory ______________ light bulbs.
① waves ② saving ③ produces ④ opens ⑤ basement

2 The plane ______________ safely.
① sneezed ② landed ③ belonged ④ closed ⑤ sailed

Review Test 07

Day 13 + Day 14 | 월 일 |

A 우리말에 맞게 빈 칸에 알맞은 단어를 쓰세요.

1 ______________ John for the accident 사고에 대해 John을 비난하다

2 ______________ a light 전등을 비추다

3 a ______________ place 낯선 장소

4 rich ______________ 비옥한 토양

5 ______________ her hand 그녀의 손을 잡다

6 open an ______________ 봉투를 열다

7 ______________ a lecture 강의를 하다

8 break ______________ 탈옥하다

9 ______________ paper 종이를 재활용하다

10 a ______________ mistake 어리석은 실수

B 다음 영어 풀이에 알맞은 어휘를 〈보기〉에서 고르세요.

보기	speech	calendar	neighbor	event	wolf

1 ____________ : something that happens or is held for a particular purpose

2 ____________ : charts or sheets showing days and months of a year

3 ____________ : someone who lives near or next to you

4 ____________ : a wild animal that looks like a dog and is related to foxes

5 ____________ : a talk given to an audience

C 다음 단어의 관계가 A:B=C:D가 되도록 알맞은 단어를 골라 빈 칸에 적으세요.

1 ________________ : tired = sleep : sleepy

① tire ② tiring ③ tires
④ tir ⑤ tireded

2 ________________ : schedule = fix : watch

① regular ② busy ③ cancel
④ tomorrow ⑤ go

3 dark : bright = child : ________________

① children ② baby ③ childish
④ woman ⑤ adult

4 safe : ________________ = kind : kindness

① safer ② safety ③ save
④ safeties ⑤ safely

5 book : novel = bird : ________________

① elephant ② animal ③ wing
④ parrot ⑤ dog

D 문맥에 맞게 다음 문장을 완성하세요.

1 Hyunsuk set •	• a a special event next Monday.
2 The man was criticized •	• b light bulbs.
3 Our school will hold •	• c down to the basement.
4 The factory produces •	• d for his bad behavior.
5 They walked •	• e the alarm for 6 a.m.

E 문장을 읽고 문맥에 적절한 단어를 고르세요.

1 The only way to (connect/conclude) the two villages is to build a new highway.

2 They compete (next/against) each other to win the prize.

3 He (seemed/set) nervous when he was waiting for the exam.

4 Dan's father used to own the watch. Now it (delivers/belongs) to Dan.

5 Eating healthy food can (reduce/deliver) the risks of heart disease.

F 문장의 빈칸에 알맞은 단어를 〈보기〉에서 찾아 쓰세요. (필요하면 형태를 고치세요.)

보기	battle	gain	dense	dew	ashamed

1 Jill was ____________ of her rude behavior at the meeting yesterday.
Jill은 어제 모임에서 자신의 무례한 행동이 창피했다.

2 A brief ____________ between the two countries developed into a major war.
두 나라 사이에 벌어진 짧은 전투는 대규모 전쟁으로 확대 되었다.

3 The flowers in the garden were wet with the morning ____________.
정원의 꽃들이 아침 이슬로 젖어 있었다.

4 Hojin searched all the newspapers to ____________ information on the product.
호진은 모든 그 제품에 대한 정보를 얻기 위해 모든 신문을 조사했다.

5 Because of the rain, it was difficult to walk through the ____________forest.
비 때문에 그 빽빽한 숲을 통해 걷는 것은 힘들었다.

G 그림에 해당하는 낱말을 〈보기〉에서 골라 쓰세요.

1
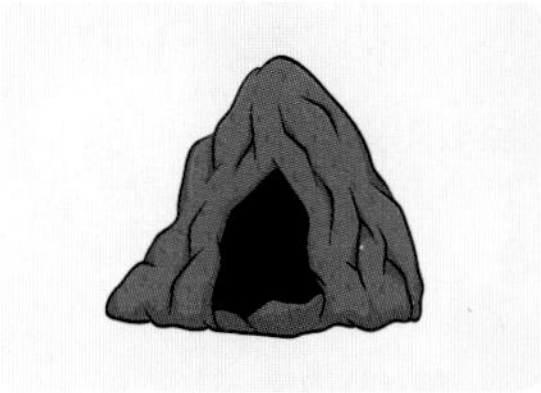
(   )

2
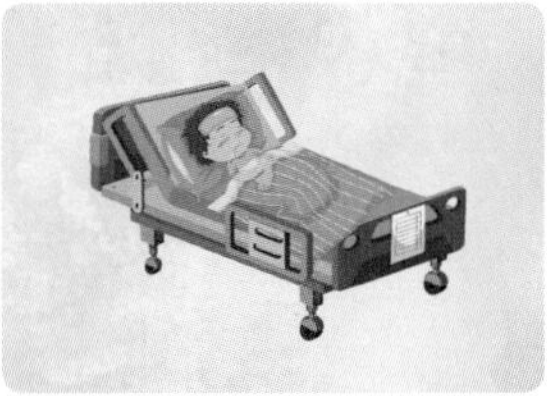
(   )

3

(   )

4

(   )

5

(   )

6

(   )

보기 garbage melt wave cave sneeze ill

Study More

'연결하다, 잇다' 와 비슷한 뜻을 가진 단어들

- join, link, associate, tie, unite, combine

The two cities are **joined** by a highway. 그 두 도시는 고속도로로 연결되어 있다.

Some people **associate** winter with skiing. 어떤 사람들은 겨울을 스키타기와 연관시킨다.

A camel was **tied** to a tree. 낙타 한 마리가 나무에 묶여 있었다.

He wanted to **combine** his experience with my knowledge.
그는 자신의 경험과 나의 지식을 결합하기를 원했다.

Day 15

MP3

351 **divide** [diváid]
동 나누다 divide-divided-divided 명 division 나누기, 분배
divide a cake into 3 pieces 케익을 세 조각으로 나누다

352 **popular** [pápjələr]
형 인기 있는, 대중적인 명 popularity 인기, 대중성
a popular American dish 인기 있는 미국 음식

353 **such** [sʌtʃ]
형 그러한, ~와 같은, 매우 ~한
such a great idea 아주 훌륭한 생각 such as ~와 같은

354 **announce** [ənáuns]
동 발표하다, 알리다 announce-announced-announced
announce a marriage 결혼을 발표하다

355 **campaign** [kæmpéin]
명 캠페인 동 캠페인을 벌이다 campaign-campaigned-campaigned
conduct a campaign 캠페인을 벌이다

356 **chapter** [tʃǽptər]
명 (책의) 장
the first chapter 첫 번째 장 a chapter on sailing 항해에 관한 장

357 **common** [kámən]
형 흔한, 보통의 유 usual 흔히 있는, 일상적인
a common name 흔한 이름 a common mistake 흔히 있는 실수

358 **cycle** [sáikl]
명 주기, 순환기, 자전기
a life cycle 생활 주기 a cycle track 자전거 도로

359 **draw** [drɔː]
동 그리다 draw-drew-drawn
draw pictures 그림을 그리다 draw a triangle 삼각형을 그리다

360 **exam** [igzǽm]
명 시험
take an exam 시험을 보다 pass an exam 시험에 통과하다

361 **fortune** [fɔ́ːrtʃən]
명 운, 재산, 부 형 fortunate 운이 좋은
have good fortune 운이 좋다 make a fortune 재산을 모으다

362 **however** [hauévər]
부 그러나, 그렇지만
However, he didn't come back. 그러나 그는 돌아오지 않았다.

363 **kill** [kil]
동 죽이다 kill-killed-killed
kill pigs 돼지들을 죽이다 kill time 시간을 보내다

Daily Test

| 월 일 |

A 우리말에 맞게 빈 칸에 알맞은 단어를 쓰세요.

1 Let's ______________ this pie into three pieces. 이 파이를 세 조각으로 나누자.

2 His novel is ______________ among teenagers. 그의 소설은 10대 사이에서 인기가 좋다.

3 Colors ______________ as green and red are my favorites. 녹색과 빨간색 같은 색은 내가 가장 좋아하는 색깔이다.

4 Tim and Linda ______________ their marriage last week. 지난 주 Tim과 Linda는 그들의 결혼을 발표했다.

5 Calm down. It's a ______________ mistake. 진정해. 이건 흔히 있는 실수야.

6 I rode a bike at a ______________ track. 나는 자전거 도로에서 자전거를 탔다.

7 Kihyuk likes to ______________ cartoons during his free time. 기혁은 쉬는 동안에 만화를 그리는 것을 좋아한다.

8 Some students didn't pass the graduation ______________. 몇몇 학생들은 졸업 시험을 통과하지 못했다.

9 Mr. Park made a ______________ from selling cakes. Mr. Park은 케이크를 팔아 거금을 모았다.

10 ______________, the weather has changed. 그러나, 날씨가 바뀌었다.

B 빈 칸에 알맞은 단어를 고르세요.

1 The anti-smoking ______________ will run from July 10 to August 1.

① making ② popular ③ campaign ④ announce ⑤ fortune

2 Let's read the title of the first ______________.

① dew ② chapter ③ mistake ④ draw ⑤ beauty

3 ______________ two birds with one stone.

① Common ② Kill ③ Fly ④ Pass ⑤ Divide

Day 15

MP3

364 **mall** [mɔːl]

명 쇼핑몰

a shopping mall 쇼핑몰　　at a mall 쇼핑몰에서

365 **merry** [méri]

형 즐거운, 명랑한

a merry voice 명랑한 목소리　　a merry face 명랑한 얼굴

366 **past** [pæst]

명 과거　형 지나간　　반 present 현재, 현재의

in the past 과거에　　over the past four years 지난 4년 동안에

367 **beauty** [bjúːti]

명 아름다움, 미인

the beauty of nature 자연의 아름다움　　a great beauty 굉장한 미인

368 **puzzle** [pʌ́zl]

명 퍼즐　동 어리둥절하게 하다　puzzle-puzzled-puzzled

a word puzzle 단어 퍼즐　　be very puzzled 매우 어쩔 줄 모르다

369 **scholar** [skɑ́lər]

명 학자　　형 scholarly 학구적인, 학술적인

a great scholar in history 역사 분야에서 위대한 학자

370 **shy** [ʃai]

형 부끄러움을 많이 타는

a shy girl 부끄러운 소녀　　a shy face 부끄러운 얼굴

371 **south** [sauθ]

명 남쪽　형 남쪽의　　*southern 형 남쪽의, 남부의

the South Pole 남극　　a south wind 남풍

372 **healthy** [hélθi]

형 건강한, 건강에 좋은　healthy-healthier-healthiest

a healthy habit 건강한 습관　　healthy food 건강에 좋은 음식

373 **suit** [sjuːt]

명 정장, 활동복　동 맞다, 적합하다　suit-suited-suited

a swimsuit 수영복　　suit your purposes 목적에 적합하다

374 **symbol** [símbəl]

명 상징, 기호

a symbol of peace 평화의 상징　　a scientific symbol 과학 기호

375 **talk** [tɔːk]

동 말하다, 이야기하다　talk-talked-talked

talk about the weather 날씨에 대해 이야기하다　　talk big 과장해서 말하다

Daily Test

| 월 일 |

A 우리말에 맞게 빈 칸에 알맞은 단어를 쓰세요.

1 Let's go to the ______________. 쇼핑몰에 가자.

2 This ______________ song makes me happy. 이 즐거운 노래는 날 행복하게 해준다.

3 Lisa was a great ______________ when she was young.
Lisa는 어렸을 때 굉장한 미인이었다.

4 She did a crossword ______________ with her brother.
그녀는 오빠와 함께 십자말 풀이를 했다.

5 My mother is a famous ______________ in physics.
우리 엄마는 물리학 분야에서 유명한 학자이다.

6 When Peter was young, he was a quiet and ______________ boy.
Peter가 어렸을 때, 그는 조용하고 부끄러움 많은 소년이었다.

7 There are a variety of animals in ______________ Africa.
남아프리카에는 다양한 동물들이 있다.

8 Suzy is a ______________ person. 수지는 건강한 사람이다.

9 Sohyun looks good in a ______________. 소현이는 정장이 잘 어울린다.

10 They ______________ about their dreams. 그들은 꿈에 대해서 얘기를 나눴다.

B 빈 칸에 알맞은 단어를 고르세요.

1 She was a singer in the ______________.
① future ② yesterday ③ next month ④ today ⑤ past

2 The pigeon is a ______________ of peace.
① draw ② picture ③ symbol ④ beautiful ⑤ cycle

Day 16

MP3

376 **enter** [éntər]
동 들어가다, 입력하다 enter-entered-entered
enter the classroom 교실에 들어가다 enter your ID ID를 입력하다

377 **square** [skwɛər]
형 정사각형 모양의 명 정사각형, 광장
a square room 정사각형 방 a square in town 마을 안 광장

378 **adventure** [ədvéntʃər]
명 모험 형 adventurous 모험적인
an exciting adventure 흥미진진한 모험

379 **arrive** [əráiv]
동 도착하다 arrive-arrived-arrived 명 arrival 도착
arrive on time 정각에 도착하다 arrive at the airport 공항에 도착하다

380 **bill** [bil]
명 고지서, 청구서, 지폐
the telephone bill 전화비 고지서 a ten-dollar bill 10달러 지폐

381 **cage** [keidʒ]
명 새장, 우리 *pen 명 (가축의) 우리
a bird cage 새장 escape from a cage 우리에서 도망치다

382 **conversation** [kɑ̀nvərséiʃən]
명 대화
the topic of conversation 대화의 주제

383 **culture** [kʌ́ltʃər]
명 문화 형 cultural 문화의
a different culture 다른 문화 Asian culture 아시아 문화

384 **during** [djú(ː)əriŋ]
전 ~동안
during winter vacation 겨울방학 동안

385 **feather** [féðər]
명 깃털
light as a feather 깃털처럼 가벼운 a gold feather 황금 깃털

386 **happiness** [hǽpinis]
명 행복
find true happiness 참된 행복을 찾다

387 **important** [impɔ́ːrtənt]
형 중요한 명 importance 중요성
important information 중요한 정보

388 **low** [lou]
형 낮은 low-lower-lowest
a low chair 낮은 의자 a low temperature 낮은 온도

Daily Test

| 월 일 |

A 우리말에 맞게 빈 칸에 알맞은 단어를 쓰세요.

1 Helen ______________ middle school last year. Helen은 작년에 중학교에 입학했다.

2 Sue's new blanket has stars and ______________ on it.
Sue의 새 담요는 별과 정사각형으로 꾸며져 있었다.

3 This book is about a boy's ______________ in Africa.
이 책은 한 소년의 아프리카에서의 모험에 관한 것이다.

4 Mr. Park ______________ late for the meeting. Mr. Park은 회의에 늦게 도착하였다.

5 We had a long ______________ during dinner. 저녁 식사 동안 우리는 긴 대화를 나눴다.

6 Each country has a different ______________. 각 나라들은 다른 문화를 가지고 있다.

7 We went to Spain ______________ summer vacation.
우리는 여름 방학 중에 스페인에 다녀왔다.

8 A positive attitude is the key to ______________. 긍정적인 태도가 행복의 비결이다.

9 A healthy diet is very ______________ for your body.
건강한 식단은 여러분의 몸을 위해서 매우 중요하다.

10 Billy, your English grade is too ______________. Billy, 너의 영어 성적이 너무 낮구나.

B 빈 칸에 알맞은 단어를 고르세요.

1 Birds of a ______________ flock together.
① feather ② culture ③ fly ④ leg ⑤ wing

2 The electricity ______________ for this month is very high.
① money ② bill ③ square ④ dollar ⑤ paper

3 The lion escaped from the ______________ last night.
① culture ② adventure ③ strange ④ sunset ⑤ cage

Day 16

MP3

389 **mental** [méntəl]
형 정신의, 마음의, 정신적인
mental health 정신 건강 mental disease 정신병

390 **palace** [pǽlis]
명 궁전
a beautiful palace 아름다운 궁전 live in a palace 궁전에 살다

391 **poem** [póuəm]
명 시 *poet 명 시인 *poetry 명 시, 시가
write a poem 시를 쓰다 read a poem loudly 크게 시를 읽다

392 **price** [prais]
명 값, 가격
a high price 높은 가격 the price of a coat 코트의 가격

393 **remove** [rimúːv]
동 치우다, 제거하다 remove-removed-removed
remove the virus 바이러스를 제거하다

394 **seed** [siːd]
명 씨앗
a flower seed 꽃씨 plant the seed 씨앗을 심다

395 **skip** [skip]
동 (일 등을) 거르다, 건너뛰다 skip-skipped-skipped
skip the next chapter 다음 장을 건너뛰다 skip dinner 저녁을 거르다

396 **value** [vǽljuː]
명 가치, 유용성 형 valuable 가치 있는
the value of this gold ring 이 금반지의 가치 value of life 삶의 가치

397 **sweat** [swet]
명 땀 동 땀을 흘리다
covered with sweat 땀으로 젖은 a cold sweat 식은땀

398 **sunset** [sʌ́nsèt]
명 해질녘, 일몰 반 sunrise 일출
at sunset 해질 녘에 the view of the sunset 해질 녘의 풍경

399 **task** [tæsk]
명 일, 과제 *duty 명 의무, 직무, 업무
a difficult task 어려운 일 finish a task 과제를 끝내다

400 **thief** [θiːf]
명 도둑 복 thieves
a necklace thief 목걸이 도둑 catch a thief 도둑을 잡다

Daily Test

| 월 일 |

A 우리말에 맞게 빈 칸에 알맞은 단어를 쓰세요.

1 We will visit Buckingham ______________ next Sunday.
우리는 다음주 일요일에 버킹엄 궁전을 방문할 것이다.

2 She wrote a number of ______________ about nature.
그녀는 자연에 대한 시 여러 편을 썼다.

3 What's the ______________ of this cup? 이 컵의 가격은 얼마인가요?

4 Could you ______________ this book from my desk?
내 책상에서 이 책 좀 치워줄래요?

5 Jack is planting ______________ in the garden. Jack은 정원에 씨앗을 심고 있다.

6 The teacher ______________ the next question. 선생님은 다음 질문을 생략하셨다.

7 We should know the ______________ of good education.
우리는 좋은 교육의 가치를 알아야 한다.

8 We arrived home at ______________. 우리는 해질녘에 집에 도착했다.

9 Start with an easy ______________. 쉬운 일부터 시작하세요.

10 He caught the car ______________ last night. 그는 지난 밤 그 자동차 도둑을 잡았다.

B 빈 칸에 알맞은 단어를 고르세요.

1 She needs to relax for her ______________ health.
① mental ② remove ③ crazy ④ enter ⑤ happy

2 Micky was covered with ______________ when he woke up.
① sun ② sweat ③ square ④ sea ⑤ cloud

Review Test 08

Day 15 + Day 16 | 월 일 |

A 우리말에 맞게 빈 칸에 알맞은 단어를 쓰세요.

1 ________________ a marriage 결혼을 발표하다

2 the first ________________ 첫 번째 장

3 a ________________ mistake 흔히 있는 실수

4 a ________________ voice 명랑한 목소리

5 a ________________ of peace 평화의 상징

6 ________________ on time 정각에 도착하다

7 the topic of ________________ 대화의 주제

8 find true ________________ 참된 행복을 찾다

9 ________________ the virus 바이러스를 제거하다

10 the view of the ________________ 해질 녘의 풍경

B 다음 영어 풀이에 알맞은 어휘를 〈보기〉에서 고르세요.

보기	campaign	cycle	cage	palace	price

1 ____________ : a series of actions designed to achieve a particular goal

2 ____________ : the amount of money you pay to buy something

3 ____________ : the official home where a king, queen, or president lives

4 ____________ : a container made of metal wires or bars to keep birds or animals in

5 ____________ : a period or amount of time in which the same events repeat

C 다음 단어의 관계가 A:B=C:D가 되도록 알맞은 단어를 골라 빈 칸에 적으세요.

1 divide : ________________ = bake : baked

① divided ② division ③ divides
④ dividely ⑤ dividid

2 ________________ : beautiful = taste : tasty

① ugly ② beauties ③ beauty
④ pretty ⑤ beautifully

3 health : ________________ = wealth : wealthy

① healthies ② healthy ③ healthily
④ healths ⑤ healthes

4 ________________ : room = build : house

① enter ② dining ③ small
④ bed ⑤ run

5 value : ________________ = fortune : fortunate

① valueible ② values ③ valued
④ invaluable ⑤ valuable

D 문맥에 맞게 다음 문장을 완성하세요.

1 His novel is popular •	• a are my favorites.
2 Sue's new blanket has •	• b thief last night.
3 Colors such as green and red •	• c stars and squares on it.
4 He caught the car •	• d in the garden.
5 Jack is planting seeds •	• e among teenagers.

E 문장을 읽고 문맥에 적절한 단어를 고르세요.

1 Our team scored three goals (among/during) the second half of the match.

2 Joe has a(n) (important/popular) meeting tomorrow.

3 Tim already forgot about his (puzzle/past) mistakes.

4 Kiyoung likes to watch sports games. (Then/However), he does not like playing any sport.

5 Fortunately, the price of the coat was much (lower/loner) than I expected.

F 문장의 빈칸에 알맞은 단어를 〈보기〉에서 찾아 쓰세요. (필요하면 형태를 고치세요.)

보기	fortune	scholar	adventure	mental	shy

1 The company made a ____________ in business software.
그 회사는 영업용 소프트웨어에서 거액을 벌었다.

2 A healthy diet and regular exercise are good for your ____________ health.
건강한 식단과 규칙적인 운동은 여러분의 정신 건강을 위해서 좋습니다.

3 The Little Zoe is ____________ around guests.
꼬마 Zoe는 손님들이 있으면 부끄러워한다.

4 Although he is 17 years old, going to the USA alone is an ____________ for him.
그는 17살이긴 하지만, 미국에 혼자 가는 것은 그에게 모험이다.

5 Many ____________ gathered to discuss the topic.
많은 학자들이 그 주제에 대해 토론하기 위해 모였다.

G 그림과 낱말이 잘못 짝지어진 것을 고르세요. .... (   )

ⓐ

draw

ⓑ

healthy

ⓒ

popular

ⓓ

enter

H 낱말과 어울리는 그림을 연결하세요.

1 skip •

• ⓐ

2 sweat •

• ⓑ

Study More

during '~하는 동안, ~(때)에'의 용법

- during은 대개 특정한 '기간' 혹은 '때'를 나타낼 때 사용한다.
  She studied Spanish **during** the winter. 그녀는 겨울에 스페인어를 공부했다.
- during은 특정적이지 않은 기간을 나타내는 표현과는 사용하지 않는다.
  She studied Spanish during one year. (X) *이런 경우는 for를 사용한다.
  She studied Spanish **for** one year. 그녀는 일년 동안 스페인어를 공부했다.

Day 17

MP3

401 **exhibition** [èksəbíʃən]
명 전시회 / 동 exhibit 전시하다
an art exhibition 미술 전시회 / on exhibition 전시 중인

402 **nation** [néiʃən]
명 국가, 나라 / 유 country 나라
a strong nation 강대국 / fight for the nation 나라를 위해 싸우다

403 **tie** [tai]
명 넥타이 동 묶다 tie-tied-tied
a red tie 빨간 넥타이 / tie your shoelaces 신발끈을 묶다

404 **destination** [destineiʃn]
명 행선지, 도착지 / 유 goal 목표, 목적지
reach your destination 목적지에 이르다

405 **auditorium** [ɔ̀:ditɔ́:riəm]
명 강당
in an auditorium 강당에서 / a school auditorium 학교 강당

406 **choir** [kwáiər]
명 합창단
a church choir 교회 성가대 / sing in a choir 합창단에서 노래하다

407 **create** [kriéit]
동 창조하다 명 창조 create-created-created
create a new hair style 새로운 머리스타일을 창조하다

408 **disease** [dizí:z]
명 질병 / 유 illness 병, 아픔
heart disease 심장병 / catch a disease 질병에 걸리다

409 **drop by** [drɑp bai]
동 (~에)들르다 / 유 stop by ~에 잠시 들르다
drop by the office 사무실에 들르다

410 **everywhere** [évrihwɛ̀ər]
부 모든 곳에, 어디든지
follow everywhere 모든 곳을 따라다니다

411 **fry** [frai]
동 (기름에) 볶다, 튀기다 fry-fried-fried
fry eggs and bacon 달걀과 베이컨을 볶다

412 **interview** [íntərvjù:]
동 인터뷰하다 명 인터뷰, 면접
interview a famous actress 유명한 여배우를 인터뷰하다

413 **luggage** [lʌ́gidʒ]
명 (여행용) 짐, 수하물
pack luggage 짐을 싸다 / lose luggage 짐을 잃어버리다

Daily Test

| 월 일 |

A 우리말에 맞게 빈 칸에 알맞은 단어를 쓰세요.

1 There will be an Asian art ______________ at City Hall next week.
다음 주에 시청에서 아시아 미술 전시회가 있을 예정이다.

2 There are many island ______________ in the Pacific.
태평양에는 많은 섬나라들이 있다.

3 After a long flight, we finally arrived at the ______________.
긴 비행 후에, 우리는 마침내 목적지에 도착했다.

4 A graduation ceremony will be held in the ______________ tomorrow.
졸업식은 내일 강당에서 있을 예정입니다.

5 Mike wants to ______________ a new movie. Mike는 새로운 영화를 만들고 싶어한다.

6 I'll ______________ by your house next week. 다음주에 너희 집에 들를게.

7 My sister always follows me ______________ I go.
내 여동생은 항상 어디든지 나를 따라다닌다.

8 Sally is ______________ some potatoes in oil. Sally는 기름에 감자를 볶고 있다.

9 I have a job ______________ in an hour. 한 시간 뒤에 취업 면접이 있어요.

10 Peter is busy packing his ______________ for the trip.
Peter는 여행 짐을 싸느라 바쁘다.

B 빈 칸에 알맞은 단어를 고르세요.

1 Jackson ______________ his son's shoelaces.
① tried ② interview ③ fried ④ tied ⑤ still

2 He got heart ______________.
① interview ② exhibition ③ choir ④ shape ⑤ disease

3 Sarah sings in a church ______________.
① choir ② chair ③ people ④ stage ⑤ club

Day 17

MP3

414 **musician** [mju(:)zíʃən]
명 음악가
become a great musician 위대한 음악가가 되다

415 **shake** [ʃeik]
동 흔들다, 흔들리다 shake-shook-shaken
shake your head 머리를 흔들다 shake in the wind 바람에 흔들리다

416 **playground** [pléigràund]
명 운동장
in the playground 운동장에서 a school playground 학교 운동장

417 **pouch** [pautʃ]
명 주머니 유 pocket 호주머니, 포켓
a small pouch 작은 주머니 money in a pouch 주머니 속 돈

418 **reuse** [riːjúːz]
동 재사용하다 reuse-reused-reused
reuse paper 종이를 재사용하다

419 **service** [sə́ːrvis]
명 (고객에 대한) 서비스
an excellent repair service 훌륭한 수리 서비스

420 **wrap** [ræp]
동 싸다, 포장하다 wrap-wrapped-wrapped 유 pack 포장하다
wrap John's birthday presents John의 생일선물을 포장하다

421 **still** [stil]
부 여전히, 아직도 형 가만히 있는
still miss him 여전히 그를 그리워하다 stand still 가만히 서있다

422 **tear** [tiər]
명 눈물 동 찢다 tear-tore-torn
in tears 눈물을 흘리며 tear up 갈기갈기 찢다

423 **third** [θəːrd]
형 세 번째의
the third floor 3층 on the third day of March 3월의 셋째 날

424 **cruel** [krúːəl]
형 잔혹한, 잔인한 유 brutal 잔혹한, 악랄한
a cruel war 잔혹한 전쟁 be cruel to animals 동물에게 잔인하다

425 **heavily** [hévəli]
부 심하게, 세게, 무겁게
rain heavily 비가 세차게 오다 cough heavily 기침을 심하게 하다

Daily Test

| 월 일 |

Ⓐ 우리말에 맞게 빈 칸에 알맞은 단어를 쓰세요.

1 My dream is to become a great classical ______________.
내 꿈은 위대한 클래식 음악가가 되는 것이다.

2 The trees are ______________ in the wind. 나무들이 바람에 흔들리고 있다.

3 Students are playing soccer in the ______________.
학생들은 운동장에서 축구를 하고 있다.

4 Grandmother made a small black ______________ for me.
할머니가 나를 위해 검정색 작은 주머니를 만들어 주셨다.

5 The computer repair ______________ was really bad.
컴퓨터 수리 서비스는 매우 안 좋았다.

6 The woman ______________ the box in pink paper.
그 여자는 분홍색 종이로 상자를 포장했다.

7 Cindy is ______________ in America. Cindy는 여전히 미국에 있다.

8 His office is on the ______________ floor. 그의 사무실은 3층에 있다.

9 Many people suffered under the ______________ king.
많은 사람들이 그 잔인한 왕 아래서 고통을 받았다.

10 Snow was falling ______________ yesterday. 어제 눈이 심하게 왔다.

Ⓑ 빈 칸에 알맞은 단어를 고르세요.

1 Minji ______________ up Jack's letter.
① teared ② tore ③ tearing ④ tored ⑤ tear

2 We ______________ bottles to protect the environment.
① useful ② tear ③ reuse ④ service ⑤ heavy

Day 18

MP3

426 **senior** [síːnjər]
형 상위의 명 연장자, 선배 반 junior 하급의, 부하의, 하급자 부하
a senior student 상급생 senior to ~보다 연상인

427 **century** [séntʃəri]
명 세기, 100년
the twentieth century 20세기 two centuries 200년

428 **action** [ǽkʃən]
명 행동, 조치 동 act 행동하다
take action 조치를 취하다 a quick action 신속한 행동

429 **another** [ənʌ́ðər]
형 다른, 또 하나의 대 하나 더
another question 또 다른 질문 one after another 차례대로

430 **blend** [blend]
동 섞다, 혼합하다 blend-blended-blended 유 mix 섞다, 섞이다
blend the flour with the milk 밀가루와 우유를 섞다

431 **vase** [veis]
명 꽃병
flowers in a vase 꽃병에 꽂힌 꽃들 break a vase 꽃병을 깨뜨리다

432 **complete** [kəmplíːt]
동 완성하다, 끝내다 형 완벽한 complete-completed-completed
complete the task 일을 끝내다 a complete success 완벽한 성공

433 **disappoint** [dìsəpɔ́int]
동 실망시키다 disappoint-disappointed-disappointed
disappoint a friend 친구를 실망시키다

434 **emotion** [imóuʃən]
명 감정 유 feeling 감정
strong emotions 격한 감정 hide your emotions 감정을 숨기다

435 **focus** [fóukəs]
명 초점, 주목 동 집중하다 focus-focused-focused
the focus of this meeting 이 모임의 초점 focus on ~에 초점을 맞추다

436 **global** [glóubəl]
형 세계적인, 지구 전체의
a global event 세계적인 행사 global warming 지구 온난화

437 **lesson** [lésən]
명 수업, 교습, 교훈
take lessons 수업을 받다 take piano lessons 피아노 교습을 받다

438 **move** [muːv]
동 움직이다, 옮기다, 이사하다 move-moved-moved
move the table 식탁을 옮기다 move house 이사하다

Daily Test

| 월 일 |

A 우리말에 맞게 빈 칸에 알맞은 단어를 쓰세요.

1 This tower is more than a ______________ old. 이 탑은 100년이 더 넘었다.

2 Thank you for your quick ______________ on this accident. 이 사고에 대한 신속한 조치에 대해 감사드립니다.

3 ______________ the eggs, sugar, and salt together. 달걀과 설탕, 소금을 함께 섞으세요.

4 I gave a white ______________ to my mom. 나는 엄마께 흰 꽃병을 드렸다.

5 You should ______________ your homework before 9 p.m. 9시 전까지 숙제를 마쳐야 한다.

6 She was ______________ at the result of the math test. 그녀는 수학 시험 결과에 대해 실망했다.

7 I don't want to show my ______________. 나는 내 감정을 드러내는 것을 원하지 않는다.

8 Mina ______________ on solving the math problem. 미나는 그 수학 문제를 푸는 것에 집중했다.

9 We have no ______________ today. 우리는 오늘 수업이 없다.

10 Can you ______________ this chair? 이 의자 좀 옮겨줄래요?

B 빈 칸에 알맞은 단어를 고르세요.

1 Alex is three years ______________ to me.

① young ② old ③ senior ④ up ⑤ juniors

2 Do you want ______________ piece of cheese cake?

① another ② others ③ having ④ focus ⑤ pure

3 The World Cup is a(n) ______________ event.

① disappoint ② global ③ focus ④ still ⑤ easy

Day 18

MP3

439 tight [tait]
형 꼭 끼는, 단단한 tight-tighter-tightest 부 tightly 꽉, 단단히
a tight skirt 꽉 끼는 치마 a tight knot 단단한 매듭

440 project [prádʒekt]
명 과제, 계획
a research project 연구 과제 finish a project 과제를 마치다

441 pure [pjuər]
형 순수한, 깨끗한 반 impure 순수하지 못한, 불순물이 섞인
pure gold 순금 pure water 깨끗한 물

442 violent [váiələnt]
형 폭력적인 명 violence 폭력
violent movies 폭력적인 영화들 violent actions 폭력적인 행동

443 servant [sə́:rvənt]
명 하인, 종업원
a faithful servant 충실한 하인 call a servant 하인을 부르다

444 silent [sáilənt]
형 말이 없는, 조용한 명 silence 침묵
keep silent 침묵을 지키다 a silent moment 조용한 순간

445 steal [sti:l]
동 훔치다 steal-stole-stolen 유 rob 털다, 도둑질하다
steal a book 책을 훔치다 steal money 돈을 훔치다

446 straw [strɔ:]
명 짚, 빨대
a straw hat 밀짚 모자 a straw basket 밀짚 바구니

447 temple [témpl]
명 절, 사원
a temple in the town 마을에 있는 절 go to the temple 절에 가다

448 time [taim]
명 시간, 시대, 횟수
for a long time 오랜 시간 동안 prehistoric times 선사 시대

449 purpose [pə́:rpəs]
명 목적, 의도
the purpose of the meeting 모임의 목적

450 volunteer [vὰləntíər]
동 자원하다 명 자원봉사자 volunteer-volunteered-volunteered
volunteer for ~에 자원하다 volunteer at school 학교에서 자원봉사 하다

Daily Test

| 월 일 |

A 우리말에 맞게 빈 칸에 알맞은 단어를 쓰세요.

1 The jeans are too ______________ for me. 그 청바지는 내게 너무 꽉 낀다.

2 We will start a new ______________ next month.
우리는 다음 달에 새로운 프로젝트를 시작할 것이다.

3 This ring is made of ______________ gold. 이 반지는 순금으로 만들어졌다.

4 There are many ______________ TV programs these days.
요즘 폭력적인 TV 프로그램들이 많이 있다.

5 The king ordered his ______________ to build a new bridge.
왕은 하인들에게 새로 다리를 만들라고 명령했다.

6 The room is so ______________. 이 방은 매우 조용하다.

7 The man ______________ the car. 그 남자는 차를 훔쳤다.

8 Would you like a ______________ for your coke? 콜라에 빨대를 꽂아 드릴까요?

9 Suho goes to the ______________ to pray. 수호는 절에 기도하러 간다.

10 Lily and Amy do ______________ work on Saturdays.
Lily와 Amy는 토요일마다 자원 봉사 활동을 한다.

B 빈 칸에 알맞은 단어를 고르세요.

1 Long ______________ no see.
① time ② day ③ week ④ month ⑤ year

2 The ______________ of this meeting is to elect a new representative.
① position ② popularity ③ purpose ④ population ⑤ pause

Review Test 09

A 우리말에 맞게 빈 칸에 알맞은 단어를 쓰세요.

1 reach your ________________ 목적지에 이르다

2 sing in a ________________ 합창단에서 노래하다

3 ________________ by the office 사무실에 들르다

4 the ________________ of the meeting 모임의 목적

5 the ________________ floor 3층

6 ________________ the flour with the milk 밀가루와 우유를 섞다

7 ________________ a friend 친구를 실망시키다

8 ________________ actions 폭력적인 행동

9 go to the ________________ 절에 가다

10 ________________ at school 학교에서 자원봉사 하다

B 다음 영어 풀이에 알맞은 어휘를 〈보기〉에서 고르세요.

보기	lesson	servant	nation	service	century

1 ____________ : a person whose job is working in another person's home

2 ____________ : a period of 100 years

3 ____________ : an area of land or people ruled under the same government

4 ____________ : an act or work done to help customers or other people

5 ____________ : a unit of learning activity for a particular subject or task

C 다음 단어의 관계가 A:B=C:D가 되도록 알맞은 단어를 골라 빈 칸에 적으세요.

1 exhibit : ______________ = fail : failure

① exhibition ② exhibits ③ exhibture
④ exhibitly ⑤ exhibited

2 front : back = junior : ______________

① children ② students ③ native
④ senior ⑤ exhibited

3 steal : ______________ = awake : awoke

① steals ② stealed ③ stole
④ stealled ⑤ stealt

4 heavy : ______________ = easy : easily

① heavyly ② heavily ③ heavyes
④ heavly ⑤ heaviness

5 fish : fishbowl = flower : ______________

① fence ② rose ③ flowers
④ vase ⑤ lily

D 문맥에 맞게 다음 문장을 완성하세요.

1	Sally is frying •	• a	in the playground.
2	Students are playing soccer •	• b	the math problem.
3	Mina focused on solving •	• c	pure gold.
4	This ring is made of •	• d	some potatoes in oil.
5	Would you like a straw •	• e	for your coke?

E 문장을 읽고 문맥에 적절한 단어를 고르세요.

1 The house was so (silent/tight) that she could hear footsteps downstairs.

2 Miho (stole/reused) the milk bottle as a flower base.

3 Bob (sailed/wrapped) the present for his mother with a ribbon.

4 Kate plans to (blend/complete) the project by next week.

5 It was difficult for Brian to talk about himself in an (interview/auditorium).

F 문장의 빈칸에 알맞은 단어를 〈보기〉에서 찾아 쓰세요. (필요하면 형태를 고치세요.)

보기 luggage everywhere auditorium tight emotion

1 Students gathered in the ____________ to see the violinist's performance.
학생들이 바이올린 연주자의 공연을 보기 위해 강당에 모였다.

2 There are more than ten million kinds of insects, and they live ____________ in the world.
곤충의 종류는 천만 가지가 넘으며 지구 모든 곳에 살고 있다.

3 Dad turned his head away to hide his ____________.
아빠는 자신의 감정을 감추기 위해 고개를 돌렸다.

4 Why don't you weigh your ____________ before leaving for the airport?
공항으로 가기 전에 수하물 무게를 재 보는 게 어때?

5 I think the new shoes are too ____________.
새 구두가 너무 꽉 끼는 것 같아.

G 그림에 해당하는 낱말을 〈보기〉에서 골라 쓰세요.

1

(   )

2

(   )

3

(   )

4

(   )

5

(   )

6

(   )

보기 time tears musician move tie shake

Study More

until vs. **by**

- until과 buy는 둘 다 '~까지'라는 의미를 가지고 있지만 쓰임새가 다르다.
- until은 'play, wait, sleep' 등 주로 지속적인 의미를 가진 표현들과 쓰인다.
  play football **until** dark 어두워 질 때까지 축구를 하다
- by는 'finish, stop, arrive' 등 주로 한 번에 끝나는 의미를 가진 표현들과 쓰인다.
  finish homework **by** Monday 월요일까지 프로젝트를 끝내다

Day 19

MP3

451 □ **forgive** [fərgív]

동 용서하다 forgive-forgave-forgiven

forgive him for his lie 그의 거짓말을 용서하다

452 □ **gallery** [gǽləri]

명 미술관, 화랑

an art gallery 미술관, 화랑 an exhibition gallery 전람회장

453 □ **forth** [fɔːrθ]

부 앞으로

back and forth 앞뒤로 go forth 나가다, 출발하다

454 □ **amount** [əmáunt]

명 양, 총액 유 quantity 수량, 분량

a large amount of salt 많은 양의 소금 a total amount 총액

455 □ **average** [ǽvəridʒ]

형 평균의 명 평균

an average price 평균 가격 above average 평균 이상

456 □ **coach** [koutʃ]

명 (스포츠 팀의) 코치, 감독 동 코치하다, 지도하다

a baseball coach 야구팀 코치

457 □ **decide** [disáid]

동 결정하다 decide-decided-decided 명 decision 결정

decide to ~하기로 결심하다 decide to stay 머무르기로 결정하다

458 □ **dialogue** [dáiəlɔ̀(ː)g]

명 대화 유 conversation 대화

an interesting dialogue 재미있는 대화 a long dialogue 긴 대화

459 □ **experience** [ikspí(ː)əriəns]

명 경험 동 경험하다 experience-experienced-experienced

a wonderful experience 멋진 경험

460 □ **fiction** [fíkʃən]

명 소설, 허구 반 nonfiction 실화, 논픽션

a science fiction novel 공상 과학 소설 a fiction writer 소설가

461 □ **evil** [íːvəl]

형 나쁜, 불길한

an evil heart 사악한 마음 an evil queen 사악한 여왕

462 □ **lonely** [lóunli]

형 외로운, 쓸쓸한 명 loneliness 고독, 쓸쓸함

feel lonely 외롭다 a lonely day 외로운 날

463 □ **north** [nɔːrθ]

명 북쪽 형 북쪽의 +northern 형 북부의, 북쪽의

the North Pole 북극 North Korea 북한

Daily Test

| 월 일 |

A 우리말에 맞게 빈 칸에 알맞은 단어를 쓰세요.

1 Please ______________ me for my rude behavior.
제가 당신에게 한 무례한 행동을 용서해 주세요.

2 LA has several great art ______________. LA는 몇몇 훌륭한 화랑들이 있다.

3 This USB drive can save a large ______________ of information.
이 USB는 많은 양의 정보를 저장할 수 있다.

4 My math score is always above ______________ . 내 수학 점수는 항상 평균 이상이다.

5 He ______________ to stay here for another month.
그는 이곳에 한 달 더 머무르기로 결정했다.

6 Rio had a ______________ with his old friend. Rio는 그의 오랜 친구와 대화를 나누었다.

7 My first trip to London was a wonderful ______________.
내 첫 번째 런던 여행은 매우 멋진 경험이었다.

8 She is the ______________ queen in this story. 그녀는 이 이야기에서 사악한 여왕이다.

9 Julie was ______________ after her friend left her house.
Julie는 그녀의 친구가 집을 떠난 후 외로웠다.

10 Helen lives an hour ______________ of Seoul.
Helen은 서울에서 북쪽으로 1시간 떨어진 곳에 산다.

B 빈 칸에 알맞은 단어를 고르세요.

1 The dog waved his tail back and ______________.
① fourth ② forth ③ behind ④ by ⑤ front

2 Tina is writing a science ______________ novel.
① movie ② dialogue ③ long ④ evil ⑤ fiction

3 Our new basketball ______________ is Mr. William.
① coach ② players ③ team ④ winners ⑤ ceremony

Day 19

MP3

464 **plate** [pleit]

명 접시, 판

cookies on the plate 접시 위의 쿠키 　 a paper plate 종이 접시

465 **be proud of** [bi praud ʌv]

형 ~을 자랑스러워하다 　 명 pride 자랑스러움

be proud of my family 가족을 자랑스러워하다

466 **referee** [rèfərí:]

명 심판 　 유 umpire (테니스, 야구 등의) 심판

a soccer referee 축구 경기 심판

467 **model** [mádəl]

명 기준, 모범, 모형, (상품의) 모델 　 형 모형의

a model airplane 모형 비행기 　 the latest model 최신 모델

468 **sleeve** [sli:v]

명 소매

a shirt with long sleeves 긴 소매의 셔츠

469 **sore** [sɔ:r]

형 아픈, 따가운

have a sore throat 목이 아프다 　 a sore arm 아픈 팔

470 **storm** [stɔ:rm]

명 폭풍, 태풍

a heavy storm 심한 폭풍 　 destroyed by a storm 태풍에 의해 파괴되다

471 **surprising** [sərpráiziŋ]

형 놀라운 　 부 surprisingly 놀랍게도

a surprising discovery 놀라운 발견 　 surprising news 놀라운 소식

472 **tasty** [téisti]

형 맛있는 　 유 delicious 맛있는

a tasty pie 맛있는 파이 　 enjoy a tasty meal 맛있는 식사를 즐기다

473 **victory** [víktəri]

명 승리

bring Korea victory 한국에게 승리를 안겨주다

474 **tour** [tuər]

명 여행 　 동 여행하다, 견학하다 　 tour-toured-toured

take a tour 여행을 가다 　 tour a museum 박물관을 견학하다

475 **vet** [vet]

명 수의사 (=veterinarian)

go to the vet 동물 병원에 가다 　 a skilled veterinarian 숙련된 수의사

Daily Test

| 월 일 |

Ⓐ 우리말에 맞게 빈 칸에 알맞은 단어를 쓰세요.

1 There are many ______________ on the table. 탁자 위에 접시들이 많이 있다.

2 Jenny's dream is to become a soccer ______________. Jenny의 꿈은 축구 심판이 되는 것이다.

3 Daddy and I will make a ______________ ship this Sunday. 이번 주 일요일에 아빠와 난 모형 배를 만들 것이다.

4 I love the dress with short ______________. 난 저 소매가 짧은 드레스가 맘에 들어요.

5 Kate has a ______________ foot from riding her bike. 자전거를 타고 난 뒤 Kate는 발이 아팠다.

6 The ______________ continued for a week. 폭풍이 일주일간 계속 되었다.

7 Mrs. Park made us ______________ snacks. Mrs. Park은 우리에게 맛있는 간식을 만들어주셨다.

8 Many people celebrated our team's ______________. 많은 사람들이 우리 팀의 승리를 축하했다.

9 We will take a ______________ of the United Kingdom next winter. 우리는 다음 겨울에 영국으로 여행을 갈 것이다.

10 Minhyuk took his cat to the ______________. 민혁이는 그의 고양이를 수의사에게 데려갔다.

Ⓑ 빈 칸에 알맞은 단어를 고르세요.

1 We're so ______________ of you.

① proud ② like ③ lovely ④ sore ⑤ celebrate

2 It's ______________ that the team did not win the game.

① sore ② surprising ③ happy ④ event ⑤ sleeve

Day 20

MP3

476 **be anxious about** [bi ǽŋkʃəs əbaut]
형 ~에 대해 걱정하다, 불안해하다 명 anxiety 불안
be anxious about the test 시험에 대해 불안하다

477 **step** [step]
명 걸음, 조치, 단계
step by step 한 걸음씩 take a step 조치를 취하다

478 **clap** [klæp]
동 박수치다 명 박수 clap-clapped-clapped
clap your hands in delight 기쁨에 박수치다

479 **appear** [əpíər]
동 나타나다, ~인 것 같다 appear-appeared-appeared
appear on stage 무대에 서다 appear to be rich 부자인 것 같다

480 **belief** [bilíːf]
명 믿음, 생각
general belief 일반적인 믿음 wrong belief 잘못된 믿음

481 **castle** [kǽsl]
명 성
an old castle 오래된 성 live in a castle 성에 살다

482 **death** [deθ]
명 죽음 동 die 죽다
his grandfather's death 그의 할아버지의 죽음

483 **effect** [ifékt]
명 영향, 결과 *affect 동 영향을 미치다
a positive effect 긍정적인 영향 in effect 실제로는

484 **exchange** [ikstʃéindʒ]
동 교환하다, 맞바꾸다 명 교환 exchange-exchanged-exchanged
exchange opinions 의견을 교환하다

485 **final** [fáinəl]
형 마지막의, 최종적인
the final year of middle school 중학교의 마지막 해

486 **huge** [hjuːdʒ]
형 거대한 유 enormous 거대한
a huge success 거대한 성공 a huge rock 거대한 돌

487 **lay** [lei]
동 놓다, 두다, (알을) 낳다 lay-laid-laid
lay eggs 알을 낳다 lay down a towel 수건을 내려놓다

488 **pass** [pæs]
동 지나가다, 통과시키다, 합격하다 pass-passed-passed
pass the test 시험에 통과하다 pass away 돌아가시다

Daily Test

| 월 일 |

A 우리말에 맞게 빈 칸에 알맞은 단어를 쓰세요.

1 We were ______________ about Tim's health. 우리는 Tim의 건강에 대해 걱정했다.

2 Everyone cheered and ______________. 모든 사람들이 환호하고 박수를 쳤다.

3 Look! A rainbow has ______________ on the hill. 봐봐! 무지개가 언덕 위에 나타났어.

4 People thought that Jackson's ______________ in luck was wrong.
사람들은 Jackson의 운에 대한 믿음은 잘못되었다고 생각했다.

5 I want to visit old ______________ in England. 나는 영국의 오래된 성들에 가보고 싶다.

6 The old woman's ______________ was surprising news.
그 노부인의 죽음은 놀라운 소식이었다.

7 John and I ______________ phone numbers today.
John과 나는 오늘 전화번호를 교환했다.

8 Busan is a ______________ city in Korea. 부산은 한국에 있는 거대한 도시이다.

9 Susan carefully ______________ her baby on the sofa.
Susan은 조심스럽게 그녀의 아기를 소파 위에 내려놓았다.

10 My grandfather ______________ away 4 years ago. 할아버지는 4년 전에 돌아가셨다.

B 빈 칸에 알맞은 단어를 고르세요.

1 We should take the first ______________ toward solving the problem.
① death ② level ③ step ④ castle ⑤ belief

2 This movie will have a positive ______________ on children.
① interesting ② affect ③ huge ④ effect ⑤ thinking

3 We will study in the library for the ______________ exam.
① textbook ② final ③ death ④ take ⑤ front

Day 20

MP3

489 **print** [print]
동 인쇄하다 명 활자, 출판 print-printed-printed
print a report 보고서를 인쇄하다 print four pages 네 장을 인쇄하다

490 **reach** [riːtʃ]
동 ~에 이르다, (손이) 닿다, 도착하다 reach-reached-reached
reach the terminal 터미널에 도착하다 reach for 손을 뻗다

491 **sense** [sens]
명 감각, 느낌 동 느끼다, 알아채다
the five senses 오감 a sense of freedom 해방감

492 **side** [said]
명 옆, 측면 *beside 전 ~옆에
the right side of the box 상자의 오른쪽 면 the opposite side 반대 쪽

493 **snail** [sneil]
명 달팽이
snail shells 달팽이 껍질 as slow as a snail 달팽이처럼 느린

494 **wisdom** [wízdəm]
명 지혜, 현명함
the wisdom of ancient people 옛날 사람들의 지혜

495 **suggest** [səgdʒést]
동 제안하다, 추천하다 suggest-suggested-suggested
suggest an idea 생각을 제안하다

496 **through** [θruː]
전 ~을 통해 (관통하여), ~사이로
through the window 창문을 통해 through the year 1년을 통해서

497 **voice** [vɔis]
명 목소리
a good voice 좋은 목소리 in a high voice 높은 목소리로

498 **tip** [tip]
명 조언, (뾰족한) 끝 유 hint 힌트, 조언
a useful tip 유용한 조언 the tip of the pencil 연필의 끝(촉)

499 **toward** [tɔːrd]
전 ~을 향해서, ~쪽으로
toward the west 서쪽으로 walk toward the park 공원 쪽으로 걸어가다

500 **triangle** [tráiæŋgl]
명 삼각형 형 triangular 삼각형의
draw a triangle 삼각형을 그리다 a regular triangle 정삼각형

Daily Test

| 월 일 |

A 우리말에 맞게 빈 칸에 알맞은 단어를 쓰세요.

1 Can you ______________ the photos for us? 우리를 위해 사진을 인쇄해 줄 수 있니?

2 The boy can't ______________ the top shelf. 소년은 선반 맨 위 칸까지 손이 닿지 않는다.

3 Sight is one of the five ______________. 시각은 오감 중의 하나이다.

4 There is a ______________ on the window glass. 창문 유리에 달팽이가 있다.

5 Yuna gained ______________ through the experience. 그 경험을 통해 유나는 지혜가 생겼다.

6 Can you ______________ a new French restaurant? 새로운 프랑스 식당을 추천해 줄래요?

7 I was watching him ______________ the window. 나는 창문을 통해 그를 보고 있었다.

8 I think Lina has a good ______________. 나는 Lina가 좋은 목소리를 갖고 있다고 생각한다.

9 Father always gives me useful ______________. 아빠는 내게 항상 유용한 조언들을 해주신다.

10 Her scarf is decorated with red ______________. 그녀의 스카프는 삼각형 무늬로 장식되어 있다.

B 빈 칸에 알맞은 단어를 고르세요.

1 She rolled the ball ______________ the door.

① tip ② toward ③ side ④ after ⑤ back

2 The store is on the right ______________ of the road.

① thing ② sense ③ through ④ clapping ⑤ side

Review Test 10 Day 19 + Day 20

| 월 일 |

A 우리말에 맞게 빈 칸에 알맞은 단어를 쓰세요.

1 a baseball ________________ 야구팀 코치

2 ________________ to stay 머무르기로 결정하다

3 be ________________ of my family 가족을 자랑스러워 하다

4 a regular ________________ 정삼각형

5 bring Korea ________________ 한국에게 승리를 안겨주다

6 wrong ________________ 잘못된 믿음

7 ________________ opinions 의견을 교환하다

8 a ________________ success 거대한 성공

9 ________________ the terminal 터미널에 도착하다

10 ________________ the year 1년을 통해서

B 다음 영어 풀이에 알맞은 어휘를 〈보기〉에서 고르세요.

보기	effect	death	vet	model	fiction

1 ____________ : an ideal example that can be copied for further production

2 ____________ : a person who cares for sick and injured animals

3 ____________ : the end of life and the state of being dead

4 ____________ : a written piece of work that describes imaginary events

5 ____________ : something that happens as a result of an action or event

C 다음 단어의 관계가 A:B=C:D가 되도록 알맞은 단어를 골라 빈 칸에 적으세요.

1 anxiety : ________________ = perfection : perfect

① anxious ② anxietion ③ anxiously
④ anxieties ⑤ anxioues

2 forgive : ________________ = graduate : graduated

① forgives ② mistake ③ forgot
④ forgave ⑤ forgively

3 wise : ________________ = friendly : friend

① wisely ② memory ③ wisdom
④ smart ⑤ wisous

4 ________________ : good = narrow : wide

① evil ② angel ③ true
④ book ⑤ goodness

5 three : third = four : ________________

① fourth ② fourd ③ forth
④ forted ⑤ foird

D 문맥에 맞게 다음 문장을 완성하세요.

1 LA has several •	• a and clapped.
2 There is a snail •	• b on the window glass.
3 Kate has a sore foot •	• c 4 years ago.
4 Everyone cheered •	• d great art galleries.
5 My grandfather passed away •	• e from riding her bike.

E 문장을 읽고 문맥에 적절한 단어를 고르세요.

1 The basketball player could spin the ball on the (tip/sleeve) of his finger.

2 The final kicker of the team kicked the ball (until/toward) the goal.

3 If your headache continues, I (suggest/suppose) you see a doctor.

4 He (led/laid) the book on the desk and went out.

5 Environmental pollution can have a harmful (effect/affect) on our lives.

F 문장의 빈칸에 알맞은 단어를 〈보기〉에서 찾아 쓰세요. (필요하면 형태를 고치세요.)

보기	sleeve	experience	dialogue	voice	final

1 The ____________ results will be delivered to you next Friday.
최종 결과는 다음 주 금요일에 전달될 것입니다.

2 Both countries agreed to continue the ____________.
양 국가는 대화를 계속 하기로 합의했다.

3 He has enough knowledge and ____________ to lead a football team.
그는 축구팀을 이끌기에 충분한 지식과 경험이 있다.

4 He rolled up his ____________ and began to work at the desk.
그는 소매를 걷어 부치고 책상에서 일을 하기 시작했다.

5 The girl lowered her ____________ and whispered to her father.
소녀는 목소리를 낮추고 아빠에게 속삭였다.

G 그림과 낱말이 <u>잘못</u> 짝지어진 것을 고르세요. .... (　　　　　)

ⓐ  lonely

ⓑ  plate

ⓒ  wisdom

ⓓ  storm

H 낱말과 어울리는 그림을 연결하세요.

1 side •　　　　• ⓐ 

2 castle •　　　　• ⓑ 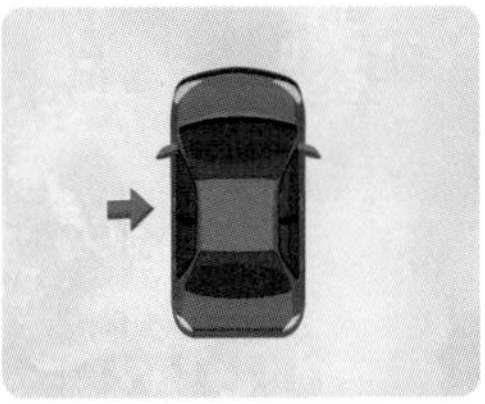

Study More

huge와 비슷한 뜻을 가진 어휘들

- enormous, vast, immense, magnificent, gigantic
  an **enormous** amount of time 막대한 시간　a **vast** number of people 어마어마한 수의 사람들
  on an **immense** scale 엄청난 규모로　a **magnificent** castle 거대한 성
  a **gigantic** dinosaur 거대한 공룡 *magnificent는 주로 크기와 정도를, gigantic은 주로 크기나 규모에 대해 많이 쓰인다.

Day 21

MP3

501 □ **hide** [haid]
동 감추다, 숨다 hide-hid-hidden
hide the key 열쇠를 숨기다 impossible to hide 숨기는 게 불가능한

502 □ **court** [kɔːrt]
명 법정, (경기장) 코트
in court 법정에서 a badminton court 배드민턴 코트

503 □ **deep** [diːp]
형 깊은 deep-deeper-deepest 명 depth 깊이
a deep river 깊은 강 deep thoughts 깊은 생각

504 □ **allow** [əláu]
동 허락하다 allow-allowed-allowed
allow A to B A가 B하는 것을 허락하다

505 □ **blank** [blæŋk]
형 공백의, 빈 명 빈칸 유 empty 빈, 아무 것도 없는
a blank page 빈 페이지 fill in the blanks 빈칸을 채우다

506 □ **bride** [braid]
명 신부
bride and groom 신랑과 신부 my lovely bride 내 사랑스러운 신부

507 □ **deaf** [def]
형 귀가 먼, 청각 장애가 있는
a deaf boy 청각 장애 소년 become deaf 청각을 잃다

508 □ **donkey** [dɑ́ŋki]
명 당나귀
ride a donkey 당나귀를 타다 a donkey cart 당나귀가 끄는 수레

509 □ **forever** [fərévər]
부 영원히 +constantly 부 끊임없이, 계속
love forever 영원히 사랑하다 last forever 영구히 계속되다

510 □ **gesture** [dʒéstʃər]
명 몸짓, 제스처
a hand gesture 손짓 use a lot of gestures 제스처를 많이 사용하다

511 □ **hunger** [hʌ́ŋgər]
명 배고픔, 굶주림, 열망 형 hungry 배고픈
feel hunger 배고픔을 느끼다 die of hunger 굶어 죽다

512 □ **necessary** [nèsəséri]
형 필요한
a necessary death 피할 수 없는 죽음 a necessary item 필요한 물품

513 □ **for free** [fər friː]
형 공짜로, 무료로
get tickets for free 공짜로 표를 얻다

Daily Test

| 월 일 |

Ⓐ 우리말에 맞게 빈 칸에 알맞은 단어를 쓰세요.

1 We ______________ the hat under the table. 우리는 탁자 밑에 모자를 숨겼다.

2 This river is too ______________. 이 강은 너무 깊다.

3 He ______________ his son to buy a new car. 그는 그의 아들이 새 차를 사는 것을 허락했다.

4 Write your name and phone number in the ______________.
빈 칸에 이름과 전화 번호를 적으세요.

5 Mr. Ryu introduced his new ______________. Mr. Ryu는 그의 새 신부를 소개했다.

6 The boy enjoyed riding the ______________. 그 소년은 당나귀 타는 것을 즐겼다.

7 I want to be your good friend ______________. 난 영원히 당신의 좋은 친구가 되고 싶어요.

8 He made a rude ______________ at the taxi driver.
그는 택시 기사에게 무례한 제스처를 해 보였다.

9 Regular exercise is ______________ for good health.
규칙적인 운동은 좋은 건강에 필요하다.

10 You can drink coffee ______________. 무료로 커피를 드실 수 있습니다.

Ⓑ 빈 칸에 알맞은 단어를 고르세요.

1 There is a tennis ______________ in the gym.
① deep ② surface ③ court ④ bride ⑤ blank

2 The woman was ______________ in the left ear.
① blind ② deaf ③ dumb ④ donkey ⑤ listening

3 Many children suffer from ______________ all over the world.
① forever ② hungry ③ gesture ④ free ⑤ hunger

Day 21

MP3

514 **promise** [prámis]
명 약속 동 약속하다 promise-promised-promised
make a promise 약속 하다 break a promise 약속을 어기다

515 **receive** [risíːv]
동 받다, 받아들이다 receive-received-received
receive a letter 편지를 받다 receive a phone call 전화를 받다

516 **sailor** [séilər]
명 선원, 뱃사람
become a sailor 선원이 되다 an English sailor 영국 선원

517 **mission** [míʃən]
명 임무, 사절단
a space mission 우주 여행 임무 carry out a mission 임무를 수행하다

518 **solar** [sóulər]
형 태양의 +lunar 형 달의, 달에 관련된
solar energy 태양 에너지 the solar system 태양계

519 **strike** [straik]
동 ~을 치다, 때리다 명 파업 strike-struck-struck
strike the wall with his fist 주먹으로 벽을 치다

520 **stripe** [straip]
명 줄무늬
striped shirts 줄무늬 셔츠 wide stripes 넓은 줄무늬

521 **title** [táitl]
명 제목
a movie title 영화 제목 the title of this book 이 책의 제목

522 **underwater** [ʌ̀ndərwɔ́ːtər]
형 물속의
underwater creatures 수중 생물 underwater camera 수중 카메라

523 **type** [taip]
명 종류, 유형 유 kind 종류, 유형
different types of books 다른 유형의 책들 a blood type 혈액형

524 **waste** [weist]
동 낭비하다 명 쓰레기, 낭비 waste-wasted-wasted
waste time 시간을 낭비하다 garden waste 정원 쓰레기

525 **virtue** [vɔ́ːrtʃuː]
명 덕목, 미덕, 선행 형 virtuous 도덕적인, 덕이 있는
a life of virtue 선한 삶 Courage is a virtue. 용기는 하나의 미덕이다.

Daily Test

| 월 일 |

A 우리말에 맞게 빈 칸에 알맞은 단어를 쓰세요.

1 Yesterday we ______________ to meet in Paris. 어제 우리는 파리에서 만나기로 약속했다.

2 Lily ______________ a doll from her grandmother. Lily는 할머니께 인형을 받았다.

3 Three ______________ are working on the ship. 세 명의 선원들이 배 위에서 일하는 중이다.

4 There are eight planets in the ______________ system. 태양계에는 8개의 행성이 있다.

5 He ______________ the table with his fist. 그는 책상을 주먹으로 쳤다.

6 I wear a shirt with blue narrow ______________. 나는 파란색 가는 줄무늬 셔츠를 입고 있다.

7 He wants to buy a new ______________ camera. 그는 새로운 수중 카메라를 사고 싶어 한다.

8 What's your blood ______________? 넌 혈액형이 무엇이니?

9 Don't ______________ your time and money. 당신의 시간과 돈을 낭비하지 마세요.

10 Joe lived a life of ______________. Joe는 선한 삶을 살았다.

B 빈 칸에 알맞은 단어를 고르세요.

1 Her new ______________ is to find the gold ring.

① title ② mission ③ sailor ④ underwater ⑤ type

2 Jiyoung can't remember the ______________ of the song.

① basic ② solar ③ stripe ④ strike ⑤ title

Day 22

MP3

526 □ **behave** [bihéiv]
동 행동하다 behave-behaved-behaved 명 behavior 행동
behave like a baby 아기처럼 행동하다

527 □ **royal** [rɔiəl]
형 국왕의
the royal family 왕실 the royal palace 왕궁

528 □ **affect** [əfékt]
동 영향을 주다, 감동시키다 affect-affected-affected
affected by the news 그 소식에 감명을 받다

529 □ **attack** [ətǽk]
동 공격하다 명 공격 attack-attacked-attacked
attack the city 도시를 공격하다 make an attack 공격을 개시하다

530 □ **capital** [kǽpitəl]
명 수도, 대문자
the capital of China 중국의 수도 write in capitals 대문자로 쓰다

531 □ **competition** [kàmpitíʃən]
명 경쟁, 시합 동 compete 경쟁하다
competition between players 선수들 간의 경쟁

532 □ **develop** [divéləp]
동 성장하다, 개발하다 develop-developed-developed
develop a new online game 새로운 온라인 게임을 개발하다

533 □ **fair** [fɛər]
형 타당한, 공정한 반 unfair 부당한, 편파적인
a fair game 공정한 경기 a fair price 타당한 가격

534 □ **gather** [gæðər]
동 모으다, 모이다 gather-gathered-gathered
gather information 정보를 모으다 gather together 함께 모이다

535 □ **harmony** [ha:rməni]
명 조화, 화합, 화음 형 harmonious 조화로운
live in harmony with ~와 좋게 지내다

536 □ **mean** [mi:n]
동 의미하다 mean-meant-meant 명 meaning 뜻, 의미
R.O.K means Republic of Korea. R.O.K는 대한민국을 뜻한다.

537 □ **noise** [nɔiz]
명 소음 형 noisy 시끄러운
make a noise 시끄럽게 하다 What's the noise? 무슨 소리야?

538 □ **peaceful** [pi:sfl]
형 평화적인
a peaceful day 평화로운 날 a peaceful solution 평화로운 해결책

Daily Test

| 월 일 |

Ⓐ 우리말에 맞게 빈 칸에 알맞은 단어를 쓰세요.

1 We visited the ______________ palace last weekend. 지난 주말 우리는 왕궁을 방문했다.

2 The storm seriously ______________ this area. 태풍은 이 지역에 심각하게 영향을 주었다.

3 They ______________ the city at night. 그들은 밤에 그 도시를 공격했다.

4 John got the first prize in the music ______________. John은 음악 경연에서 1등을 했다.

5 We ______________ a new software program in 2015.
우리는 2015년에 새로운 소프트웨어 프로그램을 개발했다.

6 I think the game was ______________. 난 그 경기가 공정했다고 생각한다.

7 My family ______________ together to watch the soccer game.
우리 가족은 축구 경기를 보기 위해 함께 모였다.

8 I don't understand what the sentence ______________.
나는 그 문장이 의미하는 바를 모르겠다.

9 Don't make a ______________ in this room. 이 방에서 시끄럽게 굴지마.

10 Today is so ______________. 오늘은 참 평화롭다.

Ⓑ 빈 칸에 알맞은 단어를 고르세요.

1 Susan ______________ like a baby.
① behavior ② behave ③ behaved ④ behavely ⑤ behaving

2 Seoul is the ______________ of Korea.
① capital ② affect ③ attack ④ fair ⑤ nation

3 I live in ______________ with my neighbors.
① noise ② steam ③ gather ④ shape ⑤ harmony

Day 22

MP3

539 punish [pʌ́niʃ]

동 벌하다, 혼을 내다 punish-punished-punished

punish theft 절도를 처벌하다 punish mildly 가볍게 벌주다

540 vacuum [vækjuəm]

명 진공, 공백

a vacuum state 진공 상태 a vacuum cleaner 진공 청소기

541 shape [ʃeip]

명 형태, 모양

a circle shape 원 모양 in the shape of a heart 하트 모양의

542 spoil [spɔil]

동 망치다 spoil-spoiled-spoiled 유 ruin 망치다

spoil the view 전망을 망치다 spoil the party 파티를 망치다

543 steam [sti:m]

명 김, 증기

a steam train 증기 기관차 steam up 김이 서리다

544 teenager [tí:nèidʒər]

명 10대

a teenager magazine 10대용 잡지

545 twin [twin]

명 쌍둥이 형 쌍둥이의

twin brothers 쌍둥이 형제 one of the twins 쌍둥이 중 한 사람

546 tradition [trədíʃən]

명 전통 형 traditional 전통적인

follow tradition 전통을 따르다 a Japanese tradition 일본 전통

547 unusual [ʌnjú:ʒuəl]

형 특이한 유 extraordinary 기이한, 보기 드문

be unusual 심상치 않다 an unusual hobby 별난 취미

548 waist [weist]

명 허리

around the waist 허리 주위에 from the waist up 허리 위로

549 weight [weit]

명 몸무게

gain weight 체중이 늘다 lose weight 살을 빼다

550 without [wiðáut]

전 ~없이

without reason 이유 없이 without food 음식 없이

Daily Test

| 월 일 |

A 우리말에 맞게 빈 칸에 알맞은 단어를 쓰세요.

1 The teacher ______________ Hana because she didn't do her homework. 선생님은 하나가 숙제를 안 했기 때문에 혼을 냈다.

2 Her bag was in the ______________ of a heart. 그녀의 가방은 하트 모양이었다.

3 His bad attitude ______________ our dinner. 그의 나쁜 태도는 우리의 저녁 식사를 망쳤다.

4 There is a ______________ train in the museum. 그 박물관에는 증기 기관차가 있다.

5 We will make a TV program for ______________. 우리는 10대들을 위한 TV 프로그램을 만들 것이다.

6 Jack and John are ______________. Jack과 John은 쌍둥이다.

7 He has an ______________ talent. 그는 심상치 않은 재능을 가졌다.

8 I bought a new ______________ belt for my brother. 난 오빠를 위해 새 허리띠를 샀다.

9 I want to lose ______________. 나는 살을 빼고 싶어.

10 People can't live ______________ water. 사람들은 물 없이 살 수 없다.

B 빈 칸에 알맞은 단어를 고르세요.

1 Sound cannot travel through a ______________.
① noise ② air ③ vacuum ④ tradition ⑤ steam

2 Wearing a Hanbok on New Year's Day is a Korean ______________.
① holiday ② unusual ③ belt ④ punished ⑤ tradition

Review Test 11 Day 21 + Day 22 | 월 일 |

A 우리말에 맞게 빈 칸에 알맞은 단어를 쓰세요.

1 ________________ A to B A가 B하는 것을 허락하다

2 gain ________________ 체중이 늘다

3 carry out a ________________ 임무를 수행하다

4 a blood ________________ 혈액형

5 garden ________________ 정원 쓰레기

6 ________________ reason 이유 없이

7 ________________ between players 선수들 간의 경쟁

8 live in ________________ with ~와 좋게 지내다

9 ________________ the party 파티를 망치다

10 a ________________ pain 허리 통증

B 다음 영어 풀이에 알맞은 어휘를 〈보기〉에서 고르세요.

보기	court	bride	title	shape	donkey

1 ____________ : a woman who is about to be married or has recently been married

2 ____________ : a horse-like animal that is also used for riding

3 ____________ : a name of a book, movie, music, poem, painting, etc

4 ____________ : a place where official judgments based on laws are made

5 ____________ : a form or outline of a thing such as a triangle or a circle

C 다음 단어의 관계가 A:B=C:D가 되도록 알맞은 단어를 골라 빈 칸에 적으세요.

1 mean : ________________ = steal : stolen

① means ② meant ③ meaning
④ meaned ⑤ mean

2 ________________ : politely = drive : safely

① behave ② polite ③ study
④ opinion ⑤ think

3 eye : blind = ear : ________________

① ears ② dumb ③ deafly
④ deaf ⑤ ankle

4 ________________ : day = daily : newspaper

① belong ② peaceful ③ danger
④ dew ⑤ cup

5 ________________ : empty = strike : hit

① ahead ② thick ③ full
④ busy ⑤ vacuum

D 문맥에 맞게 다음 문장을 완성하세요.

1	Write your name and	a	was fair.
2	You can drink	b	coffee for free.
3	There are eight planets	c	phone number in the blanks.
4	I think the game	d	an unusual talent.
5	He has	e	in the solar system.

E 문장을 읽고 문맥에 적절한 단어를 고르세요.

1 The boy was (spoiled/punished) for lying.

2 Kurt (received/allowed) 100 dollars as a prize for winning the quiz show.

3 The girl (gathered/wiped) her dolls and put them in a box.

4 It is (necessary/proud) for you to take action right now.

5 He (stressed/struck) the ball really hard.

F 문장의 빈칸에 알맞은 단어를 〈보기〉에서 찾아 쓰세요. (필요하면 형태를 고치세요.)

보기	steam	promise	affect	forever	develop

1 The writer's latest novel greatly ____________ young readers.
그 작가의 최신 소설은 젊은 독자들에게 큰 영향을 주었다.

2 The small island has a ____________ rail service.
그 작은 섬은 증기 기관차를 운영한다.

3 Joan ____________ his daughter a new skirt.
Joan은 딸에게 새 스커트를 약속했다.

4 The company spent a lot of money to ____________ the new model car.
그 회사는 새로운 자동차 모델을 개발하기 위해 많은 돈을 썼다.

5 They thought that their friendship would last ____________.
그들은 자신들의 우정이 영원히 지속될 것이라고 생각했다.

G 그림에 해당하는 낱말을 〈보기〉에서 골라 쓰세요.

1 

(　　　　　　　　)

2 

(　　　　　　　　)

3 

(　　　　　　　　)

4 

(　　　　　　　　)

5 

(　　　　　　　　)

6 

(　　　　　　　　)

보기 attack twins gesture deep tradition hide

Study More

음이 비슷한 단어 royal vs. Royal vs. loyal

- [royal] 형 국왕의, 여왕의
  the **royal** household 왕실
- [Royal] 형 왕이 있는 국가에서 '왕립' 혹은 왕과 관련된 것을 의미할 때.
  The **Royal** Library 왕립 도서관
- [loyal] 형 충실한, 충성스러운
  a **loyal** supporter 충실한 지지자

Day 23

MP3

551 **electric** [iléktrik]
형 전기의 명 electricity 전기
an electric motor 전기 모터 an electric guitar 전자 기타

552 **west** [west]
명 서쪽 형 서쪽의 부 서쪽으로 *western 형 서쪽의, 서부의
from the west 서쪽으로부터 West Africa 서아프리카

553 **alive** [əláiv]
형 살아 있는
still alive 아직 살아 있는 catch alive 생포하다

554 **background** [bǽkgràund]
명 배경
historical background 역사적 배경 a background color 배경색

555 **both** [bouθ]
형 양자의 대 둘 다(의)
both A and B A와 B 둘 다 both countries 양쪽 국가 모두

556 **ceiling** [síːliŋ]
명 천장
a ceiling fan 천장 선풍기 a kitchen ceiling 부엌 천장

557 **crash** [kræʃ]
동 충돌하다 명 사고, 굉음 crash-crashed-crashed
a car crash 자동차 사고 crash into ~와 충돌하다

558 **express** [iksprés]
형 빠른, 급행의 동 표현하다 express-expressed-expressed
express mail 특급 우편 express a feeling 감정을 표현하다

559 **friendship** [fréndʃip]
명 우정, 교우관계
a close friendship 돈독한 관계 develop a friendship 우정을 키우다

560 **housework** [háuswə̀ːrk]
명 집안 일
do the housework 집안일을 하다 routine housework 일상의 가사

561 **mystery** [místəri]
명 수수께끼, 미스터리 형 mysterious 기이한, 불가사의한
read a mystery book 추리 소설을 읽다

562 **pain** [pein]
명 고통, 통증 형 painful 아픈, 괴로운
back pain 등 통증 feel pain 통증을 느끼다, 고통스러워하다

563 **pop** [pɑp]
형 인기있는 명 팝 음악, 펑 터지는 소리
my favorite pop music 내가 좋아하는 팝 음악 go pop 뻥 하고 터지다

Daily Test

| 월 일 |

A 우리말에 맞게 빈 칸에 알맞은 단어를 쓰세요.

1 She can play the ______________ guitar. 그녀는 전자 기타를 연주할 수 있다.

2 We learned the historical ______________ of World War Ⅱ.
우리는 2차 세계 대전의 역사적 배경에 대해 배웠다.

3 ______________ Nuri and Yuna are good dancers. 누리와 유나는 둘 다 춤을 잘 춘다.

4 I need to paint the kitchen ______________. 나는 부엌 천장에 색을 칠할 필요가 있다.

5 Two cars ______________ into each other. 두 대의 자동차가 서로 충돌했다.

6 Alex doesn't like to ______________ his feelings.
Alex는 그의 감정을 표현하는 것을 좋아하지 않는다.

7 Our ______________ will last forever. 우리의 우정은 영원히 계속될 거야.

8 Minsu does the ______________ to help his mom. 민수는 엄마를 돕기 위해 집안일을 한다.

9 There are some ______________ about the universe.
우주에 대한 몇 가지 미스터리가 있다.

10 Sally is in ______________ because she failed the exam.
Sally는 시험에서 떨어진 뒤에 고통스러워하고 있다.

B 빈 칸에 알맞은 단어를 고르세요.

1 The sun sets in the ______________.
① east ② electric ③ country ④ Korea ⑤ west

2 I don't know whether the tiger is ______________ or dead.
① live ② alive ③ lively ④ lived ⑤ lives

3 The balloon went ______________.
① pops ② pop ③ popping ④ popped ⑤ popes

Day 23

MP3

564 □ **really** [rí(:)əli]
부 실제로, 진짜로, 정말로, 아주
really happen 실제로 일어나다 really busy 몹시 바쁜

565 □ **several** [sévərəl]
형 몇몇의 대 몇몇
several cities 몇몇 도시들 several problems 몇몇 문제들

566 □ **similar** [símələr]
형 비슷한 반 dissimilar 다른, 같지 않은
similar in size 크기가 비슷한 similar interests 비슷한 흥미

567 □ **stage** [steidʒ]
명 단계, 무대
an early stage 초기 단계 appear on the stage 무대에 등장하다

568 □ **talent** [tǽlənt]
명 재능 형 talented 재능있는
a talent for math 수학적 재능 a special talent 특별한 재능

569 □ **thirsty** [θə́ːrsti]
형 목이 마른
hungry and thirsty 배고프고 목이 마른 a thirsty boy 목이 마른 소년

570 □ **trade** [treid]
명 무역 동 무역하다 유 commerce 무역, 상업
international trade 국제 무역 foreign trade 외국 무역

571 □ **view** [vjuː]
명 관점, 견해, 경관
have a different view 다른 관점을 갖다 a point of view 관점

572 □ **vote** [vout]
명 투표 동 투표하다 vote-voted-voted
hold a vote 투표를 실시하다 vote for ~에 투표하다

573 □ **cool** [kuːl]
형 시원한, 서늘한 유 chilly 쌀쌀한, 추운
cool weather 서늘한 날씨 a cool drink 시원한 음료

574 □ **while** [hwail]
접 ~하는 동안에
for a while 잠시 동안 stand for a while 잠시 동안 서 있다

575 □ **with** [wið]
전 ~와 함께
have lunch with friends 친구들과 점심을 먹다

Daily Test

| 월 일 |

A 우리말에 맞게 빈 칸에 알맞은 단어를 쓰세요.

1 We ______________ miss Yuna. 우리는 정말 유나가 그립다.

2 I received ______________ letters from Tim. 나는 Tim에게 편지 몇 통을 받았다.

3 Alice and I have ______________ hobbies. Alice와 나는 비슷한 취미들을 갖고 있다.

4 Sue has a ______________ for dancing. Sue는 춤에 재능이 있다.

5 Do you feel ______________? 목이 마르니?

6 Fair ______________ is very important. 공정 무역은 매우 중요하다.

7 The ______________ of the ocean from the house is great.
그 집에서 보는 바다 전망은 멋있다.

8 Today's weather is so ______________. 오늘 날씨는 시원하다.

9 ______________ you are making cookies, I will buy some juice.
네가 쿠키를 만드는 동안에 난 주스를 사올게.

10 Minsuk lives ______________ his little brother in Seoul.
민석이는 어린 남동생과 서울에서 함께 살고 있다.

B 빈 칸에 알맞은 단어를 고르세요.

1 He is performing on the ______________.
① situation ② stage ③ view ④ ceiling ⑤ pain

2 Jimin ______________ for a new president.
① several ② traded ③ voted ④ crashed ⑤ both

Day 24

MP3

576 **forget** [fərgét]
동 잊다 forget-forgot-forgotten 형 forgetful 잘 잊어먹는
forget the promise 약속을 잊다 forget to call 전화하는 것을 까먹다

577 **pardon** [páːrdn]
명 용서 동 용서하다
beg your pardon 당신의 용서를 구하다 Pardon me. 죄송합니다.

578 **wood** [wud]
명 나무, 목재 ⁺wooden 형 나무로 된, 목재의
a wood table 나무 탁자 cut wood 나무를 패다

579 **career** [kəríər]
명 직업, 경력
an interesting career 흥미로운 직업 a teaching career 교육 경력

580 **beside** [bisáid]
전 ~옆에
beside the table 탁자 옆에 beside the bakery 빵집 옆에

581 **college** [kálidʒ]
명 대학 유 university 대학
a college student 대학생 enter college 대학에 들어가다

582 **east** [iːst]
명 동쪽 형 동쪽의 ⁺eastern 형 동쪽에 위치한, 동부의
go east 동쪽으로 가다 along the East Sea 동해안을 따라서

583 **flat** [flæt]
형 평평한, 바람이 빠진
flat ground 평평한 땅 a flat tire 바람 빠진 타이어

584 **heaven** [hévən]
명 천국 ⁺haven 명 안식처
the kingdom of heaven 천국 pictures of heaven 천국 그림

585 **honest** [ánist]
형 정직한 반 dishonest 정직하지 않은
an honest boy 정직한 소년 to be honest with you 솔직히 말해서

586 **neat** [niːt]
형 정돈된, 깔끔한 neat-neater-neatest
a neat room 깔끔한 방 neat and tidy 깔끔하고 정돈된

587 **attend** [əténd]
동 참석하다 attend-attended-attended 명 attendance 참석
attend a party 파티에 참석하다 attend school 학교에 다니다

588 **prize** [praiz]
명 상, 상품
win the first prize 일등상을 받다 the Nobel Prize 노벨상

Daily Test

| 월 일 |

Ⓐ 우리말에 맞게 빈 칸에 알맞은 단어를 쓰세요.

1 She ______________ Tim's birthday. 그녀는 Tim의 생일을 잊었다.

2 I was making a ______________ chair for my son.
나는 아들을 위해 나무 의자를 만드는 중이었다.

3 Jieun wants to have a long and successful ______________.
지은이는 장기간 성공적인 경력을 쌓고 싶어 한다.

4 There is a supermarket ______________ the bakery. 빵집 옆에 슈퍼마켓이 있다.

5 My brother is a ______________ student. 우리 형은 대학생이다.

6 The park is to the ______________ of the gym. 공원은 체육관 동쪽에 있다.

7 Mrs. Lee likes ______________ shoes. Mrs. Lee는 굽이 없는 신발을 좋아한다.

8 I want to be ______________ with you. 난 당신에게 솔직해지고 싶어요.

9 Her desk is always ______________ and tidy. 그녀의 책상은 언제나 깔끔하고 정돈되어 있다.

10 John will ______________ the party tomorrow. John은 내일 파티에 참석할 것이다.

Ⓑ 빈 칸에 알맞은 단어를 고르세요.

1 Jimmy begged for ______________.
① east ② pardon ③ honest ④ view ⑤ neat

2 She looks like an angel from ______________.
① flat ② east ③ ground ④ talent ⑤ heaven

3 Jack and Leah got the first ______________ in the music contest.
① spirit ② prize ③ beside ④ pardon ⑤ play

Day 24

MP3

589 **review** [rivjúː]
동 비평하다, 검토하다 명 복습, 비평 review-reviewed-reviewed
review a movie 영화를 비평하다 review a report 보고서를 검토하다

590 **shark** [ʃɑːrk]
명 상어
be afraid of sharks 상어를 두려워하다

591 **spill** [spil]
동 엎지르다, 쏟다 spill-spilled(spilt)-spilled(spilt)
spill milk 우유를 엎지르다 spill salt 소금을 엎지르다

592 **spirit** [spírit]
명 정신, 마음, 자세 *spirits 명 기분, 마음
a spirit of leadership 지도자의 자세 be in low spirits 기분이 우울하다

593 **text** [tekst]
명 본문, 글 동 문자 메시지를 보내다
hidden message in the text 글 속에 숨겨진 메시지

594 **tongue** [tʌŋ]
명 혀, 언어, 말씨
mother tongue 모국어 have a gentle tongue 말씨가 부드럽다

595 **vest** [vest]
명 조끼
wear a black vest 검은 조끼를 입다 a life vest 구명복

596 **skin** [skin]
명 피부
healthy skin 건강한 피부 have dark skin 까무잡잡한 피부를 가지다

597 **volume** [váljuːm]
명 음량, 권, 용량, 용적
turn down the volume 음량을 줄이다

598 **worm** [wəːrm]
명 벌레
catch a worm 벌레를 잡다 see a dead worm 죽은 벌레를 보다

599 **yet** [jet]
부 아직
haven't finished yet 아직 끝내지 않았다 not yet 아직도 ~않다

600 **ugly** [ʌ́gli]
형 못생긴, 싫은, 불쾌한 ugly-uglier-ugliest
look very ugly 매우 못생겨 보이다 an ugly task 골치 아픈 일

Daily Test

| 월 일 |

A 우리말에 맞게 빈 칸에 알맞은 단어를 쓰세요.

1 The book got a good ______________. 그 책은 좋은 비평을 얻었다.

2 There are big ______________ in the aquarium. 수족관에 큰 상어들이 있다.

3 Yuna is usually in good ______________. 유나는 대개 기분이 좋다.

4 ______________ me when you wake up. 일어나면 문자 보내줘.

5 Peter has a gentle ______________. Peter는 말씨가 부드럽다.

6 You should wear a life ______________ when you swim in the sea.
바다에서 수영할 때는 구명복을 입어야 한다.

7 I want to have healthy ______________. 난 건강한 피부를 갖고 싶다.

8 Can you turn down the ______________ on the radio?
라디오 볼륨을 줄여 줄 수 있나요?

9 The early bird catches the ______________. 일찍 일어나는 새가 벌레를 잡는다.

10 They say Linda is really ______________. 그들은 Linda가 정말 못생겼다고 말한다.

B 빈 칸에 알맞은 단어를 고르세요.

1 Don't cry over ______________ milk.
① spilt ② tongue ③ vest ④ held ⑤ texted

2 She hasn't started to do her homework ______________.
① already ② while ③ yet ④ for ⑤ during

Review Test 12

Day 23 + Day 24 | 월 일 |

A 우리말에 맞게 빈 칸에 알맞은 단어를 쓰세요.

1 a teaching ________________ 교육 경력

2 a car ________________ 자동차 사고

3 a special ________________ 특별한 재능

4 international ________________ 국제 무역

5 stand for a ________________ 잠시 동안 서 있다

6 ask for a ________________ 용서를 빌다

7 ________________ the table 탁자 옆에

8 a ________________ tire 바람 빠진 타이어

9 mother ________________ 모국어

10 turn down the ________________ 음량을 줄이다

B 다음 영어 풀이에 알맞은 어휘를 〈보기〉에서 고르세요.

보기	ceiling	friendship	prize	college	skin

1 ____________ : the top inside surface of a room or covered space

2 ____________ : a natural and protective covering of your body

3 ____________ : a school one goes to after graduation from high school

4 ____________ : the relationship between friends or the state of being friends

5 ____________ : something you get for winning a game or competition

C 다음 단어의 관계가 A:B=C:D가 되도록 알맞은 단어를 골라 빈 칸에 적으세요.

1 forget : ________________ = take : taken

① forgotten ② forgot ③ forgets
④ forgetted ⑤ forgetting

2 ________________ : electrictiy = active : activity

① electricities ② eletricive ③ electronic
④ electric ⑤ electricically

3 ________________ : meeting = tell : joke

① attend ② good ③ regular
④ attending ⑤ late

4 warm : ________________ = smart : foolish

① hottest ② summer ③ weather
④ mild ⑤ cool

5 honest : ________________ = near : far

① honesty ② dishonest ③ honestly
④ unhonest ⑤ honested

D 문맥에 맞게 다음 문장을 완성하세요.

1	We learned the historical background	a	when you wake up.
2	There are some mysteries	b	of World War II.
3	Text me	c	about the universe.
4	Her desk is	d	always neat and tidy.
5	There are big	e	sharks in the aquarium.

E 문장을 읽고 문맥에 적절한 단어를 고르세요.

1 Yesterday, people in this town (voted/viewed) for a new mayor.

2 Donkeys and horses look (square/similar) to each other.

3 We haven't been to the museum (already/yet).

4 Drawing pictures can be a way to (express/expect) yourself.

5 Swimming in the sea without wearing a life (volume/vest) is dangerous.

F 문장의 빈칸에 알맞은 단어를 〈보기〉에서 찾아 쓰세요. (필요하면 형태를 고치세요.)

보기	both	ceiling	review	wood	alive

1 A:Which shirt would you like? B: I'd like ____________.
A:어떤 셔츠가 마음에 드니? B:양쪽 다 좋아.

2 Yunho, why don't you ____________ your essay before you hand it in?
윤호야, 네 에세이를 제출하기 전에 한 번 검토하는 게 어때?

3 There are no more animals ____________ on this island.
이 섬에는 더 이상 살아있는 동물들이 없다.

4 This house has a ____________ floor.
이 집은 바닥이 나무로 되어있다.

5 The basketball player's head almost touched the ____________ of the room.
그 농구선수의 머리가 방 천장에 거의 닿았다.

G **그림과 낱말이 <u>잘못</u> 짝지어진 것을 고르세요.** ························ (　　　　)

ⓐ

housework

ⓑ

pardon

ⓒ

thirsty

ⓓ
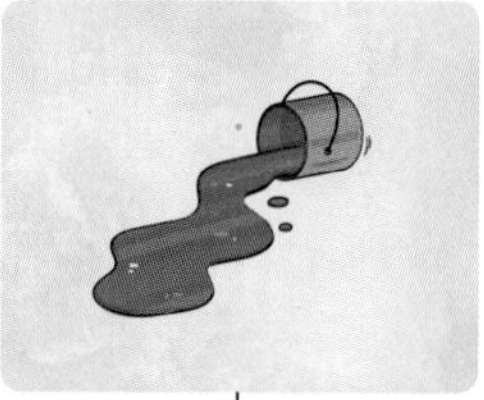
spilt

H **낱말과 어울리는 그림을 연결하세요.**

1 worm •　　　　• ⓐ

2 ugly •　　　　• ⓑ

Study More

yet의 용법

- [부정문,의문문] : '아직'
  I haven't had lunch **yet.** 나는 아직까지 점심을 먹지 못했어.
- [접속사] : '그렇지만, 그런데도'
  Her explanation was simple **yet** effective. 그녀의 설명은 간결했지만 효과적이었다.

Day 25

MP3

601 **hold** [hould]
동 잡다, 쥐다 명 잡기 hold-held-held
hold hands 손을 잡다 take hold of ~을 잡다

602 **sticky** [stíki]
형 끈적거리는
sticky with sweat 땀으로 끈적거리는 a sticky handle 끈적한 손잡이

603 **choice** [tʃɔis]
명 선택 *choose 동 선택하다
the best choice 최상의 선택 the right choice 올바른 선택

604 **along** [əlɔ́(:)ŋ]
전 ~을 따라서 부 ~와 함께
come along (with) ~와 함께 가다 along the street 거리를 따라서

605 **branch** [bræntʃ]
명 나뭇가지, 지사, 지점
the branches of a pine tree 소나무 가지들

606 **tough** [tʌf]
형 거친, 강인한 tough-tougher-toughest
a tough man 강인한 남자 tough meat 질긴 고기

607 **end up ~ing** [end ʌp ~iŋ]
결국 ~하게 되다
end up losing the game 결국 게임에 지게 되다

608 **freeze** [fri:z]
동 얼어붙다, 얼리다 freeze-froze-frozen *frozen 형 냉동된, 얼린
freeze over 완전히 얼어붙다 freeze to the ground 땅에 얼어붙다

609 **hole** [houl]
명 구멍, 굴
a deep hole 깊은 구멍 drill a hole 구멍을 뚫다

610 **information** [ìnfərméiʃən]
명 정보
good information 좋은 정보 collect information 정보를 수집하다

611 **be nervous about** [bi nə́:rvəs əbout]
~에 대해 불안해하다, 초조해하다
be nervous about the future 미래에 대해 불안해하다

612 **pat** [pæt]
동 (애정을 담아) 쓰다듬다, 토닥거리다 pat-patted-patted
pat him on the back 그의 등을 쓰다듬다

613 **reason** [rí:zən]
명 이유, 이성, 판단력 유 cause 원인, 이유
know the reason 이유를 알다 give a reason 이유를 들다

Daily Test

| 월 일 |

A 우리말에 맞게 빈 칸에 알맞은 단어를 쓰세요.

1 Tim and I ______________ hands while walking in the park.
Tim과 나는 손을 잡고 공원을 걸었다.

2 He was ______________ with sweat after the soccer game.
축구 경기 후 그는땀으로 끈적거렸다.

3 She has a difficult ______________ to make. 그녀는 어려운 선택을 해야 한다.

4 The birds are sitting on a tree ______________. 새들이 나뭇가지 위에 앉아있다.

5 We think Kevin is a very ______________ man. 우리는 Kevin이 매우 강한 남자라고 생각한다.

6 The boy ______________ the math exam again. 소년은 결국 수학 시험을 다시 치게 되었다.

7 Harry dug a big ______________ in the ground. Harry는 땅에 큰 구멍을 팠다.

8 There is a lot of ______________ about healthy food in this book.
이 책에는 건강에 좋은 음식에 관한 정보들이 많이 있다.

9 He ______________ his dog on the head. 그는 그의 강아지 머리를 쓰다듬었다.

10 I don't know the ______________ why he couldn't come to the party.
나는 그가 파티에 오지 못한 이유를 모른다.

B 빈 칸에 알맞은 단어를 고르세요.

1 Can you come ______________ with us?
① along ② tough ③ through ④ against ⑤ to

2 Water ______________ at 0℃.
① frozen ② freezes ③ freezing ④ freeze ⑤ freezeses

3 She was ______________, so her leg started to shake.
① nervous ② adventure ③ solar ④ dew ⑤ cry

Day 25

MP3

614 **sharp** [ʃɑːrp]

형 날카로운 sharp-sharper-sharpest 동 sharpen 날카롭게 하다

use a sharp knife 날카로운 칼을 사용하다 sharp teeth 날카로운 이빨

615 **sign** [sain]

명 신호, 징조 동 서명하다, 신호를 보내다 sign-signed-signed

a sign of stress 스트레스의 징후 sign the paper 서류에 서명하다

616 **spread** [spred]

동 펴다, 펼치다, 펴서 바르다 명 확산 spread-spread-spread

spread a newspaper 신문을 펼치다 spread rumors 소문을 퍼뜨리다

617 **language** [lǽŋgwidʒ]

명 언어

speak two languages 2개 국어를 하다 language skill 언어 능력

618 **whisper** [wispə(r)]

동 속삭이다, 소근거리다

whisper in your ear 귀에 대고 속삭이다

619 **control** [kəntróul]

명 지배, 통제 동 통제하다, 제어하다 control-controlled-controlled

out of control 통제 불능의 control your feelings 감정을 통제하다

620 **village** [vílidʒ]

명 마을, 촌락

a mountain village 산간 마을 a big village 큰 마을

621 **weather** [wéðər]

명 날씨 유 climate 기후

a weather report 일기 예보 bad weather 나쁜 날씨

622 **yard** [jɑːrd]

명 마당, 뜰, 운동장, 제조장

plant a tree in the back yard 뒷마당에 나무를 심다

623 **customer** [kʌ́stəmər]

명 고객

a regular customer 단골 손님 customer service 고객 서비스

624 **modern** [mádərn]

형 현대적인 반 ancient 고대의, 오래된

modern life 현대 생활 modern history 현대사

625 **escape** [iskéip]

동 탈출하다, ~을 벗어나다 명 탈출 escape-escaped-escaped

escape from the enemy 적들로부터 도망치다

Daily Test

| 월 일 |

Ⓐ 우리말에 맞게 빈 칸에 알맞은 단어를 쓰세요.

1 Lions have _______________ teeth. 사자는 날카로운 이빨을 갖고 있다.

2 The _______________ on the door said "closed". 그 문 표지판에는 '휴업'이라고 쓰여 있었다.

3 The bird _______________ its wings. 새는 그의 날개를 펼쳤다.

4 _______________ your feelings is the most important thing.
감정을 통제하는 것이 가장 중요하다.

5 My grandmother lives in a quiet _______________. 우리 할머니는 조용한 마을에 사신다.

6 Let's check the _______________ report. 일기예보를 확인해보자.

7 There is a swing in the _______________. 마당에 그네가 있다.

8 Linda is one of my store's _______________ customers.
Linda는 우리 가게의 단골손님 중 한 명이다.

9 I study _______________ Art History these days. 나는 요즘 현대 미술사에 대해서 배우고 있다.

10 Sam _______________ from the enemy at night. Sam은 밤에 적들로부터 도망쳤다.

Ⓑ 빈 칸에 알맞은 단어를 고르세요.

1 My sister learns three _______________: French, Chinese and English.
① languages ② countries ③ weathers ④ reasons ⑤ languages

2 The little girl _______________ something into her father's ear.
① signed ② surprised ③ disappointed ④ whispered ⑤ cycled

Day 26

MP3

626 **fail** [feil]

동 실패하다 명 실패 fail-failed-failed

fail a test 시험에 떨어지다 fail to win the game 경기에 이기지 못하다

627 **slide** [slaid]

동 미끄러지다 명 미끄럼틀 slide-slid-slid

slide down 미끄러져 내려가다 go down the slide 미끄럼틀을 타다

628 **object** [ɑ́bdʒikt]

명 물건, 목표 동 반대하다 object-objected-objected

the object in the basket 바구니 속 물건 object to ~에 반대하다

629 **appreciate** [əpríːʃièit]

동 고마워 하다, 알아보다 appreciate-appreciated-appreciated

appreciate your help 도움에 감사하다

630 **chance** [tʃæns]

명 기회, 가능성 유 opportunity 기회

take a chance 기회를 잡다 by chance 우연히

631 **cross** [krɔ(:)s]

동 건너다 cross-crossed-crossed

cross the bridge 다리를 건너다 cross your arms 팔짱을 끼다

632 **explain** [ikspléin]

동 설명하다 explain-explained-explained

explain the rules of the game 경기 규칙을 설명하다

633 **fund** [fʌnd]

명 기금, 자금

raise funds 기금을 모으다 a charity fund 자선 기금

634 **judge** [dʒʌdʒ]

동 판단하다, 심사하다 명 판사 judge-judged-judged

judge a singing contest 노래 대회를 심사하다

635 **musical** [mjúːzikəl]

형 음악적인, 음악의

a musical director 음악 감독 musical talent 음악적 재능

636 **narrate** [nǽreit]

동 이야기를 하다 narrate-narrated-narrated

narrate his experiences 자신의 경험을 얘기하다

637 **polar** [póulər]

형 북극/남극의, 극지방의

a polar bear 북극곰 a polar explorer 극지방 탐험가

638 **report** [ripɔ́ːrt]

명 보도, 보고서 동 알리다, 보고하다 report-reported-reported

newspaper report 신문 보도 report the accident 사고를 보도하다

Daily Test

| 월 일 |

A 우리말에 맞게 빈 칸에 알맞은 단어를 쓰세요.

1 He ______________ the science exam. 그는 과학시험에 낙제했다.

2 The ______________ of his desire is the telescope. 그가 가지고 싶어하는 물건은 만원경이다.

3 I really ______________ your help. 당신의 도움에 정말 감사드립니다.

4 There's a ______________ of snow tomorrow. 내일 눈이 올 가능성이 있다.

5 Rose ______________ the street. Rose는 길을 건넜다.

6 Our science teacher ______________ how to conduct the experiment.
과학 선생님이 실험을 어떻게 하는지에 대해 설명하신다.

7 My sister has great ______________ talent. 우리 언니는 음악적 재능이 뛰어나다.

8 Cherry ______________ her adventures to the audience.
Cherry는 그녀의 모험에 대해서 청중에게 이야기했다.

9 ______________ bears are large and white. 북극곰은 크고 하얗다.

10 The newspaper ______________ on the accident. 그 신문은 그 사고에 대해 보도했다.

B 빈 칸에 알맞은 단어를 고르세요.

1 The boys are going down the ______________.
① polar ② slide ③ narrate ④ traffic ⑤ medium

2 The club will raise charity ______________.
① funds ② clubs ③ report ④ object ⑤ trick

3 Don't ______________ a book by its cover.
① text ② cross ③ wait ④ judge ⑤ fail

Day 26

MP3

639 search [sə:rtʃ]
동 찾다, 수색하다 명 찾기, 수색 search-searched-searched
search for ~을 찾다 search for the treasure 보물을 찾다

640 legal [lí:gəl]
형 법적인 반 illegal 불법의
legal knowledge 법적 지식 legal advice 법적 조언

641 trust [trʌst]
명 신뢰, 신임 동 신뢰하다 trust-trusted-trusted
have trust in people 사람들을 신뢰하다 Trust me! 믿어줘!

642 statue [stǽtʃu:]
명 조각상
the statue made of stone 돌로 만든 조각상

643 tiny [táini]
형 아주 작은 tiny-tinier-tiniest
tiny bugs 아주 작은 벌레들 tiny insects 아주 작은 곤충들

644 traffic [trǽfik]
명 교통(량), 차량들
heavy traffic 극심한 교통량 a traffic jam 교통 정체

645 trick [trik]
명 속임수 동 속이다 trick-tricked-tricked
play a trick 장난을 치다 a mean trick 비열한 속임수

646 desirable [dizaiərəbl]
형 바람직한, 가치 있는 명 desire 갈망, 욕심
a desirable result 바람직한 결과

647 message [mésidʒ]
명 메시지
deliver a message 메시지를 전달하다

648 wonderful [wʌ́ndərfəl]
형 신나는, 훌륭한 유 excellent 훌륭한, 아주 좋은
a wonderful time in Korea 한국에서의 신나는 시간

649 expression [ikspréʃən]
명 표현, 표정
a good expression 좋은 표현 facial expression 얼굴의 표정

650 medium [mí:diəm]
형 중간의 명 매체, 수단 복 media
a medium-sized car 중간 크기의 자동차 the news media 뉴스 매체

Daily Test

| 월 일 |

A 우리말에 맞게 빈 칸에 알맞은 단어를 쓰세요.

1 We helped to ______________ for the missing child. 우리는 미아 찾는 것을 도왔다.

2 The man is carving a ______________. 그 남자는 상을 조각하고 있다.

3 Jungmin is a ______________ baby. 정민은 아주 작은 아기다.

4 There is heavy ______________ on this street at night. 이 거리는 밤에 교통량이 많다.

5 Jinsu played a ______________ on his sister. 진수는 그의 여동생에게 장난을 쳤다.

6 It is ______________ that you apply to the school as soon as possible. 너는 그 학교에 가능한 빨리 지원하는 것이 바람직하다.

7 Eunsoo left a ______________ for Jinju. 은수는 진주에게 메시지를 남겼다.

8 We had a ______________ time in LA. 우리는 LA에서 신나는 시간을 보냈다.

9 She has a variety of facial ______________. 그녀는 다양한 표정이 있다.

10 Cindy wears a ______________ length white dress. Cindy는 중간 길이의 하얀 드레스를 입고 있다.

B 빈 칸에 알맞은 단어를 고르세요.

1 We have ______________ in Minsu.

① believe ② trust ③ traffic ④ message ⑤ search

2 We want to get some ______________ advice.

① statue ② expression ③ legal ④ narration ⑤ tiny

Review Test 13 Day 25 + Day 26 | 월 일 |

A 우리말에 맞게 빈 칸에 알맞은 단어를 쓰세요.

1 come ______________ (with) ~와 함께 가다

2 the news ______________ 뉴스매체

3 be ______________ about the future 미래에 대해 불안해하다

4 out of ______________ 통제 불능의

5 ______________ history 현대사

6 take a ______________ 기회를 잡다

7 ______________ a singing contest 노래 대회를 심사하다

8 have ______________ in people 사람들을 신뢰하다

9 deliver a ______________ 메시지를 전달하다

10 a good ______________ 좋은 표현

B 다음 영어 풀이에 알맞은 어휘를 〈보기〉에서 고르세요.

보기	evening	information	object	yard	musical

1 ______________ : facts or knowledge about something you get through search or discovery

2 ______________ : an area of land which is usually outside a house or a building

3 ______________ : of or relating to music such as a musical instrument

4 ______________ : a thing that has a shape and can be touched

5 ______________ : the period between late afternoon and night

C 다음 단어의 관계가 A:B=C:D가 되도록 알맞은 단어를 골라 빈 칸에 적으세요.

1 spread : ________________ = think : thought

① spreaded ② spread ③ spreads
④ spreaden ⑤ spreading

2 ________________ : test = destroy : building

① great ② difficult ③ match
④ English ⑤ fail

3 legal : ________________ = regular : irregular

① unlegal ② underlegal ③ illegal
④ exlegal ⑤ delegal

4 ________________ : Korean = subject : math

① Chinese ② Hanbok ③ sweet
④ language ⑤ textbook

5 choose : ________________ = serve : service

① chose ② friend ③ choice
④ character ⑤ choosen

D 문맥에 맞게 다음 문장을 완성하세요.

1	He was sticky with sweat •	• a	the weather report.
2	Let's check •	• b	large and white.
3	Our science teacher explains •	• c	how to conduct the experiment.
4	Polar bears are •	• d	on the street at night.
5	There is heavy traffic •	• e	after the soccer game.

E 문장을 읽고 문맥에 적절한 단어를 고르세요.

1 The students (reported/replied) the accident to the police.

2 If you want to join the team, you need to (sign/signal) your name on the line.

3 I (narrated/waited) for the bus for half an hour.

4 We really (freeze/appreciate) your help with our history project.

5 The boy helped the old woman to (cross/suggest) the street safely.

F 문장의 빈칸에 알맞은 단어를 〈보기〉에서 찾아 쓰세요. (필요하면 형태를 고치세요.)

보기	customer	narrate	hole	tough	reason

1 The famous actor ____________ his trip to Indonesia on TV.
그 유명한 영화배우는 TV에서 자신의 인도네시아 여행에 대해 이야기했다.

2 Jack always greets his ____________ with a smile.
Jack은 항상 웃는 얼굴로 손님들을 맞이한다.

3 The dog made a small ____________ in the fence.
그 개는 울타리에 작은 구멍을 만들었다.

4 The turtle's shell is very hard and ____________.
거북의 등껍질은 매우 단단하고 거칠다.

5 There is no ____________ not to study as many languages as you can.
가능한 많은 외국어를 공부하지 않을 이유가 없다.

G 그림에 해당하는 낱말을 〈보기〉에서 골라 쓰세요.

1 

( )

2 

( )

3 

( )

4 

( )

5 

( )

6 

( )

보기 branch pat hold slide freeze sharp

Study More

비슷한 단어 legal vs. regal

- [legal] : '법률의, 법적인'
  legal advice 법률 상담 a legal document 법률 문서 *illegal 불법적인 an illegal act 불법 행위
- [regal] : '제왕의, 왕의, 장엄한'
  regal power 제왕의 권력 the regal office 왕위

Day 27

MP3

651	**be curious about** [bi kjú(:)əriəs əbáut]	~에 대해 호기심이 많다 — 명 curiosity 호기심 be curious about space 우주에 대해 호기심이 많다
652	**splash** [splæʃ]	동 (물, 흙탕물 등을) 튀기다, 끼얹다 — splash-splashed-splashed splash water on his face 그의 얼굴에 물을 끼얹다
653	**portrait** [pɔ́ːrtrit]	명 초상화, 인물사진 paint a portrait 초상화를 그리다 / a self-portrait 자화상
654	**degree** [digríː]	명 (온도 또는 각도) 도, 학위 14 degrees below zero 영하 14도 / a bachelor's degree 학사학위
655	**comfortable** [kʌ́mfərtəbl]	형 편안한 — 유 cozy 아늑한, 편안한 a comfortable chair 편안한 의자 / a comfortable night 편안한 밤
656	**excellent** [éksələnt]	형 훌륭한, 우수한 excellent service 훌륭한 서비스 / an excellent movie 훌륭한 영화
657	**flea** [fliː]	명 벼룩 a flea market 벼룩시장 / get rid of fleas 벼룩을 제거하다
658	**harvest** [háːrvist]	명 수확 동 수확하다 — harvest-harvested-harvested a good harvest 풍작, 풍년 / harvest apples 사과를 수확하다
659	**liberty** [líbərti]	명 자유, 해방 fight for liberty 자유를 위해 싸우다 / celebrate liberty 해방을 기념하다
660	**major** [méidʒər]	형 주요한, 일류의 동 전공하다 — major-majored-majored major changes 주요한 변화들 / major in ~을 전공하다
661	**look for** [luk fər]	동 ~을 찾다, 구하다 — 유 seek 찾다, 추구하다 look for a diamond ring 다이아몬드 반지를 찾다
662	**pity** [píti]	명 연민, 동정(심), 유감 What a pity! 불쌍해라! / feel pity for ~에게 동정심을 느끼다
663	**respond** [rispánd]	동 반응하다, 대답하다 — respond-responded-responded respond to a letter 편지에 답장하다

Daily Test

| 월 일 |

A **우리말에 맞게 빈 칸에 알맞은 단어를 쓰세요.**

1 Kyungsu is ______________ about space. 경수는 우주에 대해 호기심이 많다.

2 Don't ______________ water on me. 나에게 물을 튀기지마.

3 The woman is painting a ______________. 그 여자는 초상화를 그리고 있다.

4 This bed looks very ______________. 이 침대는 매우 편안해 보인다.

5 I think his performance was ______________. 나는 그의 공연이 훌륭했다고 생각한다.

6 The ______________ festival will be held next Friday. 다음 주 금요일에 추수 감사제가 열릴 것이다.

7 Many people fought for ______________ in the past. 과거에는 많은 사람들이 자유를 위해 싸웠다.

8 The man is ______________ a subway station. 남자는 지하철역을 찾는 중이다.

9 It's a ______________ that Jaehyuk lost his wallet yesterday. 어제 재혁이가 지갑을 잃어버려서 유감이야.

10 We waited for Harry to ______________ to the question. 우리는 Harry가 그 질문에 대답하기를 기다렸다.

B **빈 칸에 알맞은 단어를 고르세요.**

1 My mom got a college ______________ at 40.

① splash ② excellent ③ degree ④ liberty ⑤ pity

2 Soyoung and I go to the ______________ market on Saturdays.

① respond ② flea ③ way ④ topic ⑤ wild

3 I ______________ in Physics.

① majored ② drew ③ showed ④ waited ⑤ way

Day 27

MP3

664 **show** [ʃou]
명 쇼, 공연물 동 보여주다 show-showed-showed
go to a show 쇼를 보러 가다 show your tickets 표를 보여주다

665 **oppose** [əpouz]
동 반대하다, 대립하다 oppose-opposed-opposed
oppose a suggestion 제안에 반대하다

666 **stairs** [steərs]
명 계단
go down stairs 계단을 내려가다 take the stairs 계단을 이용하다

667 **success** [səksés]
명 성공 형 successful 성공한, 성공적인
secret of success 성공의 비결 wealth and success 부와 성공

668 **topic** [tápik]
명 주제 유 subject 주제, 화제
the topic of the speech 연설의 주제

669 **journal** [dʒə́:rnəl]
명 잡지, 신문, 정기 간행물
a monthly journal 월간 잡지 a scientific journal 과학 정기 간행물

670 **one day** [wʌn dei]
언젠가, 어느 날
one day in August 8월의 어느날

671 **way** [wei]
명 길, 방향, 방법
know the way 길을 알다 a unique way 독특한 방법

672 **wild** [waild]
형 야생의 +wildlife 명 야생동물
wild animals 야생 동물들 wild flowers 야생화

673 **nickname** [níknèim]
명 별명 동 별명을 붙이다 nickname-nicknamed-nicknamed
have a new nickname 새 별명을 갖다

674 **positive** [pɑ:zətiv]
형 낙관적인, 긍정적인
a positive attitude 긍정적인 태도 a positive reply 긍정적인 회신

675 **million** [míljən]
명 백만 형 백만의, 수많은
a million 백만 millions of people 아주 많은 사람들

Daily Test

| 월 일 |

A 우리말에 맞게 빈 칸에 알맞은 단어를 쓰세요.

1 You should ______________ me your ticket. 제게 표를 보여주셔야 합니다.

2 Many people ______________ the mayor's proposal.
많은 사람들이 시장의 제안에 반대했다.

3 There is a ball at the bottom of the ______________. 계단 밑에 공 하나가 있다.

4 There is no hope of ______________. 성공할 가망이 없다.

5 What is the ______________ of this book? 이 책의 주제는 무엇인가요?

6 ______________ we will meet again. 우리 언젠가는 만날 거야.

7 She solved the problem in a unique ______________.
그녀는 문제를 독특한 방식으로 풀었다.

8 There are many ______________ animals in the safari.
사파리 안에는 많은 야생동물들이 있다.

9 She was happy to hear a ______________ response from the school.
그녀는 학교로부터 긍정적인 답신을 들어서 행복했다.

10 There are four ______________ books in our library.
우리 도서관에는 4백만 권의 책이 있습니다.

B 빈 칸에 알맞은 단어를 고르세요.

1 This ______________ is published twice a year.
① journal ② success ③ mouth ④ harvest ⑤ liberty

2 Alice's ______________ is "Snow White".
① late ② stairs ③ respond ④ nickname ⑤ media

Day 28

MP3

676 **leave** [li:v]
동 남겨두다, 출발하다 leave-left-left
leave her alone 그녀를 혼자 남겨두다 leave for ~로 출발하다

677 **warn** [wɔ:rn]
동 경고하다 warn-warned-warned 명 warning 경고, 훈계
warn about the danger 위험에 대해 경고하다

678 **beyond** [bijánd]
전 ~저편에, ~을 넘어서는
beyond the hill 언덕 저편에 beyond his ability 그의 능력 밖인

679 **celebrity** [səlébrəti]
명 연예인, 유명인
a man of celebrity 유명인사 a film celebrity 영화계 유명인사

680 **cure** [kjuər]
명 치료 동 고치다, 치료하다 cure-cured-cured
cure for cancer 암 치료 cure a patient 환자를 치료하다

681 **ease** [i:z]
명 쉬움 동 편하게 하다, 편해지다 ease-eased-eased
with ease 쉽게 ease the pain 통증을 가라앉히다

682 **front** [frʌnt]
명 앞, 정면 형 앞쪽의
in front of ~의 앞에 in front of the lake 호수 앞에

683 **happen to** [hǽpən tu]
동 우연히 ~을 하다 happen-happened-happened
happen to meet 우연히 만나다 happen to know him 마침 그를 안다

684 **march** [mɑ:rtʃ]
동 행진하다 명 행진 march-marched-marched
march down the street 거리를 따라 행진하다

685 **work out** [wə:rk aʊt]
(건강을 위해) 운동을 하다
work out at the gym regularly 체육관에서 규칙적으로 운동하다

686 **grave** [greiv]
명 무덤, 산소 유 tomb 무덤
flowers on the grave 무덤 위의 꽃 visit a grave 성묘하다

687 **pond** [pɑnd]
명 연못
fish in the pond 연못 안 물고기들 sit by the pond 연못 옆에 앉다

688 **rub** [rʌb]
동 문지르다, 비비다 rub-rubbed-rubbed
rub the table with a cloth 천으로 탁자를 문지르다

Daily Test

| 월 일 |

A 우리말에 맞게 빈 칸에 알맞은 단어를 쓰세요.

1 She ______________ us about the dangers of air pollution. 그녀는 우리에게 공기 오염의 위험에 대해 경고했다.

2 My house is ______________ the hill. 우리 집은 언덕 저편에 있다.

3 Many people want to become a ______________. 많은 사람들이 유명인사가 되길 바란다.

4 This medicine will ______________ your stomachache. 이 약이 너의 배탈을 치료해 줄 것이다.

5 These pills will help to ______________ your pain. 이 약들이 당신의 통증을 가라앉히는 것을 도와줄 것이다.

6 I ______________ to hear the rumor about him. 나는 그에 관한 소문을 우연히 들었다.

7 Soldiers are ______________ along the street. 군인들은 거리를 따라 행진하고 있다.

8 Joe ______________ regularly to stay healthy. Joe는 건강을 유지하기 위해 규칙적으로 운동한다.

9 There are three ducks in the ______________. 연못에 세 마리의 오리가 있다.

10 I ______________ the ring with a cloth. 나는 천으로 반지를 문질렀다.

B 빈 칸에 알맞은 단어를 고르세요.

1 The cat is in ______________ of the car.

① deep ② cure ③ ease ④ beyond ⑤ front

2 I put flowers on grandfather's ______________.

① grave ② celebrity ③ may ④ pond ⑤ wild

3 Don't ______________ me alone.

① march ② support ③ leave ④ show ⑤ stare

Day 28

MP3

689 **shell** [ʃel]
명 (단단한) 껍질, 조개
seashell 조개 껍데기　　shellfish 조개류

690 **situation** [sìtʃuéiʃən]
명 상황　　유 condition 상태, 상황
a dangerous situation 위험한 상황

691 **stare** [stɛər]
동 빤히 쳐다보다, 응시하다　stare-stared-stared
stare at ~을 응시하다　　stare at the wall 벽을 응시하다

692 **support** [səpɔ́ːrt]
동 지지하다, 지원하다, 부양하다　support-supported-supported
support his idea 그의 생각을 지지하다

693 **total** [tóutl]
형 전체의, 완전한　명 합계, 총액
the total number of students 총 학생의 수

694 **community** [kəmjúːnəti]
명 지역 사회, 공동체
a community center 지역 문화 센터　　a local community 지역 사회

695 **pleasant** [plézənt]
형 즐거운, 기분 좋은　　명 pleasure 즐거움
a pleasant place 기분 좋은 장소　　a pleasant mood 기분 좋은 분위기

696 **furniture** [fə́ːrnitʃər]
명 가구
office furniture 사무용 가구　　a set of furniture 가구 한 벌

697 **fence** [fens]
명 울타리
near the fence 울타리 근처　　over the fence 울타리 너머

698 **extra** [ékstrə]
형 추가의　　유 additional 추가의, 여분의
an extra table 추가 테이블　　extra homework 추가 숙제

699 **few** [fjuː]
형 거의 없는, 많지 않은
a few 어느 정도, 조금　　have few friends 친구가 거의 없다

700 **guard** [gɑːrd]
동 지키다　명 경호 요원　guard-guarded-guarded
guard the gate 정문을 지키다　　a prison guard 교도관

Daily Test

| 월 일 |

A 우리말에 맞게 빈 칸에 알맞은 단어를 쓰세요.

1 Luna likes to eat ________________. Luna는 조개를 먹는 것을 좋아한다.

2 People ________________ at the main stage. 사람들은 메인 무대를 응시했다.

3 We ________________ his opinion. 우리는 그의 의견을 지지한다.

4 I don't know the ________________ number of members in this club. 나는 이 동아리의 전체 회원 수를 모른다.

5 The new ________________ center will open tomorrow. 새 지역 문화 센터가 내일 개장할 것이다.

6 I don't have much ________________ in my room. 내 방에는 가구가 많지 않다.

7 Sheep are jumping over the ________________. 양들이 울타리를 뛰어넘고 있다.

8 We need some ________________ chairs. 우리는 여분의 의자가 더 필요하다.

9 There are a ________________ trees on the hill. 언덕 위에 나무 몇 그루가 있다.

10 Two men ________________ the gate. 두 명의 남자가 정문을 지켰다.

B 빈 칸에 알맞은 단어를 고르세요.

1 They are in a difficult ________________.
① community ② guard ③ fence ④ furniture ⑤ situation

2 I liked to hear her ________________ voice.
① pleasant ② total ③ extra ④ few ⑤ warn

Review Test 14

Day 27 + Day 28 | 월 일 |

A 우리말에 맞게 빈 칸에 알맞은 단어를 쓰세요.

1 a dangerous ________________ 위험한 상황

2 fight for ________________ 자유를 위해 싸우다

3 wealth and ________________ 부와 성공

4 know the ________________ 길을 알다

5 a ________________ 백만

6 ________________ about the danger 위험에 대해 경고하다

7 ________________ the hill 언덕 너머에

8 ________________ his idea 그의 생각을 지지하다

9 a ________________ mood 기분 좋은 분위기

10 a ________________ 어느 정도, 조금

B 다음 영어 풀이에 알맞은 어휘를 〈보기〉에서 고르세요.

보기	degree	journal	nickname	stairs	front

1 ____________ : the location or position which is directly before something

2 ____________ : a friendly or familiar name other than the real name

3 ____________ : a magazine or newspaper for a particular subject or people

4 ____________ : a unit for measuring temperature or angles

5 ____________ : a set of steps which connects different levels of a building or house

C 다음 단어의 관계가 A:B=C:D가 되도록 알맞은 단어를 골라 빈 칸에 적으세요.

1 ________________ : curiosity = healthy : health

① curious ② curiously ③ curiouses
④ curiousness ⑤ curiousy

2 leave : ________________ = ride : rode

① leaves ② lefted ③ left
④ lefted ⑤ lefting

3 comfort : ________________ = rain : rainy

① comforts ② comforted ③ comfortably
④ comfortable ⑤ comfortabile

4 draw : ________________ = go : concert

① drew ② portrait ③ monitor
④ draws ⑤ walk

5 ________________ : sofa = color : yellow

① closet ② table ③ movie
④ furniture ⑤ fruits

D 문맥에 맞게 다음 문장을 완성하세요.

1 We need •	• a	to respond to the question.
2 We waited for Harry •	• b	some extra chairs.
3 One day we will •	• c	to ease your pain.
4 These pills will help •	• d	will open tomorrow.
5 The new community center •	• e	meet again.

E 문장을 읽고 문맥에 적절한 단어를 고르세요.

1 Vitamins are known to (search/cure) and prevent many diseases.

2 Kevin's family is (looking for/looking after) a hotel to stay at.

3 The little monkey in the cage (stared/spread) at me.

4 It's a (shell/pity) that you have to leave now.

5 It was quite cold and she (splashed/rubbed) her hands together.

F 문장의 빈칸에 알맞은 단어를 〈보기〉에서 찾아 쓰세요. (필요하면 형태를 고치세요.)

보기	harvest	excellent	guard	celebrity	major

1 A group of reporters quickly surrounded the ___________ for photos.
한 무리의 기자들이 사진을 찍기 위해 그 유명인사를 에워쌌다.

2 The farmers in this village are happy to have a good ___________ this year.
이 마을의 농부들이 올해 수확이 좋아서 기뻐한다.

3 The football team took in several ___________ players.
그 축구팀은 우수한 선수들을 여러 명 영입했다.

4 Haesun played a ___________ role in the project.
해선은 그 프로젝트에서 주요한 역할을 했다.

5 This tiny software program can ___________ your computer against most computer viruses.
이 작은 소프트웨어 프로그램이 여러분의 컴퓨터를 대부분의 컴퓨터 바이러스 공격으로부터 지켜줄 것입니다.

G 그림과 낱말이 잘못 짝지어진 것을 고르세요. .... (   )

ⓐ

flea

ⓑ

slide

ⓒ

fence

ⓓ

grave

H 낱말과 어울리는 그림을 연결하세요.

1 shell •

2 march •

• ⓐ 

• ⓑ 

Study More

may의 주요 용법

- 가능성, 추측의 의미 '~일지도 모른다'
  He **may** have met Julie yesterday. 그는 어제 Julie를 만났을 지도 모른다.
- 허락, 용인의 의미 '~해도 좋다'
  You **may** go now. 이제 가도 좋다.
- 정중한 요구나 제안을 할 때 '~해도 될까요, ~해 주겠어요?'
  May I leave a bit earlier today? 오늘 조금 일찍 떠나도 될까요?

Day 29

MP3

701 **invitation** [ìnvitéiʃən]
명 초대 — 동 invite 초대하다
an invitation card 초대장 — accept an invitation 초대를 받아들이다

702 **tickle** [tíkl]
동 간지럼을 태우다, 간질간질하다 tickle-tickled-tickled
tickle your ribs 옆구리를 간지럽히다

703 **slowly** [slóuli]
부 천천히, 느리게
walk slowly 천천히 걷다 — drive slowly 느리게 운전하다

704 **broadcast** [brɔ́:dkæ̀st]
동 방송하다 명 방송 broadcast-broadcasted-broadcasted
broadcast a lecture 강연을 방송하다 — live broadcast 생방송

705 **avenue** [ǽvənjù:]
명 (도시의) 거리, -가
a hospital on Sixth Avenue 6번가에 있는 병원

706 **coin** [kɔin]
명 동전
a gold coin 금화 — pick up a coin 동전을 줍다

707 **digest** [dáidʒest]
동 소화하다 digest-digested-digested 명 digestion 소화
digest food 음식을 소화하다 — easy to digest 소화하기 쉬운

708 **foreign** [fɔ́:rin]
형 외국의, 대외의 — 반 domestic 국내의, 가정의
foreign cultures 외국 문화 — foreign visitors 외국인 방문객

709 **height** [hait]
명 높이, (사람의) 키
height and weight 키와 몸무게 — measure height 키를 재다

710 **opinion** [əpínjən]
명 의견 — 유 view 관점, 견해
in my opinion 내 의견으로는, 내 생각에는

711 **owe** [ou]
동 (돈을) 빚지고 있다, ~에게 신세지다 owe-owed-owed
owe money 빚을 지다 — owe him an apology 그에게 사과해야 한다

712 **postcard** [poʊstka:rd]
명 그림엽서, 엽서
send a postcard 엽서를 보내다 — a picture postcard 그림 엽서

713 **public** [pʌ́blik]
형 대중의, 공공의 명 일반인, 대중
go to the public library 공공 도서관에 가다 — public opinion 여론

Daily Test

| 월 일 |

Ⓐ 우리말에 맞게 빈 칸에 알맞은 단어를 쓰세요.

1 You should check the _______________ for the date and time.
초대장의 날짜와 시간을 확인해야 한다.

2 Sally _______________ her daughter's ribs. Sally는 딸의 옆구리를 간지럽혔다.

3 She spoke English very _______________. 그녀는 매우 느리게 영어를 말했다.

4 Channel 7 will _______________ the musical at 8 o'clock.
채널 7에서 정각 8시에 그 뮤지컬을 방송 할 것이다.

5 I found a lot of _______________ in the basket. 나는 바구니에서 많은 동전을 발견했다.

6 This food is easy for children to _______________. 이 음식은 어린이들이 소화시키기 쉽다.

7 There are many _______________ tourists in Gyeongbokgung Palace.
경복궁에는 많은 외국 관광객들이 있다.

8 The tower is 30 meters in _______________. 저 탑은 30미터 높이이다.

9 I _______________ Father a lot of money. 나는 아버지께 많은 돈을 빚졌다.

10 I got a _______________ from John. 난 John으로부터 엽서 한 통을 받았다.

Ⓑ 빈 칸에 알맞은 단어를 고르세요.

1 There is a hotel on Fifth _______________.
① Broadcast ② Height ③ Avenue ④ Postcard ⑤ Ground

2 In my _______________, you should apologize to her.
① invitation ② opinion ③ coin ④ owe ⑤ fence

3 Be quiet in _______________ places.
① beyond ② digest ③ public ④ total ⑤ extra

Day 29

MP3

714 **recently** [ríːsəntli]
부 최근에 형 recent 최근의
until recently 최근까지 quite recently 아주 최근에

715 **shine** [ʃain]
동 빛나다 명 빛, 햇빛, 광택 shine-shone-shone
shine brightly 밝게 빛나다 shine away 계속 빛나다

716 **smooth** [smuːð]
형 부드러운 smooth-smoother-smoothest
smooth skin 부드러운 피부 a smooth cake 부드러운 케이크

717 **temperature** [témpərətʃər]
명 온도, 기온
an average temperature 평균 온도 the body temperature 체온

718 **own** [oun]
동 소유하다 형 자기 자신의 own-owned-owned
his own problem 그 자신의 문제 own a farm 농장을 소유하다

719 **trash** [træʃ]
명 쓰레기 유 garbage 쓰레기
a trash basket 쓰레기통 be full of trash 쓰레기로 가득 차다

720 **valley** [væli]
명 계곡, 골짜기
in a valley 골짜기에 through the valley 계곡을 가로질러

721 **walk** [wɔːk]
동 걷다 walk-walked-walked
walk along the river 강가를 걷다 walk to school 학교까지 걸어가다

722 **yell** [jel]
동 소리치다 명 고함, 외침 yell-yelled-yelled
yell with excitement 신나서 소리치다 yell at ~에게 고함치다

723 **donate** [dóuneit]
동 기부하다 donate-donated-donated 명 donation 기부
donate blood 헌혈하다 donate bags 가방을 기증하다

724 **fit** [fit]
동 (사이즈가) 맞다 형 적합한, 건강한 fit-fit-fit
fit perfectly 완벽하게 맞다 fit for the job 그 직업에 적합한

725 **path** [pæθ]
명 길 유 footpath 오솔길
a garden path 정원으로 나있는 길 block the path 길을 막다

Daily Test

| 월 일 |

A 우리말에 맞게 빈 칸에 알맞은 단어를 쓰세요.

1 I moved to Busan quite _______________. 나는 아주 최근에 부산으로 이사갔다.

2 I want to have _______________ hair and skin. 나는 부드러운 피부와 머리를 갖고 싶다.

3 She _______________ a restaurant. 그녀는 식당을 소유하고 있다.

4 Take the _______________ outside as soon as possible.
가능한 빨리 쓰레기를 밖에 내다 버려라.

5 There is a house deep in the _______________. 계곡 깊숙이 집 한 채가 있다.

6 I usually _______________ to school. 나는 보통 학교까지 걸어간다.

7 Did he _______________ at you? 그가 너에게 고함을 질렀니?

8 Jinju _______________ blood for the first time in her life.
진주는 생애 처음으로 헌혈을 했다.

9 This dress _______________ me perfectly. 이 드레스는 내게 완벽하게 맞는다.

10 Mike and I rode a bike along the cycle _______________.
Mike와 나는 자전거 길을 따라서 자전거를 탔다.

B 빈 칸에 알맞은 단어를 고르세요.

1 The sun _______________ brightly.

① owns ② shines ③ recently ④ fits ⑤ tickles

2 Today's highest _______________ was 30℃.

① slow ② day ③ valley ④ few ⑤ temperature

Day 30

MP3

726 **navy** [néivi]
명 해군 형 남색의 *air force 명 공군
join the navy 해군에 입대하다 a navy shirt 남색 셔츠

727 **pollute** [pəljúːt]
동 오염시키다 pollute-polluted-polluted 명 pollution 공해
pollute water 물을 오염시키다 pollute the air 공기를 오염시키다

728 **advise** [ədváiz]
동 충고하다 advise-advised-advised 명 advice 충고
advise strongly 강력하게 충고하다

729 **argue** [áːrgjuː]
동 언쟁을 하다, 다투다 argue-argued-argued
argue with ~와 언쟁을 벌이다 argue with my friend 친구와 다투다

730 **cost** [kɔ(ː)st]
명 비용, 값 동 (돈이) 들다 cost-cost-cost
the cost of the food 음식값 cost a lot of money 많은 돈이 들다

731 **courage** [kə́ːridʒ]
명 용기 형 courageous 용기 있는
show great courage 큰 용기를 보이다 lose courage 용기를 잃다

732 **determine** [ditə́ːrmin]
동 결정하다, 알아내다 determine-determined-determined
determine prices 가격을 결정하다

733 **fill** [fil]
동 채우다 fill-filled-filled
be filled with ~로 가득 차다 be filled with water 물로 가득 차다

734 **fur** [fəːr]
명 (일부 동물의) 털, 모피
a fur hat 모피 모자 soft fur 부드러운 털

735 **habitat** [hǽbitæ̀t]
명 서식지
a natural habitat 자연 서식지 wildlife habitats 야생 서식지

736 **ocean** [óuʃən]
명 바다, -양
swim in the ocean 해수욕하다 the Pacific Ocean 태평양

737 **discover** [diskʌ́vər]
동 발견하다 discover-discovered-discovered 명 discovery 발견
discover a new land 신대륙을 발견하다

738 **pour** [pɔːr]
동 붓다, 따르다 pour-poured-poured
pour over ~을 쏟다 pour some juice 주스를 따르다

Daily Test

| 월 일 |

A 우리말에 맞게 빈 칸에 알맞은 단어를 쓰세요.

1 Sarah wears a ______________ blouse. Sarah는 남색 블라우스를 입고 있다.

2 Mother ______________ me to go to bed early. 엄마는 내게 일찍 자러 가라고 충고하셨다.

3 Minhyuk ______________ with his mom about the matter.
민혁은 그 문제에 대해 엄마와 언쟁을 벌였다.

4 How much does it ______________? 이것은 얼마예요?

5 We think Emily showed great ______________.
우리는 Emily가 큰 용기를 보여줬다고 생각한다.

6 I can't ______________ what to do during summer vacation.
나는 여름 방학동안 무엇을 할지 못 정하겠어.

7 Sumin's rabbit has short black ______________.
수민이의 토끼는 짧은 검은 털을 갖고 있다.

8 Dolphins live in the deep ______________. 돌고래는 깊은 바다에 산다.

9 Columbus ______________ the New World, America.
콜럼버스는 아메리카 신대륙을 발견했다.

10 Amy ______________ some water into a glass. Amy가 유리잔에 물을 약간 따랐다.

B 빈 칸에 알맞은 단어를 고르세요.

1 The jar is ______________ with apples.
① advised ② cost ③ shout ④ stayed ⑤ filled

2 The river is ______________ with trash.
① polluted ② walked ③ argued ④ ocean ⑤ donated

3 This place is famous as a natural ______________ for animals.
① courage ② discovery ③ navy ④ habitat ⑤ privacy

Day 30

MP3

739 **privacy** [práivəsi]
명 사생활, 비밀 형 private 사적의
respect each other's privacy 서로의 사생활을 존중하다

740 **give up** [giv ʌp]
동 포기하다 give-gave-given
give up a goal 목표를 포기하다 give up on ~을 단념하다

741 **shout** [ʃaut]
동 외치다, 호통을 치다 shout-shouted-shouted
shout for joy 환호성을 지르다 shout at boys 소년들에게 호통치다

742 **signal** [sígnəl]
명 신호
give a signal 신호를 보내다 a danger signal 위험 신호

743 **stay** [stei]
동 머무르다 명 머무름, 체류 stay-stayed-stayed
stay inside 안에서 머무르다 a short stay 단기 체류

744 **therefore** [ðέərfɔ̀:r]
부 그러므로, 그 결과 유 so 그래서
Therefore, I'm very happy. 그러므로 난 매우 행복하다.

745 **toe** [tou]
명 발가락
a little toe 새끼발가락 from top to toe 머리에서 발끝까지

746 **unique** [ju:ní:k]
형 독특한 유 distinctive 독특한
a unique fashion style 독특한 패션 스타일

747 **whale** [hweil]
명 고래
whale watching 고래 구경 a whale calf 고래새끼

748 **wonder** [wʌ́ndər]
명 놀라움, 경탄 동 궁금해하다 wonder-wondered-wondered
feel wonder 경탄하다 wonder if ~를 궁금해하다

749 **medical** [médikəl]
형 의학의, 의료의
a medical college 의과 대학 medical records 진료 기록

750 **imagine** [imǽdʒin]
동 상상하다 imagine-imagined-imagined
imagine your future 미래를 상상하다 Can you imagine! 진짜야!

Daily Test

| 월 일 |

A 우리말에 맞게 빈 칸에 알맞은 단어를 쓰세요.

1 You should respect Tim's ______________. 너는 Tim의 사생활을 존중해야 한다.

2 Peter started to ______________ loudly. Peter는 크게 소리치기 시작했다.

3 They gave me a danger ______________. 그들은 내게 위험 신호를 보냈다.

4 I'll ______________ at home until you come back.
당신이 돌아올 때까지 난 집에 있을 거에요.

5 I got up late and ______________ I was late for school.
나는 늦잠을 잤고 그 결과 나는 학교에 지각했다.

6 Can you touch your ______________? 발가락을 만질 수 있나요?

7 Sarah wears a ______________ purple hat. Sarah는 독특한 보라색 모자를 쓰고 있다.

8 We ______________ how she solved the problem.
우리는 그녀가 어떻게 그 문제를 풀었는지 궁금하다.

9 We need to check her ______________ condition regularly.
우리는 정기적으로 그녀의 건강상태를 확인할 필요가 있다.

10 ______________ that you are a beautiful princess.
당신이 아름다운 공주라고 상상해보세요.

B 빈 칸에 알맞은 단어를 고르세요.

1 Don't ______________ on your goal.

① for free ② therefore ③ live in ④ yell at ⑤ give up

2 People are ______________ at whales.

① staying ② signal ③ advising ④ looking ⑤ arguing

Review Test 15

Day 29 + Day 30 | 월 일 |

A 우리말에 맞게 빈 칸에 알맞은 단어를 쓰세요.

1 ________________ your ribs 옆구리를 간지럽게 하다

2 a ________________ college 의과 대학

3 ________________ money 빚을 지다

4 an average ________________ 평균 온도

5 from top to ________________ 머리에서 발끝까지

6 ________________ a goal 목표를 포기하다

7 show great ________________ 큰 용기를 보이다

8 a natural ________________ 자연 서식지

9 give a ________________ 신호를 보내다

10 feel ________________ 경탄하다

B 다음 영어 풀이에 알맞은 어휘를 〈보기〉에서 고르세요.

보기	avenue	coin	valley	privacy	ocean

1 ____________ : a large sea that covers much of the earth's surface

2 ____________ : a small, round and flat piece of metal used as money

3 ____________ : a wide street, usually with trees on each side

4 ____________ : the state of being away from other people or their attention

5 ____________ : a long and low area of land between hills and mountains

C 다음 단어의 관계가 A:B=C:D가 되도록 알맞은 단어를 골라 빈 칸에 적으세요.

1 invite : ________________ = collect : collection

① invitation ② party ③ weekend
④ invited ⑤ time

2 slow : ________________ = direct : directly

① speed ② race ③ slowly
④ movie ⑤ slowness

3 ________________ : stayed = grow : grew

① stay ② stays ③ staying
④ staied ⑤ stayies

4 ________________ : secret = earn : money

① false ② discover ③ type
④ enjoy ⑤ white

5 shine : ________________ = win : won

① shined ② shoned ③ shines
④ shone ⑤ shinese

D 문맥에 맞게 다음 문장을 완성하세요.

1	Channel 7 will broadcast •	• a	me perfectly.
2	There are many foreign tourists •	• b	some water into a glass.
3	This dress fits •	• c	the musical at 8 o'clock.
4	Amy poured •	• d	in Gyoungbokgung Palace.
5	I got up late and •	• e	therefore was late for school.

E 문장을 읽고 문맥에 적절한 단어를 고르세요.

1 The doctor (advised/argued) me to avoid salty food.

2 Her bookshelf was (tickled/filled) with books from various countries.

3 The tennis player (cost/donated) his prize money to a local school.

4 I can easily (imagine/wonder) what they will say.

5 The people in this island still keep their (necessary/unique) way of life.

F 문장의 빈칸에 알맞은 단어를 〈보기〉에서 찾아 쓰세요. (필요하면 형태를 고치세요.)

보기	trash	determine	argue	cost	smooth

1 The doctors at the hospital finally ______________ the cause of the disease.
그 병원의 의사들은 마침내 그 병의 원인을 알아냈다.

2 The surface of the wood was very ____________ and flat.
그 목재의 표면은 매우 편평하고 부드러웠다.

3 Many students volunteered to pick up the ____________ in the park.
많은 학생들이 공원의 쓰레기를 줍는 것에 자원했다.

4 The subway ticket to Gwanghwamun Station ____________ me two dollars.
광화문 역까지 가는 지하철 표는 가격이 2달러가 들었어.

5 Whenever they meet, they ____________ about football.
그들은 만날 때 마다 축구로 언쟁을 한다.

G 그림에 해당하는 낱말을 〈보기〉에서 골라 쓰세요.

1 

(　　　　　　)

2 

(　　　　　　)

3 

(　　　　　　)

4 

(　　　　　　)

5 

(　　　　　　)

6 

(　　　　　　)

보기　path　yell　digest　pollute　whale　walk

Study More

'길' 대한 다양한 어휘

- way, street, avenue, route, road, path

way 사람, 차 등이 다니는 길, 도로, (*highway 고속도로)

avenue 큰 길 (*특히 양쪽으로 나무가 늘어서 있는 길)

road 주로 차가 다닐 수 있게 만든 길, 도로 명으로서 ~가

street 거리, 차도, 거리 명으로서 ~가

route 경로, 한 곳에서 다른 곳으로 가기 위한 길

path 주로 사람들이 지나는 작은 길

Index

T

U

V

W

Y

Answer Key

정답 및 해설

Answer Key

Day 01

Daily Test 1 P. 09

A
1 mud
2 best
3 candles
4 bug
5 curly
6 dance
7 dinosaur
8 elderly
9 equal
10 absent

B
1 ① cooked
2 ② anyone
3 ④ afraid

Daily Test 2 P. 11

A
1 gift
2 hotel
3 glasses
4 hugged
5 job
6 leg
7 Mars
8 menu
9 apologized
10 narrow

B
1 ⑤ famous
2 ② absent

Day 02

Daily Test 1 P. 13

A
1 friendly
2 bakery
3 must
4 alarm
5 basis
6 cafeteria
7 damaged
8 dress
9 end
10 far

B
1 ① away
2 ② comb
3 ② desert

Daily Test 2 P. 15

A
1 film
2 died
3 gentle
4 hates
5 insects
6 lazy
7 miracle
8 advantages
9 need
10 joy

B
1 ⑤ harmful
2 ② knife

Review Test 01

Day 01 + Day 02 P. 16

A
1 afraid
2 equal
3 famous
4 basis
5 best
6 must
7 cafeteria
8 damage
9 lazy
10 harmful

B
1 bakery
2 menu
3 die
4 dress
5 desert

C
1 ② absent
2 ⑤ apologized
3 ① die
4 ④ bakery
5 ③ disadvantage

D
1 a
2 d
3 e
4 b
5 c

E
1 comb
2 ended

3 far
4 gentle
5 hate

해석

1. 그녀는 머리를 빗기 위해 빗을 찾고 있었다.
2. 수업이 끝나자마자, 학생들은 교실 밖으로 뛰어 나갔다.
3. 새로운 쇼핑 센터는 너무 멀어서 걸어 갈 수 없다.
4. 그 키가 큰 남자의 상냥한 미소는 그의 주변 사람들을 행복하게 했다.
5. 나는 거미가 무서워요. 나는 그들을 보는 것도 싫어요.

F

1 Mars
2 curly
3 insects
4 narrow
5 friendly

G

1 candle
2 dinosaur
3 hug
4 mud
5 alarm
6 desert

Day 03

Daily Test 1 P. 21

A

1 part
2 repaired
3 around
4 bookmark
5 bitter
6 cloth
7 cousins
8 facts
9 variety
10 handsome

B

1 ③ copy
2 ④ down
3 ④ fashion

Daily Test 2 P. 23

A

1 hall
2 hero
3 lamp
4 machine
5 nature
6 never
7 outdoor
8 pen
9 photos
10 false

B

1 ① guest
2 ② limit

Day 04

Daily Test 1 P. 25

A

1 correct
2 pretty
3 award
4 careless
5 class
6 elementary
7 exact
8 skirt
9 gold
10 gloves

B

1 ④ about
2 ③ flight
3 ① balance

Daily Test 2 P. 27

A

1 household
2 hunted
3 items
4 lot
5 parents
6 understand
7 clever
8 quickly
9 ready
10 mosquito

B

1 ③ leaned
2 ② passport

Review Test 02

Day 03 + Day 04 P. 28

A

1 passport
2 bookmark
3 fact
4 limit
5 nature
6 ready
7 exact

8 lean
9 understand
10 photo

B
1 cousin
2 guest
3 lamp
4 glove
5 item

C
1 ③ copied
2 ① correct
3 ④ cleverest
4 ⑤ false
5 ② repair

D
1 e
2 c
3 a
4 b
5 d

E
1 pretty
2 long
3 never
4 about
5 lot

해석

1. 나는 엄마의 생신선물을 예쁜 종이로 쌌다.
2. 내가 그 책을 읽는 데는 꽤 오래 걸렸다.
3. 그 남자는 그가 그렇게 아름다운 그림은 전에 본적이 없다고 말했다.
4. 오늘 밤 우리는 그 과학 문제에 대해 얘기할 거에요.
5. 이 책은 프랑스에 대한 많은 지식을 전해준다.

F
1 bitter
2 flight
3 hero
4 careless
5 elementary

G
ⓒ run

H
1 ⓑ
2 ⓐ

Day 05

Daily Test 1 P. 33

A
1 romance
2 forecast
3 amazing
4 battery
5 bowed
6 close
7 concert
8 diary
9 even
10 heated

B
1 ③ dug
2 ① fare
3 ② collecting

Daily Test 2 P. 35

A
1 human
2 jogs
3 level
4 lizard
5 months
6 powder
7 quiet
8 remember
9 return
10 pimple

B
1 ① mind
2 ④ recipe

Day 06

Daily Test 1 P. 37

A
1 loudly
2 admire
3 aware
4 build
5 comedy
6 daily
7 engineer
8 especially
9 excited
10 fine

B
1 ① difficulty
2 ② bin
3 ④ hard

Daily Test 2 P. 39

A
1 inform
2 lie
3 leaves
4 monster
5 polite

6 powerful
7 relieved
8 rude
9 sad
10 sandcastle

B
1 ③ plan
2 ⑤ knocked

Review Test 03

Day 05 + Day 06 P. 40

A
1 forecast
2 lie
3 mind
4 powerful
5 polite
6 fine
7 admire
8 especially
9 relieve
10 sand

B
1 diary
2 concert
3 jog
4 comedy
5 battery

C
1 ② difficulty
2 ⑤ planned
3 ① return
4 ④ collect
5 ③ leaves

D
1 e
2 d
3 c
4 b
5 a

E
1 bowed
2 knocks
3 remember
4 Heat
5 excited

해석

1. 그는 교장선생님께 정중히 인사했다.
2. 그는 절대로 방에 들어오기 전에 문을 두드리지 않았다.
3. George는 그가 그의 학생증을 어디에 두었는지 기억나지 않았다.
4. 그 수프는 지금 차갑구나. 먹기 전에 그것을 데우렴.
5. 무대 위 그 가수의 공연은 관중들을 열광시켰다.

F
1 amazing
2 rude
3 lizards
4 recipe
5 loudly

G
1 closed
2 dig
3 pimples
4 quiet
5 difficulty
6 sad

Day 07

Daily Test 1 P. 45

A
1 standing
2 advice
3 ancient
4 company
5 curry
6 dramas
7 environment
8 fantastic
9 gray
10 guessed

B
1 ④ line
2 ② base
3 ② breath

Daily Test 2 P. 47

A
1 humorous
2 lake
3 lock
4 motto
5 pills
6 process
7 sale
8 sauce
9 science
10 smart

B
1 ③ danger
2 ③ regret

Day 08

Daily Test 1 P. 49

A
1 spend
2 miss
3 aisle
4 bacteria
5 relax
6 empty
7 example
8 trouble
9 floor
10 Hang

B
1 ④ dessert
2 ② Cheer
3 ② couple

Daily Test 2 P. 51

A
1 kingdom
2 list
3 mask
4 note
5 posed
6 ordinary
7 rules
8 scared
9 shadow
10 sleepy

B
1 ① instead
2 ③ raised

Review Test 04

Day 07 + Day 08 P. 52

A
1 pose
2 environment
3 motto
4 regret
5 smart
6 trouble
7 aisle
8 sleepy
9 instead
10 shadow

B
1 company
2 mask
3 drama
4 couple
5 curry

C
1 ① dangerous
2 ③ spent
3 ⑤ stand
4 ④ ordinary
5 ④ lock

D
1 c
2 b
3 e
4 a
5 d

E
1 advice
2 instead
3 guess
4 list
5 example

해석
1. 수지는 스페인어 공부에 대한 선생님의 충고를 받아들였다.
2. 오늘 날, 사람들은 아침에 밥 대신 빵을 먹는다.
3. 여기 오늘의 새 단어가 있습니다. 이 단어의 뜻을 추측해 볼 수 있나요?
4. 만약 네가 지금 쇼핑을 간다면, 네가 살 필요가 있는 물품들의 목록을 만드는 건 어때?
5. Sam은 친절한 학생이다. 예를 들어, 그는 그의 친구들을 돕는 걸 좋아한다.

F
1 line
2 humorous
3 ancient
4 process
5 raised

G
ⓒ desert

H
1 ⓐ
2 ⓑ

Day 09

Daily Test 1 P. 57

A
1 memory
2 alike
3 article
4 asleep
5 cause
6 chat
7 decrease

8 Emperor
9 grass
10 ground

B
1 ② costume
2 ③ fat
3 ④ recommend

Daily Test 2 P. 59

A
1 hints
2 lead
3 lend
4 ordered
5 preparing
6 record
7 scene
8 War
9 snakes
10 songs

B
1 ② possible
2 ① captain

Day 10

Daily Test 1 P. 61

A
1 overcome
2 snowy
3 among
4 change
5 confident
6 short
7 drawer
8 flood
9 giant
10 serious

B
1 ④ hosted
2 ① classical
3 ② begged

Daily Test 2 P. 63

A
1 light
2 Marathon
3 nodded
4 palm
5 praised
6 rolling
7 schedule
8 difference
9 steak
10 straight

B
1 ⑤ laughed
2 ② prison

Review Test 05

Day 09 + Day 10 P. 64

A
1 prison
2 alike
3 cause
4 order
5 prepare
6 schedule
7 among
8 laugh
9 palm
10 straight

B
1 costume
2 giant
3 emperor
4 captain
5 steak

C
1 ② overcame
2 ④ impossible
3 ① recommend
4 ⑤ difference
5 ② seriously

D
1 c
2 b
3 e
4 a
5 d

E
1 fat
2 hint
3 lend
4 praised
5 decreased

해석
1. 윤지는 살찌지 않기 위해 많은 운동을 하고 있다.
2. Tommy, 이 질문은 너무 어려워. 힌트를 좀 주겠니?
3. 한나야, 나는 내 필통을 가져 오는 걸 잊어버렸어. 연필 좀 빌려줄래?
4. 그 선생님은 그의 학생들이 교실을 깨끗하게 치운 것에 대해 칭찬했다.
5. 날씨가 추워졌기 때문에, 아침에 뛰는 사람들의 수가 줄어들었다.

F
1 nodding
2 confident

3 host
4 articles
5 drawer

G
1 war
2 snowy
3 light
4 marathon
5 roll
6 flood

Day 11

Daily Test 1

P. 69

A
1 mushrooms
2 pale
3 avoid
4 blankets
5 coffee
6 downloaded
7 enough
8 field
9 glory
10 have

B
1 ② access
2 ③ ability
3 ② diet

Daily Test 2

P. 71

A
1 master
2 medal
3 midnight
4 pot
5 relationship
6 save
7 soon
8 stamps
9 stress
10 style

B
1 ⑤ mayor
2 ③ piece

Day 12

Daily Test 1

P. 73

A
1 cute
2 manner
3 special
4 aloud
5 borrowed
6 climate
7 complains
8 effort
9 favor
10 guide

B
1 ② basic
2 ④ full
3 ③ increased

Daily Test 2

P. 75

A
1 attracted
2 muscles
3 point
4 quite
5 riddle
6 screen
7 solve
8 accident
9 sample
10 sudden

B
1 ① floating
2 ④ protected

Review Test 06

Day 11 + Day 12

P. 76

A
1 ability
2 blanket
3 have
4 relationship
5 sooner
6 riddle
7 complain
8 attract
9 quite
10 sample

B
1 mayor
2 climate
3 pot
4 basic
5 piece

C
1 ① accessible
2 ④ attracted
3 ② cute
4 ⑤ accident
5 ③ effort

D
1 b

2 e
3 c
4 a
5 d

E
1 avoids
2 favor
3 increased
4 enough
5 download

해석
1. 병원에 다녀 온 뒤, 그녀는 고기 먹는 것을 피했다.
2. Dan, 제가 부탁을 해도 될까요? 저는 이 상자들을 위층으로 옮겨야 해요.
3. Pam은 더 많은 돈을 벌기 위해 일의 속도를 높였다.
4. 그는 새 자동차를 살 충분한 돈이 없었다.
5. 만약 당신이 그 동아리에 가입하고 싶다면, 우리 웹사이트에 있는 지원서를 다운로드 받으세요.

F
1 complains
2 borrow
3 special
4 protect
5 manner

G
ⓐ favor

H
1 ⓐ
2 ⓑ

Day 13

Daily Test 1 P. 81

A
1 speech
2 next
3 battled
4 blamed
5 cave
6 connects
7 event
8 flash
9 gain
10 ill

B
1 ④ tried
2 ② ashamed
3 ③ dense

Daily Test 2 P. 83

A
1 wolves
2 melts
3 mild
4 parrot
5 pork
6 reduce
7 seems
8 adults
9 surface
10 took

B
1 ⑤ rope
2 ② soil

Day 14

Daily Test 1 P. 85

A
1 criticized
2 against
3 basement
4 belong
5 calendar
6 colorful
7 dew
8 envelope
9 safe
10 jail

B
1 ③ canceled
2 ① deliver
3 ③ garbage

Daily Test 2 P. 87

A
1 waves
2 neighbor
3 partner
4 recycle
5 sailed
6 set
7 sneezed
8 stupid
9 strange
10 interesting

B
1 ③ produces
2 ② landed

Review Test 07

Day 13 + Day 14 P. 88

A
1 blame
2 flash
3 strange
4 soil
5 take
6 envelope
7 deliver
8 jail
9 recycle
10 stupid

B
1 event
2 calendar
3 neighbor
4 wolf
5 speech

C
1 ① tire
2 ③ cancel
3 ⑤ adult
4 ② safety
5 ④ parrot

D
1 e
2 d
3 a
4 b
5 c

E
1 connect
2 against
3 seemed
4 belongs
5 reduce

해석

1. 그 두 마을을 연결하는 유일한 방법은 새로운 고속도로를 만드는 것이다.
2. 그들은 서로 상을 타기 위해 경쟁했다.
3. 그는 그가 시험을 기다리고 있을 때 불안해 보였다.
4. Dan의 아버지는 그만의 시계를 지니곤 했다. 지금 그의 시계는 Dan의 것이다.
5. 건강한 음식을 먹는 것은 심장병의 위험을 줄여줄 수 있다.

F
1 ashamed
2 battle
3 dew
4 gain
5 dense

G
1 cave
2 ill
3 melt
4 garbage
5 sneeze
6 wave

Day 15

Daily Test 1 P. 93

A
1 divide
2 popular
3 such
4 announced
5 common
6 cycle
7 draw
8 exam
9 fortune
10 However

B
1 ③ campaign
2 ② chapter
3 ② Kill

Daily Test 2 P. 95

A
1 mall
2 merry
3 beauty
4 puzzle
5 scholar
6 shy
7 South
8 healthy
9 suit
10 talked

B
1 ⑤ past
2 ③ symbol

Day 16

Daily Test 1 P. 97

A
1 entered
2 squares
3 adventure
4 arrived
5 conversation
6 culture
7 during
8 happiness
9 important
10 low

B

1 ① feather
2 ② bill
3 ⑤ cage

Daily Test 2 P. 99

A

1 Palace
2 poems
3 price
4 remove
5 seeds
6 skipped
7 value
8 sunset
9 task
10 thief

B

1 ① mental
2 ② sweat

Review Test 08

Day 15 + Day 16 P. 100

A

1 announce
2 chapter
3 common
4 merry
5 symbol
6 arrive
7 conversation
8 happiness
9 remove
10 sunset

B

1 campaign
2 price
3 palace
4 cage
5 cycle

C

1 ① divided
2 ③ beauty
3 ② healthy
4 ① enter
5 ⑤ valuable

D

1 e
2 c
3 a
4 b
5 d

E

1 during
2 important
3 past
4 However
5 lower

해석

1. 우리 팀은 경기의 후반전에서 세 골을 넣었다.
2. Joe는 내일 중요한 회의가 있다.
3. Tim은 이미 그의 지난 실수들을 잊었다.
4. 기영은 운동 경기를 보는 걸 좋아한다. 그러나 그는 어떤 운동도 하는 것은 좋아하지 않는다.
5. 운 좋게도, 그 코트의 가격은 내가 기대한 것 보다 훨씬 쌌다.

F

1 fortune
2 mental
3 shy
4 adventure
5 scholars

G

ⓒ popular

H

1 ⓐ
2 ⓑ

Day 17

Daily Test 1 P. 105

A

1 exhibition
2 nations
3 destination
4 auditorium
5 create
6 drop
7 everywhere
8 frying
9 interview
10 luggage

B

1 ④ tied
2 ⑤ disease
3 ① choir

Daily Test 2 P. 107

A

1 musician
2 shaking
3 playground
4 pouch
5 service

6 wrapped
7 still
8 third
9 cruel
10 heavily

B
1 ② tore
2 ③ reuse

Day 18

Daily Test 1 P. 109

A
1 century
2 action
3 Blend
4 vase
5 complete
6 disappointed
7 emotion
8 focused
9 lessons
10 move

B
1 ③ senior
2 ① another
3 ② global

Daily Test 2 P. 111

A
1 tight
2 project
3 pure
4 violent
5 servants
6 silent
7 stole
8 straw
9 temple
10 volunteer

B
1 ① time
2 ③ purpose

Review Test 09

Day 17 + Day 18 P. 112

A
1 destination
2 choir
3 drop
4 purpose
5 third
6 blend
7 disappoint
8 violent
9 temple
10 volunteer

B
1 servant
2 century
3 nation
4 service
5 lesson

C
1 ① exhibition
2 ④ senior
3 ③ stole
4 ② heavily
5 ④ vase

D
1 d
2 a
3 b
4 c
5 e

E
1 silent
2 reused
3 wrapped
4 complete
5 interview

해석
1. 집이 너무 조용해서 그녀는 아래층의 발자국 소리도 들을 수 있었다.
2. 미호는 우유 병을 꽃병으로써 다시 사용했다.
3. Bob은 그녀의 엄마를 위한 선물을 리본으로 포장했다.
4. Kate는 다음 주까지 그 프로젝트를 끝낼 계획이다.
5. Brian은 인터뷰에서 스스로에 대해 말하는 게 어려웠다.

F
1 auditorium
2 everywhere
3 emotions
4 luggage
5 tight

G
1 musician
2 shake
3 tears
4 tie
5 move
6 time

Day 19

Daily Test 1 P. 117

A
1 forgive
2 galleries
3 amount
4 average
5 decided
6 dialogue
7 experience
8 evil
9 lonely
10 north

B
1 ② forth
2 ⑤ fiction
3 ① coach

Daily Test 2 P. 119

A
1 plates
2 referee
3 model
4 sleeves
5 sore
6 storm
7 tasty
8 victory
9 tour
10 vet

B
1 ① proud
2 ② surprising

Day 20

Daily Test 1 P. 121

A
1 anxious
2 clapped
3 appeared
4 belief
5 castles
6 death
7 exchanged
8 huge
9 laid
10 passed

B
1 ③ step
2 ④ effect
3 ② final

Daily Test 2 P. 123

A
1 print
2 reach
3 senses
4 snail
5 wisdom
6 suggest
7 through
8 voice
9 tips
10 triangles

B
1 ② toward
2 ⑤ side

Review Test 10

Day 19 + Day 20 P. 124

A
1 coach
2 decide
3 proud
4 triangle
5 victory
6 belief
7 exchange
8 huge
9 reach
10 through

B
1 model
2 vet(erinarian)
3 death
4 fiction
5 effect

C
1 ① anxious
2 ④ forgave
3 ③ wisdom
4 ① evil
5 ① fourth

D
1 d
2 b
3 e
4 a
5 c

E
1 tip
2 toward
3 suggest

4 laid
5 effect

해석

1. 그 농구 선수는 그의 손가락 끝으로 공을 돌릴 수 있었다.
2. 그 팀의 마지막 키커는 골대를 향해 공을 찼다.
3. 당신의 두통이 계속된다면, 나는 병원에 갈 것을 권합니다.
4. 그는 책상 위에 그 책을 두었고 외출했다.
5. 환경 오염은 우리 삶에 심각한 영향을 줄 수 있다.

F
1 final
2 dialogue
3 experience
4 sleeves
5 voice

G
ⓒ wisdom

H
1 ⓑ
2 ⓐ

Day 21

Daily Test 1 P. 129

A
1 hid
2 deep
3 allowed
4 blanks
5 bride
6 donkey
7 forever
8 gesture
9 necessary
10 for free

B
1 ③ court
2 ② deaf
3 ⑤ hunger

Daily Test 2 P. 131

A
1 promised
2 received
3 sailors
4 solar
5 struck
6 stripes
7 underwater
8 type
9 waste
10 virtue

B
1 ② mission
2 ⑤ title

Day 22

Daily Test 1 P. 133

A
1 royal
2 affected
3 attacked
4 competition
5 developed
6 fair
7 gathered
8 means
9 noise
10 peaceful

B
1 ③ behaved
2 ① capital
3 ⑤ harmony

Daily Test 2 P. 135

A
1 punished
2 shape
3 spoiled
4 steam
5 teenagers
6 twins
7 unusual
8 waist
9 weight
10 without

B
1 ③ vacuum
2 ⑤ tradition

Review Test 11

Day 22 + Day 23 P. 136

A
1 allow
2 weight
3 mission
4 type
5 waste
6 without
7 competition
8 harmony
9 spoil
10 waist

B
1 bride
2 donkey
3 title

4 court
5 shape

C
1 ② meant
2 ① behave
3 ④ deaf
4 ② peaceful
5 ⑤ vacuum

D
1 c
2 b
3 e
4 a
5 d

E
1 punished
2 received
3 gathered
4 necessary
5 struck

해석
1. 그 소년은 거짓말을 해서 벌을 받았다.
2. Kurt는 그 퀴즈 쇼에서 우승해서 상으로 100달러를 받았다.
3. 그 소녀는 그녀의 인형을 모아서 상자에 넣었다.
4. 당신이 지금 조치를 취하는 것이 꼭 필요합니다.
5. 그는 정말 세게 공을 쳤다.

F
1 affected
2 steam
3 promised
4 develop
5 forever

G
1 deep
2 gesture
3 hide
4 attack
5 tradition
6 twins

Day 23

Daily Test 1 P. 141

A
1 electric
2 background
3 Both
4 ceiling
5 crashed
6 express
7 friendship
8 housework
9 mysteries
10 pain

B
1 ⑤ west
2 ② alive
3 ② pop

Daily Test 2 P. 143

A
1 really
2 several
3 similar
4 talent
5 thirsty
6 trade
7 view
8 cool
9 while
10 with

B
1 ② stage
2 ③ voted

Day 24

Daily Test 1 P. 145

A
1 forgot
2 wood
3 career
4 beside
5 college
6 east
7 flat
8 honest
9 neat
10 attend

B
1 ② pardon
2 ⑤ heaven
3 ② prize

Daily Test 2 P. 147

A
1 review
2 sharks
3 spirits
4 Text
5 tongue
6 vest
7 skin
8 volume
9 worm
10 ugly

B
1 ① spilt
2 ③ yet

Review Test 12

Day 23 + Day 24 P. 148

A
1 career
2 crash
3 talent
4 trade
5 while
6 pardon
7 beside
8 flat
9 tongue
10 volume

B
1 ceiling
2 skin
3 college
4 friendship
5 prize

C
1 ① forgotten
2 ④ electric
3 ① attend
4 ⑤ cool
5 ② dishonest

D
1 b
2 c
3 a
4 d
5 e

E
1 voted
2 similar
3 yet
4 express
5 vest

해석
1. 어제 이 마을의 사람들은 새로운 시장에 투표했다.
2. 당나귀와 말은 서로 비슷해 보인다.
3. 우리는 아직 그 박물관에 가지 않았어요.
4. 그림을 그리는 것은 너를 표현하는 방법이 될 수 있어.
5. 구명조끼 없이 바다에서 수영하는 것은 위험합니다.

F
1 both
2 review
3 alive
4 wood
5 ceiling

G
ⓑ pardon

H
1 ⓑ
2 ⓐ

Day 25

Daily Test 1 P. 153

A
1 held
2 sticky
3 choice
4 branch
5 tough
6 ended up taking
7 hole
8 information
9 patted
10 reason

B
1 ① along
2 ② freezes
3 ① nervous

Daily Test 2 P. 155

A
1 sharp
2 sign
3 spread
4 Controlling
5 village
6 weather
7 yard
8 regular
9 Modern
10 escaped

B
1 ⑤ languages
2 ④ whispered

Day 26

Daily Test 1 P. 157

A
1 failed
2 object
3 appreciate
4 chance
5 crossed
6 explains
7 musical
8 narrated

9 Polar
10 reported

B
1 ② slide
2 ① funds
3 ④ judge

Daily Test 2 P. 159

A
1 search
2 statue
3 tiny
4 traffic
5 trick
6 desirable
7 message
8 wonderful
9 expressions
10 medium

B
1 ② trust
2 ③ legal

Review Test 13

Day 25 + Day 26 P. 160

A
1 along
2 media
3 nervous
4 control
5 modern
6 chance
7 judge
8 trust
9 message
10 expression

B
1 information
2 yard
3 musical
4 object
5 evening

C
1 ② spread
2 ⑤ fail
3 ③ illegal
4 ④ language
5 ③ choice

D
1 e
2 a
3 c
4 b
5 d

E
1 reported
2 sign
3 waited
4 appreciate
5 cross

해석
1. 학생들은 경찰서에 그 사고를 알렸다.
2. 만약 당신이 그 팀에 들어가길 원한다면, 당신은 그 선 위에 당신의 이름을 서명해야 해요.
3. 나는 30분 동안 그 버스를 기다렸어요.
4. 우리는 우리의 역사 프로젝트에 대한 당신의 도움에 정말 감사 드립니다.
5. 그 소년은 그 늙은 여인이 안전하게 거리를 건너 가도록 도와드렸다.

F
1 narrated
2 customers
3 hole
4 tough
5 reason

G
1 branch
2 freeze
3 hold
4 pat
5 sharp
6 slide

Day 27

Daily Test 1 P. 165

A
1 curious
2 splash
3 portrait
4 comfortable
5 excellent
6 harvest
7 liberty
8 looking for
9 pity
10 respond

B
1 ③ degree
2 ② flea
3 ① majored

Daily Test 2 P. 167

A
1 show
2 opposed
3 stairs
4 success
5 topic
6 One day

7 way
8 wild
9 positive
10 million

B
1 ① journal
2 ④ nickname

Day 28

Daily Test 1 P. 169

A
1 warned
2 beyond
3 celebrity
4 cure
5 ease
6 happened
7 marching
8 works out
9 pond
10 rubbed

B
1 ⑤ front
2 ① grave
3 ③ leave

Daily Test 2 P. 171

A
1 shellfish
2 stared
3 support
4 total
5 community
6 furniture
7 fence
8 extra
9 few
10 guarded

B
1 ⑤ situation
2 ① pleasant

Review Test 14

Day 27 + Day 28 P. 172

A
1 situation
2 liberty
3 success
4 way
5 million
6 warn
7 beyond
8 support
9 pleasant
10 few

B
1 front
2 nickname
3 journal
4 degree
5 stairs

C
1 ① curious
2 ③ left
3 ④ comfortable
4 ② portrait
5 ④ furniture

D
1 b
2 a
3 e
4 c
5 d

E
1 cure
2 looking for
3 stared
4 pity
5 rubbed

해석

1. 비타민은 많은 질병을 치료하고 막아주는 걸로 알려져 있다.
2. Kevin의 가족은 머무를 호텔을 찾는 중이다.
3. 우리 속 그 작은 원숭이는 나를 쳐다보고 있었다.
4. 당신이 지금 떠나야만 해서 유감이에요.
5. 꽤 추웠고 그녀는 그녀의 손을 함께 비볐다.

F
1 celebrity
2 harvest
3 excellent
4 major
5 guard

G ⓑ slide

H
1 ⓑ
2 ⓐ

Day 29

Daily Test 1 P. 177

A
1 invitation
2 tickled
3 slowly

4 broadcast
5 coins
6 digest
7 foreign
8 height
9 owed
10 postcard

B
1 ③ Avenue
2 ② opinion
3 ③ public

Daily Test 2 P. 179

A
1 recently
2 smooth
3 owns
4 trash
5 valley
6 walk
7 yell
8 donated
9 fits
10 path

B
1 ② shines
2 ⑤ temperature

Day 30

Daily Test 1 P. 181

A
1 navy
2 advised
3 argued
4 cost
5 courage
6 determine
7 fur
8 ocean
9 discovered
10 poured

B
1 ⑤ filled
2 ① polluted
3 ④ habitat

Daily Test 2 P. 183

A
1 privacy
2 shout
3 signal
4 stay
5 therefore
6 toes
7 unique
8 wonder
9 medical
10 Imagine

B
1 ⑤ give up
2 ④ looking

Review Test 15

Day 29 + Day 30 P. 184

A
1 tickle
2 medical
3 owe
4 temperature
5 toe
6 give up
7 courage
8 habitat
9 signal
10 wonder

B
1 ocean
2 coin
3 avenue
4 privacy
5 valley

C
1 ① invitation
2 ③ slowly
3 ① stay
4 ② discover
5 ④ shone

D
1 c
2 d
3 a
4 b
5 e

E
1 advised
2 filled
3 donated
4 imagine
5 unique

해석
1. 그 의사는 내게 짠 음식을 피하라고 충고했다.
2. 그녀의 책장은 다양한 나라의 책들로 가득 차 있었다.
3. 그 테니스 선수는 그의 상금을 지역 학교에 기부했다.
4. 나는 쉽게 그들이 무엇을 말할 지 상상할 수 있어요.
5. 이 섬의 사람들은 그들의 독특한 생활 방식을 여전히 지키고 있다.

F

1 determined
2 smooth
3 trash
4 cost
5 argue

G

1 digest
2 path
3 walk
4 yell
5 pollute
6 whale

WORD MAX 2 5300

Workbook

WorldCom Edu

Workbook

WORD MAX 2 5300

WorldCom Edu

Workbook

Day 01

| 월 일 |

영어 단어에 해당하는 한국어 뜻을 함께 적으세요.

absent	결석한	absent	결석한
mud	진흙, 진창		
be afraid of	~을 무서워하다, ~을 두려워하다		
anyone	누군가, 누구나, 아무도		
best	최고, 최선; 최상의, 가장 훌륭한		
candle	양초		
bug	벌레, (가벼운) 유행성 질병		
cook	요리사; 요리하다		
curly	곱슬곱슬한		
dance	춤; 춤을 추다		
dinosaur	공룡		
elderly	연세가 드신		
equal	같은, 동일한; 같다		
famous	유명한		
finger	손가락		
gift	선물		
hotel	호텔		
glasses	안경		
hug	껴안다		
job	직업, 일, 책임		
leg	다리		
Mars	화성		
menu	(식당, 식사의) 메뉴		
apologize	사과하다		
narrow	좁은		

다음 단어에 해당하는 영어 단어 또는 우리말을 쓰세요.

O____개 X____개

영어	한국어
mud	
famous	
apologize	
anyone	
equal	
finger	
absent	
curly	
menu	
elderly	
bug	
cook	
Mars	
hotel	
candle	
job	
gift	
be afraid of	
dinosaur	
leg	
hug	
best	
narrow	
dance	
glasses	

한국어	영어
형 결석한	
명 손가락	
형 ~을 무서워하다, ~을 두려워하다	
명 화성	
명 최고, 최선 형 최상의, 가장 훌륭한	
명 양초	
명 같은, 동일한 동 같다	
형 유명한	
명 곱슬곱슬한	
명 호텔	
명 공룡	
명 연세가 드신	
동 껴안다	
명 선물	
대 누군가, 누구나, 아무도	
명 직업, 일, 책임	
명 요리사 동 요리하다	
동 사과하다	
명 다리	
명 벌레, (가벼운) 유행성 질병	
명 춤 동 춤을 추다	
형 좁은	
명 진흙, 진창	
명 안경	
명 (식당, 식사의) 메뉴	

Workbook

Day 02

| 월 일 |

영어 단어에 해당하는 한국어 뜻을 함께 적으세요.

friendly	친절한, 상냥한	friendly	친절한, 상냥한
bakery	빵집		
must	~해야 한다, ~임이 틀림없다		
alarm	자명종, 경보기; 놀라게 하다		
away	떨어져, 사라져		
basis	기초, 근거		
cafeteria	카페테리아(셀프 서비스 식당) 구내식당		
comb	빗; 빗다		
damage	손상; 손상을 주다		
desert	사막		
dress	드레스,옷; 옷을 입다		
end	끝내다		
far	멀리; 먼		
film	영화, 카메라 필름		
die	죽다		
gentle	온화한, 순한, 조용한		
harmful	해로운		
hate	몹시 싫어하다, 미워하다		
insect	곤충		
joy	기쁨		
knife	칼; 칼로 베다		
lazy	게으른		
miracle	기적		
advantage	이점, 이익		
need	필요로 하다; 필요		

다음 단어에 해당하는 영어 단어 또는 우리말을 쓰세요.

O____개 X____개

영어	한국어
cafeteria	
need	
lazy	
basis	
film	
end	
away	
knife	
miracle	
alarm	
insect	
desert	
must	
hate	
far	
dress	
harmful	
die	
bakery	
advantage	
gentle	
joy	
damage	
comb	
friendly	

한국어	영어
명 빵집	
부 멀리 형 먼	
명 영화, 카메라 필름	
형 친절한, 상냥한	
동 필요로 하다 명 필요	
동 끝내다	
동 죽다	
명 이점, 이익	
명 자명종, 경보기 동 놀라게 하다	
명 드레스,옷 동 옷을 입다	
형 온화한, 순한, 조용한	
조 ~해야 한다, ~임이 틀림없다	
명 칼 동 칼로 베다	
명 사막	
형 해로운	
명 기초, 근거	
동 몹시 싫어하다, 미워하다	
부 떨어져, 사라져	
명 기적	
명 손상 동 손상을 주다	
명 곤충	
명 카페테리아(셀프 서비스 식당) 구내식당	
명 기쁨	
명 빗 동 빗다	
형 게으른	

Workbook

Day 03

| 월 일 |

영어 단어에 해당하는 한국어 뜻을 함께 적으세요.

copy	복사(본); 복사하다	copy	복사(본); 복사하다
part	일부, 부분, 부품		
repair	수리하다		
around	주위에; 주변에		
bookmark	책갈피, 북마크; 북마크를 하다		
bitter	맛이 쓴, 쓰라린		
cloth	천, 옷감		
cousin	사촌		
down	아래로		
fact	사실		
variety	여러가지, 갖가지		
fashion	유행, 패션		
handsome	잘생긴, 멋진		
guest	손님		
hall	(모임이나 공연을 위한) 공간, 건물, 홀		
hero	영웅		
lamp	등, 램프		
limit	한계; 제한하다		
machine	기계		
nature	자연, 본성		
never	결코 ~않는		
outdoor	야외의		
false	틀린		
pen	펜		
photo	사진		

다음 단어에 해당하는 영어 단어 또는 우리말을 쓰세요.

O____개 X____개

영어	한국어
part	
hall	
photo	
handsome	
pen	
fashion	
outdoor	
guest	
copy	
variety	
repair	
bitter	
hero	
fact	
lamp	
around	
bookmark	
limit	
cousin	
machine	
nature	
cloth	
down	
never	
false	

한국어	영어
명 복사(본) 동 복사하다	
명 일부, 부분, 부품	
명 손님	
명 유행, 패션	
명 펜	
명 천, 옷감	
명 (모임이나 공연을 위한) 공간, 건물, 홀	
명 여러가지, 갖가지	
동 수리하다	
형 틀린	
부 주위에 전 주변에	
명 등, 램프	
명 사실	
부 아래로	
명 영웅	
명 기계	
명 책갈피, 북마크 동 북마크를 하다	
부 결코 ~않는	
명 한계 동 제한하다	
형 잘생긴, 멋진	
형 맛이 쓴, 쓰라린	
명 사진	
명 자연, 본성	
형 야외의	
명 사촌	

Workbook

Day 04

| 월 일 |

영어 단어에 해당하는 한국어 뜻을 함께 적으세요.

correct	맞는, 정확한; 바로잡다	correct	맞는, 정확한; 바로잡다
pretty	이쁜, 매력적인		
be about to	~을 막 하려고 하다		
balance	균형; 균형을 유지하다		
award	상; 수여하다		
careless	부주의한, 경솔한		
class	학급, 수업		
elementary	초급의		
exact	정확한		
skirt	치마		
flight	비행		
gold	금; 금빛의		
glove	장갑		
household	가정		
hunt	사냥; 사냥하다		
item	항목, 물품		
lean	기울다, ~에 기대다		
a lot of	많은		
mosquito	모기		
parents	부모		
passport	여권		
understand	이해하다		
clever	영리한, 똑똑한		
quickly	빨리, 빠르게		
ready	준비된		

다음 단어에 해당하는 영어 단어 또는 우리말을 쓰세요.　　　　O____개　X____개

영어	한국어
correct	
household	
ready	
pretty	
exact	
hunt	
item	
elementary	
lean	
gold	
be about to	
a lot of	
glove	
quickly	
balance	
mosquito	
understand	
skirt	
flight	
award	
parents	
careless	
clever	
passport	
class	

한국어	영어
~을 막 하려고 하다	
형 이쁜, 매력적인	
명 가정	
명 금 형 금빛의	
명 비행	
명 모기	
형 맞는, 정확한 동 바로잡다	
형 준비된	
명 치마	
대 많은	
명 사냥 동 사냥하다	
명 균형 동 균형을 유지하다	
부 빨리, 빠르게	
형 초급의	
명 학급, 수업	
명 여권	
형 부주의한, 경솔한	
동 기울다, ~에 기대다	
형 영리한, 똑똑한	
명 장갑	
형 정확한	
명 부모	
명 상 동 수여하다	
동 이해하다	
명 항목, 물품	

Day 05

| 월 일 |

영어 단어에 해당하는 한국어 뜻을 함께 적으세요.

dig	파다	dig	파다
romance	연애(감정), 로맨스		
forecast	예측; 예측하다		
amazing	놀라운		
battery	건전지, 배터리		
bow	고개를 숙이다, 절하다		
close	가까이의, 친한; 닫다		
concert	연주회, 콘서트		
diary	일기		
even	~조차(도), 훨씬; 짝수의		
fare	요금		
collect	모으다, 수집하다		
heat	열, 더위; 가열하다		
human	인간의		
jog	조깅하다		
level	정도, 수준, 단계		
lizard	도마뱀		
mind	마음, 정신		
month	월, 달		
pimple	여드름		
powder	가루		
quiet	조용한, 한적한		
recipe	조리법, 요리법		
remember	기억하다		
return	돌아오다, 돌려주다		

다음 단어에 해당하는 영어 단어 또는 우리말을 쓰세요. O____개 X____개

영어	한국어
diary	
level	
human	
concert	
remember	
romance	
jog	
mind	
fare	
forecast	
lizard	
return	
month	
amazing	
pimple	
even	
recipe	
battery	
dig	
powder	
close	
collect	
quiet	
bow	
heat	

한국어	영어
명 연애(감정), 로맨스	
명 예측 동 예측하다	
명 요금	
동 조깅하다	
부 ~조차(도), 훨씬 형 짝수의	
명 정도, 수준, 단계	
동 돌아오다, 돌려주다	
형 놀라운	
형 인간의	
동 파다	
동 기억하다	
명 일기	
명 도마뱀	
형 가까이의, 친한 동 닫다	
명 가루	
명 연주회, 콘서트	
명 조리법, 요리법	
명 건전지, 배터리	
명 마음, 정신	
동 모으다, 수집하다	
명 월, 달	
동 고개를 숙이다, 절하다	
명 여드름	
형 조용한, 한적한	
명 열, 더위 동 가열하다	

Workbook

Day 06

| 월 일 | 영어 단어에 해당하는 한국어 뜻을 함께 적으세요.

difficulty	어려움	difficulty	어려움
loud	(소리가) 큰, 시끄러운		
admire	존경하다, 칭찬하다		
bin	쓰레기통		
be aware of	~을 알고 있다, ~을 알아차리다		
build	짓다, 건설하다		
comedy	코미디, 희극		
daily	매일의		
engineer	기사, 기술자		
especially	특히, 유난히		
excite	들뜨게 하다, 흥분시키다		
fine	좋은; 벌금		
hard	단단한, 굳은; 열심히, 힘껏		
inform	알리다, 통지하다		
knock	두드리다, 노크하다; 노크 소리		
lie	거짓말		
leaf	낙엽, 잎		
monster	괴물		
polite	예의바른, 정중한		
plan	계획; 계획을 짜다		
powerful	강한, 강력한		
relieve	안도시키다, 완화하다		
rude	무례한		
sad	슬픈		
sand	모래		

다음 단어에 해당하는 영어 단어 또는 우리말을 쓰세요.

O____개 X____개

영어	한국어
excite	
inform	
difficulty	
sad	
rude	
knock	
loud	
fine	
admire	
relieve	
lie	
bin	
especially	
powerful	
be aware of	
leaf	
sand	
comedy	
build	
monster	
polite	
hard	
daily	
engineer	
plan	

한국어	영어
형 매일의	
명 괴물	
동 존경하다, 칭찬하다	
동 알리다, 통지하다	
명 낙엽, 잎	
명 쓰레기통	
형 좋은 명 벌금	
명 계획 동 계획을 짜다	
명 코미디, 희극	
동 짓다, 건설하다	
형 예의바른, 정중한	
명 거짓말	
명 어려움	
형 단단한, 굳은 부 열심히, 힘껏	
동 안도시키다, 완화하다	
형 (소리가) 큰, 시끄러운	
동 들뜨게 하다, 흥분시키다	
형 강한, 강력한	
명 기사, 기술자	
형 슬픈	
명 노크 소리 동 두드리다, 노크하다	
형 ~을 알고 있다 ~을 알아차리다	
명 모래	
형 무례한	
부 특히, 유난히	

Workbook

Day 07

| 월 일 | 영어 단어에 해당하는 한국어 뜻을 함께 적으세요.

stand	서다	stand	서다
line	선		
advice	조언, 충고		
ancient	고대의		
base	기초, 기반		
breath	입김, 숨		
company	회사, 단체		
curry	카레, 카레 요리		
drama	드라마, 연극		
environment	자연환경, (주변의) 환경		
fantastic	환상적인		
gray	회색의; 회색		
guess	추측하다; 추측		
humorous	유머가 넘치는, 재미있는		
lake	호수		
danger	위험		
lock	잠그다; 자물쇠		
motto	좌우명		
pill	알약		
process	과정, 절차		
regret	후회하다; 후회		
sale	판매, 세일		
sauce	소스, 향신료		
science	과학		
smart	현명한, 똑똑한		

다음 단어에 해당하는 영어 단어 또는 우리말을 쓰세요.

O____개 X____개

영어	한국어
ancient	
advice	
lake	
line	
smart	
humorous	
sauce	
stand	
danger	
environment	
base	
lock	
breath	
motto	
guess	
company	
pill	
drama	
process	
curry	
gray	
regret	
fantastic	
sale	
science	

한국어	영어
명 조언, 충고	
명 과정, 절차	
동 추측하다 명 추측	
형 유머가 넘치는, 재미있는	
명 알약	
형 고대의	
형 회색의 명 회색	
명 과학	
명 카레, 카레 요리	
동 서다	
형 환상적인	
명 좌우명	
명 입김, 숨	
명 소스, 향신료	
명 호수	
명 기초, 기반	
형 현명한, 똑똑한	
명 자연환경, (주변의) 환경	
명 위험	
동 잠그다 명 자물쇠	
명 선	
동 후회하다 명 후회	
명 회사, 단체	
명 판매, 세일	
명 드라마, 연극	

Workbook

Day 08

| 월 일 |

영어 단어에 해당하는 한국어 뜻을 함께 적으세요.

spend	쓰다, 소비하다	spend	쓰다, 소비하다
dessert	디저트, 후식		
miss	그리워하다		
aisle	통로		
bacteria	박테리아, 세균		
cheer	환호하다, 응원하다; 환호		
couple	두 개의, 둘의		
relax	휴식을 취하다, 긴장을 풀다		
empty	텅 빈; 비우다		
example	예시, 본보기		
trouble	문제, 골칫거리		
floor	층, 바닥		
hang	걸다		
instead of	~대신에		
kingdom	왕국		
list	목록; 목록을 작성하다		
mask	가면, 탈		
note	메모, 편지		
raise	들어올리다, 올리다, 모으다		
pose	자세를 취하다; 자세		
ordinary	보통의, 일반적인		
rule	규칙		
scare	겁주다, 겁내다		
shadow	그림자		
sleepy	졸린		

다음 단어에 해당하는 영어 단어 또는 우리말을 쓰세요.

O____개 X____개

영어	한국어
dessert	
miss	
instead of	
sleepy	
aisle	
list	
hang	
floor	
bacteria	
shadow	
spend	
kingdom	
mask	
trouble	
cheer	
couple	
raise	
note	
pose	
relax	
rule	
ordinary	
empty	
scare	
example	

한국어	영어
명 가면, 탈	
동 쓰다, 소비하다	
명 예시, 본보기	
명 왕국	
형 보통의, 일반적인	
명 환호 동 환호하다, 응원하다	
전 ~대신에	
명 메모, 편지	
명 디저트, 후식	
명 규칙	
명 두 개의, 둘의	
명 목록 동 목록을 작성하다	
명 층, 바닥	
명 그림자	
동 그리워하다	
형 텅 빈 동 비우다	
동 겁주다, 겁내다	
명 통로	
동 들어올리다, 올리다, 모으다	
명 문제, 골칫거리	
명 박테리아, 세균	
동 자세를 취하다 명 자세	
형 졸린	
동 휴식을 취하다, 긴장을 풀다	
동 걸다	

Workbook

Day 09

| 월 일 |

영어 단어에 해당하는 한국어 뜻을 함께 적으세요.

recommend	추천하다	recommend	추천하다
memory	기억(력), 추억		
alike	비슷한; 비슷하게		
article	기사, 물품		
asleep	잠이 든, 자고 있는		
cause	~을 일으키다; 이유, 원인		
chat	담소를 나누다, 수다를 떨다		
costume	의상, 복장		
decrease	감소하다; 감소		
emperor	황제		
fat	지방; 뚱뚱한		
grass	풀, 잔디		
ground	땅, 용지		
hint	힌트, 암시		
lead	안내하다		
lend	빌려주다		
possible	가능한		
order	명령하다, 주문하다; 명령		
captain	주장, 선장		
prepare	준비하다		
record	녹음하다, 기록하다; 기록, 음반		
scene	(영화, 연극 등의) 장면, 경치, 풍경		
war	전쟁		
snake	뱀		
song	노래		

다음 단어에 해당하는 영어 단어 또는 우리말을 쓰세요.

O____개 X____개

영어	한국어
memory	
hint	
song	
alike	
emperor	
lead	
snake	
lend	
recommend	
article	
possible	
grass	
asleep	
cause	
order	
chat	
captain	
record	
fat	
costume	
prepare	
scene	
decrease	
war	
ground	

한국어	영어
동 담소를 나누다, 수다를 떨다	
명 황제	
명 (영화, 연극 등의) 장면, 경치, 풍경	
형 가능한	
명 기억(력), 추억	
명 뱀	
형 비슷한 부 비슷하게	
명 땅, 용지	
동 준비하다	
명 힌트, 암시	
명 이유, 원인 동 ~을 일으키다	
동 추천하다	
명 기록, 음반 동 녹음하다, 기록하다	
동 안내하다	
명 풀, 잔디	
명 주장, 선장	
명 기사, 물품	
동 빌려주다	
동 감소하다 명 감소	
형 잠이 든, 자고 있는	
명 전쟁	
명 명령 동 명령하다, 주문하다	
명 지방 형 뚱뚱한	
명 노래	
명 의상, 복장	

Workbook

Day 10

| 월 일 |

영어 단어에 해당하는 한국어 뜻을 함께 적으세요.

overcome	극복하다	overcome	극복하다
host	주최자; (행사, 파티 등을) 주최하다		
snowy	눈이 오는		
among	~의 사이에		
beg	간청(애원)하다, 구걸하다		
change	변하다; 변화		
classical	고전의, 고전적인		
confident	자신감 있는		
short	짧은		
drawer	서랍		
flood	홍수; 범람하다		
giant	거대한; 거인		
serious	심각한		
laugh	웃음; 웃다		
light	빛, 전등; 밝은		
marathon	마라톤		
nod	(고개를) 끄덕이다; 끄덕임		
palm	손바닥		
praise	칭찬하다; 칭찬		
prison	감옥		
roll	두루마리, 통; 굴리다, 구르다		
schedule	일정		
difference	차이		
steak	스테이크		
straight	곧은; 똑바로		

다음 단어에 해당하는 영어 단어 또는 우리말을 쓰세요. O____개 X____개

영어	한국어
snowy	
laugh	
overcome	
giant	
light	
host	
flood	
marathon	
praise	
roll	
among	
nod	
change	
palm	
drawer	
beg	
prison	
schedule	
classical	
short	
steak	
difference	
confident	
straight	
serious	

한국어	영어
형 눈이 오는	
명 끄덕임 동 (고개를) 끄덕이다	
명 서랍	
형 짧은	
명 웃음 동 웃다	
전 ~의 사이에	
명 마라톤	
형 자신감 있는	
형 심각한	
명 빛, 전등 형 밝은	
동 극복하다	
형 곧은 부 똑바로	
명 손바닥	
형 거대한 명 거인	
명 주최자 동 (행사, 파티 등을) 주최하다	
명 일정	
형 고전의, 고전적인	
명 두루마리, 통 동 굴리다, 구르다	
명 차이	
동 간청(애원)하다, 구걸하다	
명 감옥	
명 홍수 동 범람하다, 물에 잠기다	
동 칭찬하다 명 칭찬	
명 스테이크	
동 변하다 명 변화	

Workbook

Day 11

| 월 일 |

영어 단어에 해당하는 한국어 뜻을 함께 적으세요.

access	접근하다, 접속하다; 접근	access	접근하다, 접속하다; 접근
mushroom	버섯		
ability	능력, 역량		
pale	(얼굴) 창백한, 색이 옅은		
avoid	피하다		
blanket	담요		
coffee	커피		
diet	식사, 다이어트		
download	파일을 내려받다		
enough	충분한; 충분히		
field	들판, 분야		
glory	영광, 명예, 영예		
have	먹다, 마시다		
mayor	시장		
master	완전히 익히다; 대가, 주인		
medal	메달		
midnight	한밤중, 자정		
pot	냄비, 솥, 병		
piece	한 부분, 조각		
relationship	관계		
save	구하다, 모으다, 저축하다		
soon	곧, 머지않아		
stamp	우표, 도장		
stress	스트레스, 압박, 긴장		
style	방식, 스타일		

다음 단어에 해당하는 영어 단어 또는 우리말을 쓰세요. O____개 X____개

영어	한국어
mushroom	
mayor	
medal	
access	
glory	
master	
piece	
field	
ability	
enough	
pot	
have	
pale	
midnight	
avoid	
coffee	
relationship	
stress	
blanket	
save	
stamp	
style	
diet	
soon	
download	

한국어	영어
명 능력, 역량	
명 관계	
명 대가, 주인 동 완전히 익히다	
명 시장	
명 접근 동 접근하다, 접속하다	
명 버섯	
명 한 부분, 조각	
명 메달	
동 먹다, 마시다	
명 방식, 스타일	
동 파일을 내려받다	
명 냄비, 솥, 병	
명 우표, 도장	
명 한밤중, 자정	
형 (얼굴) 창백한, 색이 옅은	
명 영광, 명예, 영예	
동 구하다, 모으다, 저축하다	
명 식사, 다이어트	
동 피하다	
명 스트레스, 압박, 긴장	
명 담요	
부 곧, 머지않아	
형 충분한 부 충분히	
명 커피	
명 들판, 분야	

Workbook

Day 12

| 월 일 |

영어 단어에 해당하는 한국어 뜻을 함께 적으세요.

cute	귀여운	cute	귀여운
manner	방식, 태도, 예의		
special	특별한		
aloud	소리 내어, 큰 소리로		
basic	기본적인, 기초적인		
borrow	빌리다		
climate	기후		
complain	불평하다, 항의하다		
effort	노력, 수고		
favor	호의, 친절, 부탁		
full	가득한, 배가 부른		
guide	여행 가이드, 안내자; 안내하다		
increase	증가, 인상; 증가하다		
float	(물 위에) 뜨다, 떠다니다		
attract	끌다, 매혹하다		
muscle	근육		
point	뾰족한 끝, 요점; 가리키다, 겨루다		
protect	보호하다		
quite	꽤, 상당히		
riddle	수수께끼		
screen	화면, 스크린		
solve	해결하다, (문제를) 풀다		
accident	사고, 우연		
sample	견본, 샘플		
sudden	갑작스러운		

다음 단어에 해당하는 영어 단어 또는 우리말을 쓰세요.

O___개 X___개

영어	한국어
float	
guide	
riddle	
quite	
attract	
special	
manner	
screen	
increase	
cute	
sudden	
solve	
muscle	
aloud	
basic	
point	
borrow	
accident	
climate	
effort	
protect	
complain	
favor	
sample	
full	

한국어	영어
형 귀여운	
동 (물 위에) 뜨다, 떠다니다	
명 근육	
명 노력, 수고	
명 증가, 인상 동 증가하다	
동 해결하다, (문제를) 풀다	
형 특별한	
동 끌다, 매혹하다	
명 방식, 태도, 예의	
명 사고, 우연	
명 여행 가이드, 안내자 동 안내하다	
명 화면, 스크린	
동 불평하다, 항의하다	
동 보호하다	
부 소리 내어, 큰 소리로	
명 뾰족한 끝, 요점 동 가리키다, 겨루다	
형 갑작스러운	
명 호의, 친절, 부탁	
명 견본, 샘플	
형 기본적인, 기초적인	
부 꽤, 상당히	
동 빌리다	
명 기후	
명 수수께끼	
형 가득한, 배가 부른	

Workbook

Day 13

| 월 일 |

영어 단어에 해당하는 한국어 뜻을 함께 적으세요.

tire	타이어; 피곤하게하다, 지치다	tire	타이어; 피곤하게하다, 지치다
speech	연설		
next	다음의; 다음에, 옆에		
be ashamed of	~을 부끄러워하다		
battle	전투; 싸우다		
blame	~을 탓하다, 비난하다		
cave	동굴		
connect	연결하다		
dense	빽빽한, 밀집한		
event	사건, 행사		
flash	섬광, 번쩍임; 번쩍이다		
gain	얻다, 늘다		
ill	아픈, 병 든		
wolf	늑대		
melt	녹다, 녹이다		
mild	온화한, 순한, 따뜻한		
parrot	앵무새		
pork	돼지고기		
reduce	줄이다, 낮추다		
rope	줄, 밧줄		
seem	~처럼 보이다		
soil	흙, 토양		
adult	어른, 성인		
surface	표면, 수면		
take	잡다, 획득하다, 먹다		

다음 단어에 해당하는 영어 단어 또는 우리말을 쓰세요.

O____개 X____개

영어	한국어
speech	
wolf	
take	
tire	
connect	
melt	
surface	
mild	
cave	
ill	
next	
be ashamed of	
parrot	
gain	
soil	
pork	
reduce	
battle	
flash	
dense	
rope	
blame	
adult	
seem	
event	

한국어	영어
동 줄이다, 낮추다	
형 다음의 부 다음에, 옆에	
명 어른, 성인	
동 연결하다	
명 늑대	
명 동굴	
명 섬광, 번쩍임 동 번쩍이다	
명 흙, 토양	
명 타이어 동 피곤하게하다, 지치다	
동 잡다, 획득하다, 먹다	
형 아픈, 병 든	
동 녹다, 녹이다	
동 ~을 탓하다, 비난하다	
동 ~처럼 보이다	
명 연설	
형 빽빽한, 밀집한	
형 온화한, 순한, 따뜻한	
명 사건, 행사	
명 표면, 수면	
~을 부끄러워하다	
명 앵무새	
명 줄, 밧줄	
명 전투 동 싸우다	
명 돼지고기	
동 얻다, 늘다	

Workbook

Day 14

| 월 일 |

영어 단어에 해당하는 한국어 뜻을 함께 적으세요.

cancel	취소하다	cancel	취소하다
criticize	비난하다, 비평하다		
against	~에 반대하여		
basement	지하실		
belong to	~에 속하다		
calendar	달력		
colorful	다채로운, 화려한		
deliver	배달하다, 연설을 하다		
dew	이슬		
envelope	봉투		
safe	안전한		
garbage	쓰레기		
jail	감옥, 투옥		
land	땅; 착륙하다		
wave	파도, 파장, 흔들기; 흔들다		
neighbor	이웃 사람		
partner	동반자, 동료		
produce	생산하다		
recycle	재활용하다		
sail	항해하다, (배를) 조종하다		
set	놓다, (시계를) 맞추다, (표준, 규칙, 기록을) 세우다		
sneeze	재채기하다; 재채기		
stupid	어리석은		
strange	이상한, 낯선		
tale	이야기, 설화		

다음 단어에 해당하는 영어 단어 또는 우리말을 쓰세요.

O____개 X____개

영어	한국어
jail	
tale	
criticize	
colorful	
land	
garbage	
calendar	
strange	
cancel	
neighbor	
wave	
safe	
against	
partner	
stupid	
produce	
basement	
recycle	
deliver	
sail	
belong to	
set	
envelope	
dew	
sneeze	

한국어	영어
동 취소하다	
동 항해하다, (배를) 조종하다	
동 배달하다, 연설을 하다	
명 쓰레기	
명 이야기, 설화	
동 비난하다, 비평하다	
형 안전한	
형 이상한, 낯선	
형 다채로운, 화려한	
명 봉투	
명 지하실	
전 ~에 반대하여	
명 동반자, 동료	
동 재활용하다	
동 재채기하다 명 재채기	
명 이슬	
명 땅 동 착륙하다	
명 이웃 사람	
동 ~에 속하다	
동 놓다, (시계를) 맞추다, (표준, 규칙, 기록을) 세우다	
형 어리석은	
동 흔들다 명 파도, 파장, 흔들기	
명 감옥, 투옥	
명 달력	
동 생산하다	

Workbook

Day 15

| 월 일 |

영어 단어에 해당하는 한국어 뜻을 함께 적으세요.

divide	나누다	divide	나누다
popular	인기 있는, 대중적인		
such	그러한,~와 같은, 매우 ~한		
announce	발표하다, 알리다		
campaign	캠페인; 캠페인을 벌이다		
chapter	(책의) 장		
common	흔한, 보통의		
cycle	주기, 순환기, 자전기		
draw	그리다		
exam	시험		
fortune	운, 재산, 부		
however	그러나, 그렇지만		
kill	죽이다		
mall	쇼핑몰		
merry	즐거운, 명랑한		
past	과거; 지나간		
beauty	아름다움, 미인		
puzzle	퍼즐; 어리둥절하게 하다		
scholar	학자		
shy	부끄러움을 많이 타는		
south	남쪽; 남쪽의		
healthy	건강한, 건강에 좋은		
suit	정장, 활동복; 맞다, 적합하다		
symbol	상징, 기호		
talk	말하다, 이야기하다		

다음 단어에 해당하는 영어 단어 또는 우리말을 쓰세요.

O____개 X____개

영어	한국어
popular	
mall	
healthy	
divide	
merry	
south	
fortune	
exam	
such	
campaign	
past	
announce	
beauty	
chapter	
draw	
symbol	
puzzle	
shy	
however	
common	
scholar	
cycle	
suit	
talk	
kill	

한국어	영어
형 즐거운, 명랑한	
명 과거 형 지나간	
형 건강한, 건강에 좋은	
동 죽이다	
동 발표하다, 알리다	
명 남쪽 형 남쪽의	
동 나누다	
명 주기, 순환기, 자전기	
동 그리다	
부 그러나, 그렇지만	
명 (책의) 장	
형 인기 있는, 대중적인	
명 쇼핑몰	
명 아름다움, 미인	
명 상징, 기호	
명 운, 재산, 부	
형 부끄러움을 많이 타는	
명 시험	
형 그러한, ~와 같은, 매우 ~한	
동 말하다, 이야기하다	
명 정장, 활동복 동 맞다, 적합하다	
형 흔한, 보통의	
명 캠페인 동 캠페인을 벌이다	
명 학자	
명 퍼즐 동 어리둥절하게 하다	

Workbook

Day 16

| 월 일 |

영어 단어에 해당하는 한국어 뜻을 함께 적으세요.

enter	들어가다, 입력하다	enter	들어가다, 입력하다
square	정사각형 모양의; 정사각형, 광장		
adventure	모험		
arrive	도착하다		
bill	고지서, 청구서, 지폐		
cage	새장, 우리		
conversation	대화		
culture	문화		
during	~동안		
feather	깃털		
happiness	행복		
important	중요한		
low	낮은		
mental	정신의, 마음의, 정신적인		
palace	궁전		
poem	시		
price	값, 가격		
remove	치우다, 제거하다		
seed	씨앗		
skip	(일 등을) 거르다, 건너뛰다		
value	가치, 유용성		
sweat	땀; 땀을 흘리다		
sunset	해질녘, 일몰		
task	일, 과제		
thief	도둑		

다음 단어에 해당하는 영어 단어 또는 우리말을 쓰세요.

O____개 X____개

영어	한국어
feather	
during	
palace	
enter	
mental	
cage	
poem	
important	
seed	
low	
square	
price	
conversation	
value	
remove	
culture	
arrive	
skip	
happiness	
sunset	
thief	
task	
sweat	
adventure	
bill	

한국어	영어
명 시	
명 새장, 우리	
동 들어가다, 입력하다	
명 궁전	
동 (일 등을) 거르다, 건너뛰다	
명 모험	
형 정신의, 마음의, 정신적인	
명 도둑	
형 낮은	
명 값, 가격	
명 깃털	
형 정사각형 모양의 명 정사각형, 광장	
명 대화	
동 치우다, 제거하다	
명 씨앗	
전 ~동안	
동 도착하다	
명 해질녘, 일몰	
형 중요한	
명 가치, 유용성	
명 고지서, 청구서, 지폐	
명 문화	
명 일, 과제	
명 행복	
명 땀 동 땀을 흘리다	

Workbook

Day 17

| 월 일 |

영어 단어에 해당하는 한국어 뜻을 함께 적으세요.

exhibition	전시회	exhibition	전시회
nation	국가, 나라		
tie	넥타이; 묶다		
destination	행선지, 도착지		
auditorium	강당		
choir	합창단		
create	창조하다; 창조		
disease	질병		
drop by	(~에) 들르다		
everywhere	모든 곳에, 어디든지		
fry	(기름에) 볶다, 튀기다		
interview	인터뷰하다; 인터뷰, 면접		
luggage	(여행용) 짐, 수하물		
musician	음악가		
shake	흔들다, 흔들리다		
playground	운동장		
pouch	주머니		
reuse	재사용하다		
service	(고객에 대한) 서비스		
wrap	싸다, 포장하다		
still	여전히, 아직도; 가만히 있는		
tear	눈물; 찢다		
third	세 번째의		
cruel	잔혹한, 잔인한		
heavily	심하게, 세게, 무겁게		

다음 단어에 해당하는 영어 단어 또는 우리말을 쓰세요.

O____개 X____개

영어	한국어
choir	
auditorium	
luggage	
interview	
musician	
fry	
heavily	
exhibition	
shake	
everywhere	
third	
destination	
service	
playground	
cruel	
create	
tear	
wrap	
pouch	
disease	
nation	
reuse	
drop by	
still	
tie	

한국어	영어
명 음악가	
명 행선지, 도착지	
명 (여행용) 짐, 수하물	
명 (고객에 대한) 서비스	
명 전시회	
동 인터뷰하다 명 인터뷰, 면접	
명 질병	
형 세 번째의	
동 흔들다, 흔들리다	
명 국가, 나라	
동 재사용하다	
명 넥타이 동 묶다	
동 (기름에) 볶다, 튀기다	
동 (~에) 들르다	
명 눈물 동 찢다	
명 강당	
동 싸다, 포장하다	
명 운동장	
부 여전히, 아직도 형 가만히 있는	
명 합창단	
부 모든 곳에, 어디든지	
형 잔혹한, 잔인한	
부 심하게, 세게, 무겁게	
명 주머니	
동 창조하다 명 창조	

Workbook

Day 18

| 월 일 | 영어 단어에 해당하는 한국어 뜻을 함께 적으세요.

senior	상위의; 연장자, 선배	senior	상위의; 연장자, 선배
century	세기, 100년		
action	행동, 조치		
another	다른, 또 하나의; 하나 더		
blend	섞다, 혼합하다		
vase	꽃병		
complete	완성하다, 끝내다; 완벽한		
disappoint	실망시키다		
emotion	감정		
focus	초점, 주목; 집중하다		
global	세계적인, 지구 전체의		
lesson	수업, 교습, 교훈		
move	움직이다, 옮기다, 이사하다		
tight	꼭 끼는, 단단한		
project	과제, 계획		
pure	순수한, 깨끗한		
violent	폭력적인		
servant	하인, 종업원		
silent	말이 없는, 조용한		
steal	훔치다		
straw	짚, 빨대		
temple	절, 사원		
time	시간, 시대, 횟수		
purpose	목적, 의도		
volunteer	자원하다; 자원봉사자		

다음 단어에 해당하는 영어 단어 또는 우리말을 쓰세요.

O____개 X____개

영어	한국어
action	
tight	
century	
straw	
move	
project	
senior	
pure	
focus	
global	
temple	
violent	
emotion	
time	
servant	
another	
purpose	
volunteer	
blend	
silent	
lesson	
vase	
complete	
steal	
disappoint	

한국어	영어
명 시간, 시대, 횟수	
형 꼭 끼는, 단단한	
명 과제, 계획	
형 완벽한 동 완성하다, 끝내다	
명 행동, 조치	
명 절, 사원	
명 꽃병	
동 자원하다 명 자원봉사자	
형 상위의 명 연장자, 선배	
형 순수한, 깨끗한	
명 짚, 빨대	
명 세기, 100년	
동 실망시키다	
형 폭력적인	
형 세계적인, 지구 전체의	
명 하인, 종업원	
대 하나 더 형 다른, 또 하나의	
명 감정	
동 움직이다, 옮기다, 이사하다	
형 말이 없는, 조용한	
명 초점, 주목 동 집중하다	
명 목적, 의도	
동 섞다, 혼합하다	
동 훔치다	
명 수업, 교습, 교훈	

Workbook

Day 19

| 월 일 |

영어 단어에 해당하는 한국어 뜻을 함께 적으세요.

forgive	용서하다	forgive	용서하다
gallery	미술관, 화랑		
forth	앞으로		
amount	양, 총액		
average	평균의; 평균		
coach	(스포츠 팀의) 코치, 감독; 코치하다, 지도하다		
decide	결정하다		
dialogue	대화		
experience	경험; 경험하다		
fiction	소설, 허구		
evil	나쁜, 불길한		
lonely	외로운, 쓸쓸한		
north	북쪽; 북쪽으로		
plate	접시, 판		
be proud of	~을 자랑스러워하다		
referee	심판		
model	기준, 모범, 모형, (상품의) 모델; 모형의		
sleeve	소매		
sore	아픈, 따가운		
storm	폭풍, 태풍		
surprising	놀라운		
tasty	맛있는		
victory	승리		
tour	여행; 여행하다, 견학하다		
vet	수의사		

다음 단어에 해당하는 영어 단어 또는 우리말을 쓰세요. ○____개 ×____개

영어	한국어
forgive	
plate	
vet	
be proud of	
forth	
gallery	
referee	
experience	
model	
north	
average	
sleeve	
amount	
tour	
sore	
storm	
coach	
tasty	
decide	
surprising	
dialogue	
lonely	
victory	
evil	
fiction	

한국어	영어
형 ~을 자랑스러워하다	
동 코치하다, 지도하다 명 (스포츠 팀의) 코치, 감독	
명 수의사	
형 놀라운	
명 미술관, 화랑	
명 접시, 판	
형 외로운, 쓸쓸한	
동 용서하다	
명 소매	
명 소설, 허구	
명 여행 동 여행하다, 견학하다	
명 북쪽 형 북쪽으로	
동 결정하다	
부 앞으로	
형 아픈, 따가운	
형 평균의 명 평균	
형 맛있는	
형 모형의 명 기준, 모범, 모형, (상품의) 모델	
명 양, 총액	
형 나쁜, 불길한	
명 승리	
명 대화	
명 경험 동 경험하다	
명 심판	
명 폭풍, 태풍	

Workbook

Day 20

| 월 일 |

영어 단어에 해당하는 한국어 뜻을 함께 적으세요.

be anxious about	~에 대해 걱정하다, 불안해하다	be anxious about	~에 대해 걱정하다, 불안해하다
step	걸음, 조치, 단계		
clap	박수치다; 박수		
appear	나타나다, ~인 것 같다		
belief	믿음, 생각		
castle	성		
death	죽음		
effect	영향, 결과		
exchange	교환하다, 맞바꾸다; 교환		
final	마지막의, 최종적인		
huge	거대한		
lay	놓다, 두다, (알을) 낳다		
pass	지나가다, 통과시키다, 합격하다		
print	인쇄하다; 활자, 출판		
reach	~에 이르다, (손이) 닿다, 도착하다		
sense	감각, 느낌; 느끼다, 알아채다		
side	옆, 측면		
snail	달팽이		
wisdom	지혜, 현명함		
suggest	제안하다, 추천하다		
through	~을 통해 (관통하여), ~사이로		
voice	목소리		
tip	조언, (뾰족한) 끝		
toward	~을 향해서, ~쪽으로		
triangle	삼각형		

다음 단어에 해당하는 영어 단어 또는 우리말을 쓰세요.

O____개 X____개

영어	한국어
appear	
triangle	
print	
lay	
toward	
pass	
clap	
reach	
step	
sense	
tip	
be anxious about	
voice	
exchange	
side	
huge	
death	
belief	
snail	
wisdom	
final	
through	
castle	
suggest	
effect	

한국어	영어
형 거대한	
형 ~에 대해 걱정하다, 불안해하다	
동 제안하다, 추천하다	
명 죽음	
명 걸음, 조치, 단계	
동 ~에 이르다, (손이) 닿다, 도착하다	
명 삼각형	
동 지나가다, 통과시키다, 합격하다	
명 지혜, 현명함	
동 박수치다 명 박수	
전 ~을 향해서, ~쪽으로	
형 마지막의, 최종적인	
명 믿음, 생각	
명 조언, (뾰족한) 끝	
동 나타나다, ~인 것 같다	
명 옆, 측면	
동 인쇄하다 명 활자, 출판	
명 목소리	
명 교환 동 교환하다, 맞바꾸다	
명 달팽이	
전 ~을 통해 (관통하여), ~사이로	
명 영향, 결과	
명 감각, 느낌 동 느끼다, 알아채다	
동 놓다, 두다, (알을) 낳다	
명 성	

Workbook

Day 21

| 월 일 |

영어 단어에 해당하는 한국어 뜻을 함께 적으세요.

hide	감추다, 숨다	hide	감추다, 숨다
court	법정, (경기장) 코트		
deep	깊은		
allow	허락하다		
blank	공백의, 빈; 빈칸		
bride	신부		
deaf	귀가 먼, 청각 장애가 있는		
donkey	당나귀		
forever	영원히		
gesture	몸짓, 제스처		
hunger	배고픔, 굶주림, 열망		
necessary	필요한		
for free	공짜로, 무료로		
promise	약속; 약속하다		
receive	받다, 받아들이다		
sailor	선원, 뱃사람		
mission	임무, 사절단		
solar	태양의		
strike	~을 치다, 때리다; 파업		
stripe	줄무늬		
title	제목		
underwater	물속의		
type	종류, 유형		
waste	낭비하다; 쓰레기, 낭비		
virtue	덕목, 미덕, 선행		

다음 단어에 해당하는 영어 단어 또는 우리말을 쓰세요.　　○____개　✕____개

영어	한국어
promise	
deaf	
virtue	
receive	
blank	
donkey	
bride	
sailor	
waste	
deep	
mission	
solar	
for free	
strike	
allow	
type	
stripe	
necessary	
underwater	
forever	
title	
gesture	
court	
hide	
hunger	

한국어	영어
명 당나귀	
동 감추다, 숨다	
명 약속 동 약속하다	
명 줄무늬	
형 귀가 먼, 청각 장애가 있는	
명 종류, 유형	
명 법정, (경기장) 코트	
형 필요한	
형 물속의	
명 신부	
명 배고픔, 굶주림, 열망	
형 태양의	
형 깊은	
동 받다, 받아들이다	
명 선원, 뱃사람	
부 영원히	
동 낭비하다 명 쓰레기, 낭비	
명 파업 동 ~을 치다, 때리다	
명 덕목, 미덕, 선행	
동 허락하다	
명 몸짓, 제스처	
명 제목	
형 공백의, 빈 명 빈칸	
명 임무, 사절단	
형 공짜로, 무료로	

Workbook

Day 22

| 월 일 |

영어 단어에 해당하는 한국어 뜻을 함께 적으세요.

behave	행동하다	behave	행동하다
royal	국왕의		
affect	영향을 주다, 감동시키다		
attack	공격하다; 공격		
capital	수도, 대문자		
competition	경쟁, 시합		
develop	성장하다, 개발하다		
fair	타당한, 공정한		
gather	모으다, 모이다		
harmony	조화, 화합, 화음		
mean	의미하다		
noise	소음		
peaceful	평화적인		
punish	벌하다, 혼을 내다		
vacuum	진공, 공백		
shape	형태, 모양		
spoil	망치다		
steam	김, 증기		
teenager	10대		
twin	쌍둥이; 쌍둥이의		
tradition	전통		
unusual	특이한		
waist	허리		
weight	몸무게		
without	~없이		

다음 단어에 해당하는 영어 단어 또는 우리말을 쓰세요.

O____개 X____개

영어	한국어
behave	
peaceful	
waist	
unusual	
attack	
punish	
without	
affect	
noise	
fair	
develop	
vacuum	
tradition	
royal	
shape	
gather	
twin	
spoil	
capital	
harmony	
teenager	
steam	
competition	
mean	
weight	

한국어	영어
명 수도, 대문자	
전 ~없이	
동 공격하다 명 공격	
명 전통	
명 조화, 화합, 화음	
형 평화적인	
명 진공, 공백	
동 모으다, 모이다	
동 행동하다	
명 10대	
명 허리	
형 타당한, 공정한	
명 김, 증기	
명 쌍둥이 형 쌍둥이의	
명 몸무게	
형 국왕의	
동 벌하다, 혼을 내다	
명 경쟁, 시합	
동 망치다	
동 의미하다	
동 영향을 주다, 감동시키다	
명 형태, 모양	
형 특이한	
동 성장하다, 개발하다	
명 소음	

Workbook

Day 23

| 월 일 |

영어 단어에 해당하는 한국어 뜻을 함께 적으세요.

electric	전기의	electric	전기의
west	서쪽; 서쪽의; 서쪽으로		
alive	살아 있는		
background	배경		
both	양자의; 둘 다(의)		
ceiling	천장		
crash	충돌하다; 사고, 굉음		
express	빠른, 급행의; 표현하다		
friendship	우정, 교우관계		
housework	집안 일		
mystery	수수께끼, 미스터리		
pain	고통, 통증		
pop	인기있는; 팝 음악, 펑 터지는 소리		
really	실제로, 진짜로, 정말로, 아주		
several	몇몇의; 몇몇		
similar	비슷한		
stage	단계, 무대		
talent	재능		
thirsty	목이 마른		
trade	무역; 무역하다		
view	관점, 견해, 경관		
vote	투표; 투표하다		
cool	시원한, 서늘한		
while	~하는 동안에		
with	~와 함께		

다음 단어에 해당하는 영어 단어 또는 우리말을 쓰세요.

O____개 X____개

영어	한국어
really	
thirsty	
electric	
pop	
several	
ceiling	
talent	
pain	
similar	
both	
housework	
west	
stage	
vote	
mystery	
cool	
alive	
trade	
background	
while	
friendship	
express	
view	
crash	
with	

한국어	영어
형 전기의	
명 무역 동 무역하다	
명 우정, 교우관계	
형 비슷한	
형 인기있는 명 팝 음악, 펑 터지는 소리	
전 ~와 함께	
형 양자의 대 둘 다(의)	
형 목이 마른	
형 몇몇의 대 몇몇	
명 서쪽 형 서쪽의 부 서쪽으로	
형 빠른, 급행의 동 표현하다	
형 시원한, 서늘한	
명 고통, 통증	
명 투표 동 투표하다	
형 살아 있는	
접 ~하는 동안에	
명 수수께끼, 미스터리	
명 배경	
부 실제로, 진짜로, 정말로, 아주	
명 단계, 무대	
명 천장	
명 관점, 견해, 경관	
동 충돌하다 명 사고, 굉음	
명 집안 일	
명 재능	

Workbook

Day 24

| 월 일 | 영어 단어에 해당하는 한국어 뜻을 함께 적으세요.

forget	잊다	forget	잊다
pardon	용서; 용서하다		
wood	나무, 목재		
career	직업, 경력		
beside	~옆에		
college	대학		
east	동쪽; 동쪽의		
flat	평평한, 바람이 빠진		
heaven	천국		
honest	정직한		
neat	정돈된, 깔끔한		
attend	참석하다		
prize	상, 상품		
review	비평하다, 검토하다; 복습, 비평		
shark	상어		
spill	엎지르다, 쏟다		
spirit	정신, 마음, 자세		
text	본문, 글; 문자 메시지를 보내다		
tongue	혀, 언어, 말씨		
vest	조끼		
skin	피부		
volume	음량, 권, 용량, 용적		
worm	벌레		
yet	아직		
ugly	못생긴, 싫은, 불쾌한		

다음 단어에 해당하는 영어 단어 또는 우리말을 쓰세요. O____개 X____개

영어	한국어
beside	
career	
wood	
review	
worm	
spill	
yet	
volume	
forget	
shark	
prize	
spirit	
pardon	
ugly	
skin	
college	
text	
honest	
attend	
tongue	
east	
neat	
flat	
vest	
heaven	

한국어	영어
명 상, 상품	
전 ~옆에	
명 상어	
명 복습, 비평 동 비평하다, 검토하다	
동 잊다	
동 참석하다	
형 평평한, 바람이 빠진	
동 엎지르다, 쏟다	
명 피부	
명 나무, 목재	
형 정돈된, 깔끔한	
명 용서 동 용서하다	
명 정신, 마음, 자세	
명 동쪽 형 동쪽의	
부 아직	
형 정직한	
명 본문, 글 동 문자 메시지를 보내다	
명 직업, 경력	
명 조끼	
명 혀, 언어, 말씨	
명 대학	
명 벌레	
형 못생긴, 싫은, 불쾌한	
명 음량, 권, 용량, 용적	
명 천국	

Workbook

Day 25

| 월 일 | 영어 단어에 해당하는 한국어 뜻을 함께 적으세요.

hold	잡다, 쥐다; 잡기	hold	잡다, 쥐다; 잡기
sticky	끈적거리는		
choice	선택		
along	~을 따라서; ~와 함께		
branch	나뭇가지, 지사, 지점		
tough	거친, 강인한		
end up ~ing	결국 ~하게 되다		
freeze	얼리다, 얼어붙다		
hole	구멍, 굴		
information	정보		
be nervous about	~에 대해 불안해하다, 초조해하다		
pat	(애정을 담아) 쓰다듬다, 토닥거리다		
reason	이유, 이성, 판단력		
sharp	날카로운		
sign	신호, 징조; 서명하다, 신호를 보내다		
spread	확산; 펴다, 펼치다, 펴서 바르다		
language	언어		
whisper	속삭이다, 소근거리다		
control	지배, 통제; 통제하다, 제어하다		
village	마을, 촌락		
weather	날씨		
yard	마당, 뜰, 운동장, 제조장		
customer	고객		
modern	현대적인		
escape	탈출하다, ~을 벗어나다; 탈출		

다음 단어에 해당하는 영어 단어 또는 우리말을 쓰세요. O____개 X____개

영어	한국어
along	
sharp	
be nervous about	
spread	
reason	
branch	
sign	
information	
choice	
language	
sticky	
village	
whisper	
freeze	
control	
weather	
tough	
yard	
pat	
hold	
customer	
hole	
escape	
end up ~ing	
modern	

한국어	영어
형 끈적거리는	
동 속삭이다, 소근거리다	
형 현대적인	
형 ~에 대해 불안해하다, 초조해하다	
명 나뭇가지, 지사, 지점	
형 날카로운	
명 언어	
동 잡다, 쥐다 명 잡기	
명 정보	
명 구멍, 굴	
명 신호, 징조 동 서명하다, 신호를 보내다	
명 마을, 촌락	
명 선택	
전 ~을 따라서 부 ~와 함께	
명 고객	
동 얼리다, 얼어붙다	
명 지배, 통제 동 통제하다, 제어하다	
명 날씨	
동 (애정을 담아) 쓰다듬다, 토닥거리다	
형 거친, 강인한	
명 마당, 뜰, 운동장, 제조장	
명 이유, 이성, 판단력	
결국 ~하게 되다	
명 확산 동 펴다, 펼치다, 펴서 바르다	
명 탈출 동 탈출하다, ~을 벗어나다	

Workbook

Day 26

| 월 일 |

영어 단어에 해당하는 한국어 뜻을 함께 적으세요.

fail	실패하다; 실패	fail	실패하다; 실패
slide	미끄러지다; 미끄럼틀		
object	물건, 목표; 반대하다		
appreciate	고마워 하다, 알아보다		
chance	기회, 가능성		
cross	건너다		
explain	설명하다		
fund	기금, 자금		
judge	판단하다, 심사하다; 판사		
musical	음악적인, 음악의		
narrate	이야기를 하다		
polar	북극/남극의, 극지방의		
report	보도, 보고서; 알리다, 보고하다		
search	찾다, 수색하다; 찾기, 수색		
legal	법적인		
trust	신뢰, 신임; 신뢰하다		
statue	조각상		
tiny	아주 작은		
traffic	교통(량), 차량들		
trick	속임수; 속이다		
desirable	바람직한, 가치있는		
message	메시지		
wonderful	신나는, 훌륭한		
expression	표현 , 표정		
medium	중간의; 매체, 수단		

다음 단어에 해당하는 영어 단어 또는 우리말을 쓰세요.

O____개 X____개

영어	한국어
fund	
judge	
slide	
fail	
explain	
search	
cross	
trick	
legal	
medium	
object	
desirable	
statue	
trust	
message	
appreciate	
tiny	
chance	
wonderful	
traffic	
narrate	
expression	
musical	
report	
polar	

영어	한국어
동 실패하다 명 실패	
동 설명하다	
형 중간의 명 매체, 수단	
명 찾기, 수색 동 찾다, 수색하다	
형 아주 작은	
동 미끄러지다 명 미끄럼틀	
명 기회, 가능성	
형 신나는, 훌륭한	
동 이야기를 하다	
명 표현 , 표정	
명 메시지	
명 물건, 목표 동 반대하다	
명 교통(량), 차량들	
형 음악적인, 음악의	
명 보도, 보고서 동 알리다, 보고하다	
형 법적인	
명 기금, 자금	
동 고마워 하다, 알아보다	
명 조각상	
명 속임수 동 속이다	
형 북극/남극의, 극지방의	
명 판사 동 판단하다, 심사하다	
동 건너다	
명 신뢰, 신임 동 신뢰하다	
형 바람직한, 가치있는	

Workbook

Day 27

| 월 일 |

영어 단어에 해당하는 한국어 뜻을 함께 적으세요.

be curious about	~에 대해 호기심이 많다	be curious about	~에 대해 호기심이 많다
splash	(물, 흙탕물 등을) 튀기다, 끼얹다		
portrait	초상화, 인물사진		
degree	(온도 또는 각도) 도, 학위		
comfortable	편안한		
excellent	훌륭한, 우수한		
flea	벼룩		
harvest	수확; 수확하다		
liberty	자유, 해방		
major	주요한, 일류의; 전공하다		
look for	~을 찾다, 구하다		
pity	연민, 동정(심), 유감		
respond	반응하다, 대답하다		
show	쇼, 공연물; 보여주다		
oppose	반대하다, 대립하다		
stairs	계단		
success	성공		
topic	주제		
journal	잡지, 신문, 정기 간행물		
one day	언젠가, 어느 날		
way	길, 방향, 방법		
wild	야생의		
nickname	별명; 별명을 붙이다		
positive	낙관적인, 긍정적인		
million	백만; 백만의, 수많은		

다음 단어에 해당하는 영어 단어 또는 우리말을 쓰세요. O____개 X____개

영어	한국어
show	
oppose	
splash	
journal	
million	
harvest	
stairs	
be curious about	
topic	
respond	
success	
flea	
pity	
excellent	
liberty	
portrait	
nickname	
way	
degree	
one day	
positive	
major	
comfortable	
wild	
look for	

한국어	영어
명 (온도 또는 각도) 도, 학위	
명 주제	
명 쇼, 공연물 동 보여주다	
명 백만 형 백만의, 수많은	
동 전공하다 형 주요한, 일류의	
형 낙관적인, 긍정적인	
명 성공	
~에 대해 호기심이 많다	
동 반대하다, 대립하다	
명 초상화, 인물사진	
명 계단	
동 반응하다, 대답하다	
명 잡지, 신문, 정기 간행물	
명 자유, 해방	
동 (물, 흙탕물 등을) 튀기다, 끼얹다	
동 ~을 찾다, 구하다	
언젠가, 어느 날	
형 편안한	
명 길, 방향, 방법	
형 훌륭한, 우수한	
명 수확 동 수확하다	
명 별명 동 별명을 붙이다	
명 연민, 동정(심), 유감	
명 벼룩	
형 야생의	

Workbook

Day 28

| 월 일 |

영어 단어에 해당하는 한국어 뜻을 함께 적으세요.

leave	남겨두다, 출발하다	leave	남겨두다
warn	경고하다		
beyond	~저편에, ~을 넘어서는		
celebrity	연예인, 유명인		
cure	치료; 고치다, 치료하다		
ease	쉬움; 편하게 하다, 편해지다		
front	앞, 정면; 앞쪽의		
happen to	우연히 ~을 하다		
march	행진하다; 행진		
work out	(건강을 위해) 운동을 하다		
grave	무덤, 산소		
pond	연못		
rub	문지르다, 비비다		
shell	(단단한) 껍질, 조개		
situation	상황		
stare	빤히 쳐다보다, 응시하다		
support	지지하다, 지원하다, 부양하다		
total	전체의, 완전한; 합계, 총액		
community	지역 사회, 공동체		
pleasant	즐거운, 기분 좋은		
furniture	가구		
fence	울타리		
extra	추가의		
few	거의 없는, 많지 않은		
guard	지키다; 경호 요원		

다음 단어에 해당하는 영어 단어 또는 우리말을 쓰세요. ○____개 ×____개

영어	한국어
march	
celebrity	
shell	
stare	
leave	
fence	
rub	
community	
situation	
warn	
pond	
furniture	
beyond	
guard	
work out	
extra	
support	
cure	
grave	
total	
ease	
pleasant	
few	
front	
happen to	

한국어	영어
명 (단단한) 껍질, 조개	
명 상황	
명 치료 동 고치다, 치료하다	
동 문지르다, 비비다	
동 남겨두다, 출발하다	
명 지역 사회, 공동체	
동 빤히 쳐다보다, 응시하다	
동 경고하다	
명 합계, 총액 형 전체의, 완전한	
명 앞, 정면 형 앞쪽의	
형 즐거운, 기분 좋은	
전 ~저편에, ~을 넘어서는	
명 연못	
명 쉬움 동 편하게 하다, 편해지다	
명 가구	
동 지지하다, 지원하다, 부양하다	
명 무덤, 산소	
명 연예인, 유명인	
명 울타리	
동 우연히 ~을 하다	
형 거의 없는, 많지 않은	
(건강을 위해) 운동을 하다	
동 행진하다 명 행진	
형 추가의	
동 지키다 명 경호 요원	

Day 29

| 월 일 |

영어 단어에 해당하는 한국어 뜻을 함께 적으세요.

invitation	초대	invitation	초대
tickle	간지럼을 태우다, 간질간질하다		
slowly	천천히, 느리게		
broadcast	방송하다; 방송		
avenue	(도시의) 거리, -가		
coin	동전		
digest	소화하다		
foreign	외국의, 대외의		
height	높이, (사람의) 키		
opinion	의견		
owe	~에게 신세지다, (돈을) 빚지고 있다		
postcard	그림엽서, 엽서		
public	대중의, 공공의; 일반인, 대중		
recently	최근에		
shine	빛나다; 빛, 햇빛, 광택		
smooth	부드러운		
temperature	온도, 기온		
own	소유하다; 자기 자신의		
trash	쓰레기		
valley	계곡, 골짜기		
walk	걷다		
yell	소리치다; 고함, 외침		
donate	기부하다		
fit	적합한, 건강한; (사이즈가) 맞다		
path	길		

다음 단어에 해당하는 영어 단어 또는 우리말을 쓰세요. O___개 X___개

영어	한국어
recently	
avenue	
public	
invitation	
postcard	
shine	
smooth	
tickle	
owe	
own	
slowly	
temperature	
opinion	
trash	
broadcast	
yell	
valley	
fit	
coin	
walk	
digest	
height	
donate	
foreign	
path	

한국어	영어
명 그림엽서, 엽서	
명 초대	
동 빛나다 명 빛, 햇빛, 광택	
부 최근에	
명 동전	
명 높이, (사람의) 키	
동 (돈을) 빚지고 있다, ~에게 신세지다	
동 소리치다 명 고함, 외침	
동 걷다	
동 간지럼을 태우다, 간질간질하다	
명 계곡, 골짜기	
동 기부하다	
형 외국의, 대외의	
동 방송하다 명 방송	
명 쓰레기	
부 천천히, 느리게	
형 부드러운	
형 대중의, 공공의 명 일반인, 대중	
명 길	
동 소화하다	
명 의견	
명 온도, 기온	
동 (사이즈가) 맞다 형 적합한, 건강한	
명 (도시의) 거리, -가	
동 소유하다 형 자기 자신의	

Workbook

Day 30

| 월 일 |

영어 단어에 해당하는 한국어 뜻을 함께 적으세요.

navy	해군; 남색의	navy	해군; 남색의
pollute	오염시키다		
advise	충고하다		
argue	언쟁을 하다, 다투다		
cost	비용, 값; (돈이) 들다		
courage	용기		
determine	결정하다, 알아내다		
fill	채우다		
fur	(일부 동물의) 털, 모피		
habitat	서식지		
ocean	바다, -양		
discover	발견하다		
pour	붓다, 따르다		
privacy	사생활, 비밀		
give up	포기하다		
shout	외치다, 호통을 치다		
signal	신호		
stay	머무르다; 머무름, 체류		
therefore	그러므로, 그 결과		
toe	발가락		
unique	독특한		
whale	고래		
wonder	놀라움, 경탄; 궁금해하다		
medical	의학의, 의료의		
imagine	상상하다		

다음 단어에 해당하는 영어 단어 또는 우리말을 쓰세요.

O____개 X____개

영어	한국어
navy	
stay	
medical	
shout	
toe	
give up	
imagine	
signal	
habitat	
privacy	
whale	
pollute	
ocean	
pour	
unique	
fill	
discover	
fur	
therefore	
wonder	
advise	
toe	
cost	
discover	
shout	

한국어	영어
명 비용, 값 동 (돈이) 들다	
명 사생활, 비밀	
형 독특한	
동 충고하다	
부 그러므로, 그 결과	
명 바다, –양	
동 발견하다	
명 서식지	
동 언쟁을 하다, 다투다	
동 포기하다	
동 오염시키다	
명 용기	
동 상상하다	
동 외치다, 호통을 치다	
명 (일부 동물의) 털, 모피	
명 발가락	
동 머무르다 명 머무름, 체류	
동 결정하다, 알아내다	
형 의학의, 의료의	
명 고래	
명 놀라움, 경탄 동 궁금해하다	
명 신호	
동 채우다	
명 해군 형 남색의	
동 붓다, 따르다	

memo

memo

30일 완성 내신 • 수능 완전 정복! **Word Max** 6단계 시리즈

WORD MAX 5300

MP3 무료 다운로드 www.wcbooks.co.kr

WorldCom Edu